COUNTERNARRATIVES

Routledge
New York and London

COUNTERNARRATIVES

Cultural Studies and Critical Pedagogies in Postmodern Spaces

Henry Giroux, Colin Lankshear, Peter McLaren and Michael Peters

Published in 1996 by
Routledge
29 West 35th Street
New York, NY 10001

Published in
Great Britain by
Routledge
11 New Fetter Lane
London EC4P 4EE

Copyright © 1996 by
Routledge
Printed in the United
States of America on acid-
free paper.

Chapter 13 was originally
published in *Women and
Peace* by Betty Reardon,
SUNY Press, New York,
1994. Reprinted courtesy
of SUNY Press.

The authors acknowledge the generosity of other publishers
for allowing the publication here of previously published work,
as follows:
Chapter Four of the present work originally appeared in a slightly
different version in *Rethinking Media Literacy* by Peter McLaren
© 1995 by Peter Lang Publishing.
The section in Chapter Four, "Media Literacy as Counter-Hegemonic
Practice," contains several pages adapted from an article appearing in
Religious Education, Volume 89, Number 4, by permission from the
publisher, The Religious Education Association, 409 Prospect Street,
New Haven, CT 06511-2177.

Library of Congress Cataloging-in-Publication Data

Counternarratives : cultural studies and critical pedagogies in
    postmodern spaces / by Henry Giroux . . . [et al.].
        p. cm.
    Includes bibliographical references and index.
    ISBN 0-415-90583-4 (hardcover). — ISBN 0-415-90584-2 (pbk.)
    1. Critical pedagogy.   2. Postmodernism and education.
    3. Culture—Study and teaching (Higher)   4. Mass media criticism.
    5. Education, Higher—Political aspects.   I. Giroux, Henry A.
    LC196.C68   1996
    370.11'5—dc20   96-26336
                                            CIP

CONTENTS

PREFACE

THE PROJECT of a book which explored counternarratives impinging on education in postmodern times was initially proposed by Henry Giroux in conversation with Colin Lankshear and Peter McLaren. We eventually decided we wanted to produce a volume that drew on insights from postmodern social theory to frame and explore some significant points at which the politics of "official" and "unofficial" narratives are played out in and around formal education.

We envisaged a book that would do *serious theoretical and scholarly work* on issues and terrain that are genuinely *postmodern*, and not merely appropriate concepts from contemporary social theory to rework old themes in faintly refined ways. Furthermore, we wanted a book that gave free range to the individual and idiosyncratic voices of the contributors within the bounds of a negotiated theoretical scope, rather than risking the kinds of compromise and "ironing out" that sometimes attend collaborative authorship predicated on a quest for "univocality."

At the same time, we recognized that the book we envisaged called for input beyond what the three original collaborators alone could provide. Michael Peters joined us as fourth author. Rhonda Hammer and Michele Knobel have contributed as coauthors of (different) single chapters. The result is a book which is intended to be broad in scope, yet thematically coherent; diverse in style and focus, yet consistent in quality and rigor; fragmentory at the level of specific concerns, yet cohesive as a whole; theoretically interesting and challenging, yet fruitfully useful and suggestive for teachers who daily face the exigencies of classroom practice in a world much changed from that they knew as students and as teacher educatees.

We thank Routledge for allowing us the time we needed to complete this book, and hope that readers will find our efforts well placed.

POSTMODERN COUNTERNARRATIVES

Michael Peters and Colin Lankshear

chapter 1

INTRODUCTION

THE CONTEMPORARY social scene is flecked with a diverse array of more or less distinctively postmodern counternarratives. To understand the social present is very much a matter of recognizing and understanding the extent to which and ways in which our everyday lives are invested in and impacted and punctuated by these counternarratives and the "official" narratives against which they emerge as oppositional responses.

Subsequent chapters identify and explore some typical examples of "postmodern counternarratives." By way of introduction, however, we acknowledge that the very idea of postmodern counternarratives needs to be developed. It is as yet somewhat inchoate, and needs to be made explicit. It is also a complex idea, which needs to be clarified. In this chapter we undertake the philosophical task of distilling a working concept of counternarratives from the voluminous literatures that have developed around "postmodernity" as a theoretical construct and as lived reality. By providing this conceptual framework we clear the way for authors in later chapters to draw on their respective work in cultural studies, media criticism, sociology of education, critical pedagogy, and philosophy of technology, to frame and critique a range of counternarratives which have emerged as typical cultural productions in opposition to "official" narratives of youth, pedagogy, cultural normality or propriety, and media "truth".

As developed here, the idea of postmodern counternarratives has two dimensions. The first observes the existence of counternarratives which function generically as a critique of the modernist predilection for "grand," "master," and "meta" narratives. These take issue with the narratives which have come down to us as part of the culture of the Enlightenment. They can be construed as countercultural critique, issuing from a basic skepticism, of the philosophies of history accompanying the grand claims concerning Man, Truth, Justice and Beauty, representing the West, and "America" as the last projection of European ideals, as the apex of an unbroken, evolutionary development of two thousand years of civilization. One model of the counternarrative in this sense is Theordor Adorno and Max Horkheimer's (1972) *Dialectic of the Enlightenment*, a counternarrative which emphasises the dark side of the Enlightenment. Another model is that of Jean-François Lyotard's (1984) *The Postmodern Condition* which, utilizing a Wittgensteinian approach, emphasizes the radical incommensurability of "language-games." Counternarratives in this sense serve the strategic political function of splintering and disturbing grand stories which gain their legitimacy from foundational myths concerning the origins and development of an unbroken history of the West based on the evolutionary ideal of progress.

In addition, however, there is a second, related dimension of "counternarratives," which lies at the heart of this book and will be exemplified in following chapters. According to this, even in a postmodern age, where citizens retain some sense of the critical exhibiting a characteristic "incredulity towards metanarratives" there remain "official" narratives, whether grand or otherwise. Counternarratives, then, in a second sense counter not merely (or even necessarily) the *grand* narratives, but also (or instead) the "*official*" and "*hegemonic*" narratives of everyday life: those legitimating stories propagated for specific political purposes to manipulate public consciousness by heralding a national set of common cultural ideals. The notion of counternarratives in this sense carries with it Foucault's "counter-memory" and the idea of counter-practices, but in a specific and local sense. Such counternarratives are, as Lyotard explains, quintessentially "little stories"—the little stories of those individuals and groups whose knowledges and histories have been marginalized, excluded, subjugated or forgotten in the telling of official narratives.

In this chapter we mainly explore the notion of postmodern counternarratives in the first, or generic, sense as a backdrop to the following chapters

2

which focus on official (counter)narratives in the second, more highly, contextual sense. These address, variously, the "official" narrative of the Gulf War; official narratives of what constitutes "good youth"; official narratives of classrooms and pedagogy; and official narratives of culture—together with specific, and specifically postmodern, counternarratives spawned within the cultural and political dialectics of everyday social practice.

POSTMODERNISM

Accounts of the present state of moral, political and aesthetic discourse allege there is no agreement on a universally accepted framework for resolving claims, and little immediate prospect of one emerging. Jean-François Lyotard (1984), the French poststructuralist philosopher, describes this state of affairs in terms of a crisis of legitimation of the "traditional" modernist metanarratives. These previously served to provide foundations for knowledge, morality and aesthetics, and for the cultural institutions based upon them. Lyotard argues that the metanarratives have collapsed: what characterizes cultural postmodernity is an "incredulity towards metanarratives"—an incurable suspicion that all grand, sweeping, narratives perform their legitimation functions by masking the will-to-power and excluding the interests of others.

According to this analysis of cultural postmodernity there are now only different ethical, political and aesthetic perspectives which are based on incommensurable premises—a heterogeneity of different moral language-games. Furthermore, philosophy itself is no longer considered the master discipline that can offer foundations; a metalanguage into which the claims and demands of competing language-games can be translated and resolved. The resulting "pluralism," which is seen as characteristic of cultural postmodernity, has been explained in both Kantian and Weberian terms as an extended differentiation of value spheres, each with its own inner logic. Western culture is seen to have undergone a process of accelerated cultural differentiation, especially since the Second World War. The liberal myth of a common culture, or form of life, which functioned to assimilate difference and otherness has split into a seemingly endless proliferation of subcultures and groups. The revitalization of indigenous cultures is seen as an important part of this differentiation process. With a new respect for the integrity of traditional cultures—a respect given only grudgingly under the increasing weight of a moral force deriving historically from philosophies of decolonization—Western liberal states have begun processes of redressing past grievances and of recognizing languages, epistemologies, aesthetics, and ethics different from "their own."

What has been called the "crisis of reason" is a crisis not only of foundational approaches to knowledge and morality, but also of the foundations of our institutions. "Postmodernism" is the general, if ambiguous, term used to refer to these cultural crises. It is the broad cultural phenomenon of Western societies which best typifies this questioning and the related search for new cultural and political orientations following the collapse of foundationalism. Postmodernism is, then, allegedly a Western socio-cultural phenomenon. As Ryan (1988:559) remarks, it is to art and mass culture what poststructuralism is to philosophy and social theory. Does postmodernist art and literature "obediently fall into step with the motifs and preoccupations of institutionalized poststructural theory," as Conner (1989: 128) claims, or did poststructuralism take its lead from postmodernist developments in the arts (Huyssen, 1986)?

Postmodernism is often seen as associated in some way with advanced, or late, capitalism. To say this, however, is to raise an issue without resolving it. Is postmodernism reactionary and anti-modernist? Does it enter into a relation with the logic of late capitalism which serves simply to reinforce that logic, as Jameson (1983) claims, or does it have the double capacity to also resist that logic?

The term "postmodernism", even in its linguistic inscription, is various: post-modernism, Post-Modernism (Jencks, 1987), POSTmodernISM (Hassan, 1971), postmodernism. What do the hyphenated versions imply? What do the capitals signify?

It has been described as a method, a philosophy, an attitude, a tonality, a style, a moment, a condition, a movement and even a theory, suggesting a unitary body of presuppositions and assumptions.[1] It has variously been celebrated as "a revolution in Western culture" (Jencks, 1987: 11) which has taken place "without breaking anything more than a few eggheads," and vilified as an obscurantist epistemology of free-play which has arisen in the Western academy at that precise point in history when women and non-Western peoples have begun to speak for themelves (Mascia-Lees et.al., 1989). Similarly, it has been said that postmodernism is disqualified from *political* import because it lacks an effective theory of agency (Hutcheon, 1989: 3). Further, the debate on postmodernism has generated a number of oppositional ideological positions: pre-modernist, anti-modernist, pro-postmodernist, anti-postmodernist (Jameson, 1984b); a postmodernism of resistance versus a postmodernism of reaction (Foster, 1985).

Feminism reveals an ambivalent attitude to postmodernism. Through a concern with otherness it has, along with postcolonial discourses, sought to demonstrate how representation can "no longer be considered a politically neutral and theoretically innocent activity" (Hutcheon, 1989: 21). In this respect the so-called poststructuralist critique of the subject has found favour with a number of feminist writers who have accepted and applied these insights in novel ways (e.g., see Nicholson, 1990). Flax (1990: 43), for instance, acknowledges how postmodern discourses make us skeptical about beliefs, derived from the Enlightenment, concerning "truth", "knowledge" and the "self" that are taken for granted and have served to legitimate contemporary western culture. In her view, feminists, echoing (other) postmodernists, are beginning to suspect that all such transcendental claims reflect and reify the experience of white males. On the other hand, feminism has remained wary of accepting a pluralism in politics which robs it of its universalism.

Postmodernism cuts a swathe across disciplines, especially in the arts and humanities. There are established literatures in architecture, art, dance, music, literature, film, photography and theatre (see e.g. Trachtenberg, 1985). In addition, debates on postmodernism have occurred within anthropology, history, politics, philosophy, psychoanalysis, cultural studies, geography, education, and sociology. There are significant and growing literatures in feminist scholarship and studies of popular culture focusing on television, film and video. It is a mistake to think that these disciplines and discourses treat "postmodernism" in the same way, or to assume that they have developed in a similar fashion. Something of the depth and diversity in evidence can be gauged from the fact that during the 1970s and 1980s at least twenty major journals dedicated special issues to the topic.[2]

In the United States Irving Howe (1959) and Harry Levin (1966) used the term "postmodern" in a derogatory sense to indicate the shift to "mass society" and to detect the anti-intellectual anti-rationalist undercurrent threatening the humanism and enlightenment characteristics of the culture of modernism. It has a lineage in the study of fiction and poetry in the United States beginning in the late 1950s, and a separate genealogy in architecture dating from the work of Robert Venturi in the mid 1960s. Leslie Fieder and Susan Sontag attempted to define a postmodernism in terms of the emerging counterculture of the 1960s; William Spanos' interpretation in the early 1970s began with Heidegger's ontology; thereafter the term became somewhat more inclusive (Bertens, 1986).

5

In France, the situation is more complex. Poststructuralist thought has its origins in Alexandre Kojéve's and Jean Hyppolite's "existentialist" readings of Hegel and is foreshadowed in the "structuralism" of Lacan, Lévi-Strauss and others. Here the master discipline is linguistics (Saussure), in both its structuralist and poststructuralist modes, and in its seemingly endless developments and theoretical refinements of analysis: semiotics, schizoanalysis, deconstructionism. It draws upon Friedrich Nietzsche's critique of occidental rationality and Martin Heidegger's "destruction" of western metaphysics. Poststructuralism, evinced in the work of people like Jacques Derrida, Jean-François Lyotard, Michel Foucault and Gilles Deleuze, surfaced in the late 1960s to flourish in the French speaking world in the 1970s and in anglophone culture in the 1980s. Lyotard's (1984) *The Postmodern Condition*, a book that was first published in France in 1979, crystallized the French critique of reason following a Kantian and Wittgensteinian line of thought.

In Britain, the story is very different. Hayward and Kerr (1987: 4), for instance, claim that British academics were especially inhospitable to postmodernism in the 1980s. This resistance, they comment, may be attributed to a prudent skepticism, but also "reflected the substantial institutional investment in dominant theoretical paradigms." They see Jean Baudrillard as the key figure in popularising postmodernism. His works, like those of other French poststructuralists, appeared in English only in the early 1980s. These works were received more enthusiastically in North America and Australia (especially in journals like *Art and Text, Semiotext(e)* and *ZG)* than in Britain. It was not until 1985 that the first significant signs of engaged debate in Britain became manifest, in a weekend conference on postmodernism organized by London's Institute of Contemporary Arts. Even with the presence of Lyotard this event failed to stimulate a broad cultural debate or anything like a general theoretical project (Hayward and Kerr, 1987: 4).

The situation in Germany is interesting, if ambiguous. David Wellbery (1985:229) claims that in Germany the term "postmodernism" has not enjoyed widespread accepted usage. Having said that, however, he goes on to construe postmodernism in terms of "the institutional saturation of life," "the cybernetization and medialization of cultural communication," and "the emergence of political forces of a number of groups that have traditionally been excluded from the political forum": all of which are prominent themes in German sociology. He asserts there is no unified postmodern philosophy and cautions us against using the terms "modernism" and "postmodernism" as if they were *names* with established referents. At the same time, he identifies contextual factors surrounding Habermas' lecture "Modernity Versus Postmodernity," delivered in 1980.[3] While these do not necessarily indicate singular and definitive referents applying in Germany in the late 1970s and early 1980s, they certainly do point toward some systematicity in German thought at the highest levels concerning the themes and issues at stake in "the postmodern debate."

Postmodernism in non-Western cultures is more problematic and generalizing is difficult. Slemon (1989: 4) claims that the critical projects of postmodernist theory and postcolonial criticism "have remained more or less separate in their strategies and their foundational assumptions." In current debates the genealogy of postmodernism is often lost or forgotten, along with its cultural and geographic place. Slemon suggests, however, that

> postmodernism may yet find a way to join with, not assimilate, post-colonial critical discourse in the necessary post-modernist wave of decolonizing Western culture—decolonizing it, that is, from a residual modernism, which continues to mark for Western culture its relations with the world (Slemon, 1989: 15).

Japan and the newly industrialized countries of South Korea and Taiwan occupy an ambiguous position. While "the postmodernism debate" is essentially a Western intellectual product, it has been given a peculiarly local twist in its Japanese appropriation. According to Sugimoto (1990: 49), the "emphasis is on three aspects of the Japanese context: information revolution, consumerism and the blurring of boundaries among social groups." Sugimoto's analysis of the main proponents of postmodernist theories in Japan raises interesting questions of the extent to which European currents in the sociology of modernization and modernity (post-modernization and postmodernity) are culture-bound and ethnocentric.

Postmodernity has been described as an epochal shift or break with the so called "modern era" and with various traditionally "modern" ways of viewing ourselves and the world. The extent, significance, nature and depth of that transformation has been fiercely debated but there is general agreement that a transformation is taking place.[4]

Has the dominant mode of production remained unchanged? Following the line advanced in Ernest Mandel's (1975) *Late Capitalism*, Fredric Jameson (1983) argues that since the early 1960s we have moved into a new (and final) stage of "late" capitalism, in which the production of culture has become integrated into commodity production more generally. He would agree with Peter Bürger's (1985: 117) view that the mode of production under capitalism remains, in essence, the "private appropriation of collectively produced surplus value." Bürger criticizes the sociological concept of the "postmodern" as being historically premature, claiming that "the maximization of profit remains the driving force of social reproduction." He cautions us against premature evaluation of current changes "as signs of an epoch-making transformation."

His warnings seem especially apposite in the current historical conjuncture. The so-called New Right has gained ascendancy in the West with an attack on "big" government and the Welfare State, the rapid privatization of the residual public sector (including health, education and broadcasting), massive state asset sale programs and a celebration of individualism as the fundamental liberal moral and social philosophy. At the same time, in the wake of *perestroika, glasnost*, and Boris Yeltsin's attempt to prevent the break-up of Russia; in the moment after German reunification; in the on-going "ethnic cleansing" of what used to be called Yugoslavia; the Eastern bloc seems poised ready to join the West in a blind commitment to a "free market" economy. Does the pluralism of postmodern culture stand in opposition to a global (*universal*) consumer capitalism or does it simply flourish under these new conditions?

Something of the conceptual confusion attending this moment of transformation is indicated in the list of related hybrids generated by Charles Jencks (1987: 12): "Post-Minimalism" (Pincus-Witten), "Post-Performance" (Dennis Openheim), "Post-Civilization" (Kenneth Boulding) and "Post-Logical Positivism" (Mary Hesse). To Jencks' (1987) hybrids, we can add substantially from Krishan Kumar's (1978) summary:

> Amitai Etzioni speaks of the "post-modern era," George Lichtheim of "the post-bourgeois society," Herman Kahn of "post-scarcity society." Daniel Bell simply of

the "post-industrial society." Others, putting the point more positively have spoken of "the knowledge society" (Peter Drucker), "the personal service society" (Paul Halmos), "the service class society" (Ralf Dahrendorf), and "the technetronic era" (Zbigniew Brzezinski). Taken as a whole these labels tell us what is in the past that has now been or is being suspended—e.g., scarcity, the bourgeois order, the predominance of the economic motive; and also what can be expected to be the main principle of future society—e.g., knowledge, personal services, the electronic technology of computers and tele-communications (193–94).

While Jencks' list is primarily aesthetic and philosophical, Kumar's is overwhelmingly sociological. In this context it is interesting to note that Boris Frankel (1987) uses the term "post-industrial utopians" to examine the works of Rudolf Bahro, Alvin Toffler, Barry Jones and André Gorz. The sociological concept, focusing on the theme of the postindustrial society—later, "the information society" and, most recently, "the information superhighway"—is refined internally by reference to period.

In any event, Jencks (1987: 12) is surely mistaken in maintaining that the categories he specifies have little in common, "other than the liberating potential of their prefix." This is to ignore the interrelations between subjects, disciplines and the cultural changes they theorize, as well as the collapse of traditional boundaries of discourse—a prominent feature of postmodernism. It also rules out *a priori* the possibility of some coherent, totalizing interpretation, such as Jameson's attempt to relate cultural and aesthetic transformations systematically to economic ones.

8

THE CRITIQUE OF REASON: POSTMODERN COUNTERNARRATIVES

At the theoretical level the postmodern "transformation" has been conceptualized under the rubric of the (French) critique of reason.[5] This motif refers to postmodernism's attack on the Enlightenment notion of a universal reason. In Sabina Lovibond's (1989:6) assessment

> The Enlightenment pictured the human race as engaged in an effort towards universal moral and intellectual self-realization, and so as the subject of a universal historical experience; it also postulated a universal human *reason* in terms of which social and political tendencies could be assessed as "progressive" or otherwise (the goal of politics being defined as the realization of reason in practice). Postmodernism rejects this picture: that is to say, it rejects the doctrine of the unity of reason. It refuses to conceive of humanity as a unitary subject striving towards the goal of perfect coherence (in its common stock of beliefs) or of perfect cohesion and stability (in its political practice).

Postmodernism pits *reasons* in the plural—fragmented and incommensurable—against the universality of modernism and its conception of a unified human reason which, as the standard of rationality, underwrites all knowledge claims irrespective of time and place, and provides the ground for the unitary subject considered as the agent of historically progressive change.

The attack on "the modern" and its attendant notion of universal reason is, perhaps, most famously associated with Jean-François Lyotard. Fredric Jameson (1984a: vii) begins his foreword to *The Postmodern Condition* (Lyotard 1984) by observing that postmodernism is generally understood as involving

> a radical break, both with a dominant culture and aesthetic, and with a rather different moment of socioeconomic organization against which its structural novelties and innovations are measured: a new social and economic moment (or even system), which has variously been called media society, the "society of the spectacle" (Guy Debord), consumer society (or the "société de consommation"), the "bureaucratic society of controlled consumption" (Henri Lefebvre), or "postindustrial society" (Daniel Bell).

In the Preface to the English translation, Jameson notes how Lyotard's text was also, among other things, "a thinly veiled polemic against Jürgen Habermas' concept of a 'legitimation crisis' and vision of a 'noisefree' transparent, fully communicational society" (Jameson 1984a: vii). He further observes that *The Postmodern Condition* is, above all, a critique of Enlightenment metanarratives—*grand récits*—which in virtue of their alleged totality, universality, and absolutist status are rendered ahistorical, as though their formation took place outside of history and of social practice. Lyotard questions the dogmatic basis of these metanarratives, and exposes their "terroristic" and violent nature, by which they assert certain "Truths" from the perspective of one discourse, by silencing or excluding statements from another.

Lyotard (1984a: xxiii) uses the term "postmodern" to describe "the condition of knowledge in the most highly developed societies." Postmodernity "designates the state of our culture following the transformations which, since the end of the nineteenth century, have altered the game rules for science, literature, and the arts." Indeed, these transformations have altered the very game rules for the field, practices, and institutions of education which are responsible for producing and transmitting those of science, literature, and the arts. Most fundamentally, the game rules for the discourse of legitimation have been altered, raising a key theme of *The Postmodern Condition* bearing centrally on education.

Legitimation discourse is contextualized within the crisis of narratives. This, in turn, becomes the fulcrum for distinguishing the "modern" from the "postmodern."

> I will use the term *modern* to designate any science that legitimates itself with reference to a metadiscourse. . . making an explicit appeal to some grand narrative, such as the dialectics of the Spirit, the hermeneutics of meaning, the emancipation of the rational or working subject, or the creation of wealth (Lyotard 1984a: xxiii).

PETERS AND LANKSHEAR

From this stance Lyotard defines "postmodern" elliptically, as "incredulity toward metanarratives." The rule of consensus, which governed the Enlightenment narratives and constructed truth as a product of agreement between rational minds, has, from this standpoint, been finally rent asunder. The narrative function has been dispersed into many language elements, each with its own pragmatic valencies. We are left only with "language particles," a heterogeneity of language games. There is no neutral ground upon which to adjudicate between competing claims, no synthesizing master discourse which can reproduce the speculative unity of knowledge. The linguistic turn of twentieth-century philosophy and the social sciences does not permit the assumption of a metalinguistic neutrality or foundational epistemological privilege.

Lyotard invokes the plurality of language-games to advance an attack on the conceptions of universal reason, the unity of language, and the unified subject. There is no one reason, he argues, only *reasons*, where no one form of reason takes precedence over others. Whereas Habermas (and Critical Theory) emphasizes the bifurcation of reason into its instrumental (positivistic) and moral-practical forms, Lyotard (following Wittgenstein) and Foucault emphasizes the (postmodern) multiplicity and proliferation of forms of reason, defined by the rules of particular discourses or language-games. Each of the various types of utterance—denotative, prescriptive, performative etc.—comprises a language-game, with its own body of rules. The rules are irreducible and an incommensurability exists among different games.

Employing Wittgenstein's concept of "language-games" as a procedural method, Lyotard aims to demonstrate how the metanarrative legitimation function has been broken down and dispersed into heterogeneous language elements comprising incommensurable modes of discourse, each with its own irreducible set of rules. In a creative misappropriation of Wittgenstein, Lyotard develops a general conception of language as an agonistics, where "to speak is to fight." This conception is elevated as a model for understanding society in general. In true Wittgensteinian fashion, Lyotard argues that the rules do not have a bedrock justification. Nor do they carry with them their own legitimation.

The problem of legitimation of knowledge and education is inseparable from an analysis of capitalism. In "A Svelte Appendix to the Postmodern Question," Lyotard argues that capitalism "is one of the names of modernity." In a vein highly reminiscent of *The Postmodern Condition*, he adds that

> capitalism has been able to subordinate to itself the infinite desire for knowledge that animates the sciences, and to submit its achievements to its own criterion of technicity: the rule of performance that requires the endless optimalization of the cost/benefit (input/output) ratio. (Lyotard 1993: 25)

He speaks of the "penetration of capitalism into language," and "the transformation of language into a productive commodity" which reduces phrases to encoded messages with an exchange value—information which can be stored, retrieved, packaged, calculated, and transmitted. Lyotard acknowledges his debt to Marx, framing his analysis within the ambit of commodification (albeit a *representational* commodity system): in effect, the Marxian analysis of commodity fetishism as it applies to knowledge and education. He further recognizes the way in which the logic of performance, aimed at maximizing the overall efficiency of the system, generates socio-economic contradictions.

Lyotard, however, parts company with Marxists on the possibility of emancipation or salvation emerging inevitably from these contradictions. He eschews what Bill Readings (1993: xxiv) calls the "politics of redemption" based upon "the Marxist desire to identify alienation as a reversible ideological distortion." Instead, Lyotard wants to rethink politics and resistance in "minoritarian" terms—foregoing an authoritative reading of events based on determinate judgments—to respect the differend, and "to think justice in relation to conflict and difference" that admit of no resolution. For Lyotard, "our role as thinkers" in the situation of postmodernity "is to deepen what language there is, to critique the shallow notion of information, to reveal an irremediable opacity within language itself" (van Reijen and Veerman 1988: 302). He argues that so far as it is concerned with "the cultural," the real political task facing us is to "carry forward the resistance that writing offers to established thought, to what has already been done, to what everyone thinks, to what is well-known, to what is widely recognized, to what is "readable", to everything which can change its form and make itself acceptable to opinion in general" (ibid.). In other words, the issue for Lyotard is one of understanding and providing a critique of capitalist forms of insinuating will into reason, and the way this is manifest primarily in language.

He addresses this concern in *The Postmodern Condition* in relation to the performativity principle. This reduces difference, ignores the differend, and treats all language games as commensurable, and the whole as determinable. The logic of performance, of optimizing the system's overall performance, based on the criterion of efficiency, does violence to the heterogeneity of language games and "necessarily involves a certain level of terror: be operational (that is, commensurable) or disappear" (Lyotard 1984: xxiv). The notion of performance—with its criterion of efficiency—is *technological*. It cannot provide us with a rule for judging what is true or just or beautiful. Here, then, is a trenchant critique of capitalism, its penetration of language, and the way thought is managed, packaged, and commodified in the new postmodern technologies, insofar as they express the most recent application of capitalist rules to language.

This critique returns to the central question of legitimation of knowledge and education. If the Enlightenment idealist and humanist metanarratives have become bankrupt and must be abandoned or renounced by the State and the Corporation, wherein can legitimacy reside? Lyotard's critique of

11

capitalism suggests that the State has found its only credible goal in power. Science and education are to be legitmated, de facto through the principle of performativity: that is, through the logic of maximizing the system's performance, which becomes self-legitimating in Luhmann's sense.

Historically, *The Postmodern Condition* challenges the two great Hegelian metanarratives underlying the philosophical tradition to which Habermas belongs: namely, the emancipation of humanity and the speculative unity of knowledge. Indirectly, Lyotard's assault is against the concept of "totality" and the notion of autonomy which underwrites the sovereign subject. His argument seemingly confronts Habermas' notion of a rational society modelled on communicational processes, where so-called validity claims immanent in ordinary conversation can be redeemed at the level of discourse. In this vision and realm of a "transparent" communicational society, moral and practical claims are seen to be resolved rationally and consensually without distortion or coercion. Claims are said to be resolved through the force of pure argumentation alone. For Lyotard, this conception represents the latest, perhaps last, attempt to build a "totalizing" philosophy: it is an attempt which depends on driving together in an original way the two Hegelian metanarratives, which are themselves under suspicion. By invoking a quasi-transcendentalism and ideal of consensus, the "totalizing," emancipatory vision of a "transparent" communication society is "terroristic" and exclusory.

Habermas responds to Lyotard's charges by focusing on the alleged conservatism of the poststructuralist position. His initial response was delivered as a lecture in 1980 (Habermas 1981). "Modernity versus Postmodernity" is deliberately framed within an exhaustive binary opposition which is the hallmark of classical reason. Habermas identifies himself as the defender of "the project of modernity" against the "anti-modern" sentiments of a line of French "poststructuralist" philosophers "running from Bataille to Derrida by way of Foucault." He compares their critique of reason to the views of the "Young Conservatives" of the Weimar Republic, and talks of learning from "the mistakes of . . . extravagant programs which have tried to negate modernity." (1981: 12)

According to Richard Rorty (1985: 161), the dispute between Lyotard and Habermas goes deep.

> From Lyotard's point of view, Habermas is offering one more meta-narrative, a more general and abstract "narrative of emancipation" from the Freudian and Marxian meta-narratives. For Habermas, the problem posed by incredulity towards meta-narratives is that unmasking only makes sense if we "preserve at least one standard for (the) explanation of the corruption of *all* reasonable standards." If we have no such standard, one which escapes a "totalizing self-referential critique," then distinctions between the naked and the masked, or between theory and ideology, lose their force.

From Habermas' standpoint, to accept Lyotard's argument would be to strip ideology critique of its principal function. Unless there is a universal metadiscourse the possibility of legitimizing validity claims in a theoretical manner disappears. For Lyotard, however, the very opposite seems to be the case. Universal metadiscourses cannot effect a closure: practically and empirically they betray their own ahistoricism in the experiences of recent contemporary history (e.g. the Gulags, Auschwitz, May 1968).

In the light of recent debate (White 1988), it appears that what is at stake is *not* the idea of a universal metanarrative but, rather, whether it is possible within philosophy to ground or redeem validity claims. Habermas (1990: 128) believes there is a "mutual exclusivity of the various types of discourse or standards of rationality" amongst the spheres of the moral, aesthetic and scientific, that we can translate from one discourse to another, and that through the medium of intersubjective communication it is possible to legitimize validity claims. Lyotard, by contrast, is sceptical of the unity presupposed by Habermas' pragmatic solution. He does not think that it is possible to ground validity claims in a generalizable way given the incommensurability of types of discourse.

At an early point in the debate Lyotard (1986: 72) tries to determine the kind of unity Habermas is seeking : is it a sociocultural unity or a synthesis of heterogeneous language games? He comments:

> The first hypothesis, of a Hegelian inspiration, does not challenge the notion of a dialectically totalizing *experience*; the second is closer to the spirit of Kant's *Critique of Judgement*; but must be submitted, like the *Critique*, to that severe reexamination which postmodernity imposes on the thought of the enlightenment, on the idea of a unitary end of history and of a subject (ibid.: 73).

Lyotard's question here is at one with Foucault's interpretation of Kant. To seek to define the internal teleology of time and the direction in which the history of humanity is moving is, according to Foucault (1984), an essentially *modern* preoccupation: in Kant's sense of "modern."

We are given a clue to Foucault's position in a reading of a crucial but minor text of Kant. Foucault (1984: 21) asks: "What, then, is the event that is called the *Aufklärung* and that has determined, at least in part, what we are, what we think, and what we do today?" [Kant's original question, *Was ist Aufklärung?*, was posed in terms of the difference "today" introduces with respect to "yesterday."] In an ironic inversion, posing the question "what is modern philosophy?," Foucault answers: "Perhaps we could respond with an echo: modern philosophy is the philosophy that is attempting to answer the question raised so imprudently two centuries ago: Was ist Aufklärung? ". Foucault claims that Kant defines "Enlightenment" in a negative way, as the process that releases us from the status of immaturity. Enlightenment, then, is the moment we come of age in the use of reason, when there is no longer the need to subject ourselves to forms of traditional authority. The notion of critique is also required at exactly this point, for its role is that of defining the conditions under which the use of reason is legitimate in order to determine what can be known, what must be done, and what may be hoped.

This reading of Kant's text allows Foucault to characterize modernity as an attitude rather than an epoch (or a style) and to assert that the thread connecting us to the Enlightenment is not "faithfulness to doctrinal elements, but rather the permanent reactivation of an attitude—that is, of a philosophical ethos that could be described as a permanent critique of our historical era" (Foucault 1984: 42). Postmodernity may also be defined as an attitude—Lyotard's "incredulity towards metanarratives." Defining it in this way, contrary to Habermas' reconstituted epistemological position, does not imply that "postmodernity" necessarily comes after modernity: it may mean not modernity at its end but in the nascent state, which is constant (Lyotard 1984: 79).

POSTMODERNISM, ARCHITECTURE AND THE ARTS

Unlike Lyotard, most commentators locate the inception of postmodernism in the post-war period, beginning in the late 1950s. In a kind of parody, Charles Jencks suggests that modernism ended on 15 July 1972 at 3.32 pm: allegedly the moment that the modernist Minouru Yamasaki's Pruitt-Igoe housing project was demolished. He describes the connection between Modernist architecture and modernization as "tragic", and proffers the view that

> The Post-Modern Movement was then, and remains today, a wider social protest against modernization, against the destruction of local culture by the combined forces of rationalization, bureaucracy, large-scale development and, it is true, the Modern International Style (Jencks, 1987: 29).

For Paolo Portoghesi, the opposition between modern and postmodern architecture consists in a break with the hegemony of Euclidean geometry. Victorio Grigotti, another Italian architect, sees the advent of postmodernism in terms of the demise of all relationship between the architectural project and socio-historical progress in realizing human emancipation on a large scale. Lyotard (1989: 7) captures Grigotti's view thus:

> Postmodern architecture is condemned to generate a multiplicity of small transformations in the space it inherits, and to give up the project of a last rebuilding of the whole space occupied by humanity . . . there is no longer a horizon of universalization, of general emancipation before the eyes . . . of the postmodern architect. The disappearance of this idea of progress within rationality and freedom would explain a certain tone, style or modus which are specific to postmodern architecture.

14

Kenneth Frampton (1985) proposes a critical culture of architecture which, without rejecting entirely the thrust of modernization, nonetheless resists being totally consumed by it. Frampton calls this culture a "critical regionalism" and characterizes it in terms of six points of resistance: culture and civilization, "to become modern and yet to return to sources" (Ricoeur); the transformation of the avant-garde, emphasizing the possibility for what he calls "an anti-phallocentric, anti-Eurocentric reflective culture"; development versus place-forms, that is the creation of local, public places to set against the "increasingly privatised universal reality of the megalopolis"; culture versus nature, "inscribing the built work into the ground," "the regional inflection of buildings" in terms of climate, light, etc.; the mediation of the visual by the tactile.

Perhaps the most comprehensive assessment of postmodern architecture is offered by Heinrich Klotz (1988: 421), who lists the following defining characteristics:

1. Regionalism has replaced internationalism.
2. Fictional representation . . . has supplanted geometric abstraction.
3. The tendency toward fictional representation has led away from the late-modern tendency to view a building exclusively in terms of function, and toward seeing it as a *work of art of building* that belongs in the realm of the illusory.
4. Postmodernism relies not on the symbolic value of the machine and of construction as defining progress in architecture, but on a *multiplicity of meanings*. . .
5. Poetry has supplanted technological utopianism. Postmodernism draws from the world of the imagination rather than from the "brave new world" mentality in which velocity is equated with progress.
6. Postmodernism opposes the sterile faith in the continuous improvement of instruments and construction with *improvization* and *spontaneity*. Instead of striving for untouchable perfection, it favours the disturbed and the imperfect, which are now seen as signs of life.
7. Whereas modernism sought to free itself from history and made architecture purely a thing of the present, with postmodernism we have regained *memory*. And rather than exploit history for "interesting" effects, we can now entrust ourselves to the spirit of irony.
8. Rather than view a building as an autonomous, universally valid geometric form, we can now allow it to be relativized by its historical, regional, and topological conditions, and can appreciate the palpable individuality of the particular solution. Heroism gives way to compromise, to equitable treatment of old and new, and to respect for the given environment.
9. Instead of a dominant style, with its tendency to become dogma, a broad range of vocabularies and stylistic languages exist alongside one

15

another. Postmodernism denies the self-referential inventiveness of the Modern Movement and pays tribute to the pluralism of referential allusions.

10. Rather than identify architecture with life, postmodernism establishes anew the aesthetic distance from life. Fiction as well as function!

Critics like Jencks (1987: 12) want to distinguish subtle changes in the shape and meaning of postmodernism from other events (Pop Art, the counter-culture, feminism) which occurred around the same time, and to talk of the emergence of a Post-Modern movement in architecture at least during the mid-1970s. Jencks (1987: 13) traces the early lineage of the term "Post-Modern" as follows:

> its first cousin *postmodernismo* was referred to in 1934 by Frederico De Onis in his *Antologia de la poesia española e hispanoamericana* as a "minor reaction of modernism already latent within it," a usage that was picked up by Dudley Fitts in his *Anthology of Contemporary Latin-American Poetry,* 1942.

In the 1960s, during what Jencks calls its first cultural stage, postmodernism was a nascent blend of ad hoc protest and counter-culture: firmly anti-establishment, and defined against an orthodoxy of modernism. It was informed by specific forces: the anti-Vietnam war and student movements (the uprisings at Berkeley in 1962; the Paris revolution in 1968), the growth of postwar youth subcultures fuelled by folk and rock music, the ethnic revitalization of Black "ghetto" culture and the Civil Rights movement, the feminist movement, the Pop Art and counter-culture movements.

The postmodern situation is perhaps best characterized by new social and political conflicts involving outsider groups: women, the incarcerated, the "deviant", patients of all sorts (Wellbery, 1985: 231). To this list we can add: ethnic minorities in postcolonial contexts (Blacks and Hispanics in the US, Maori in Aotearoa, West Indians in Britain, Aborigines in Australia, and Black and "Coloured" majorities in South Africa), the gay peoples' movements, and Third World peoples in neocolonial contexts. Wellbery (1985: 231) indicates that the "environmentalist movement conforms to this paradigm as well since it is carried on in the name of an excluded 'other' (nature)." He draws on Foucault's insights to define these conflicts in terms of two characteristics. First, they question the status of the individual—asserting the right to be different against the threat of forces working to atomize social life. Second, they define themselves in opposition to forms of domination linked to the "power/knowledge" of liberal discourses. Third, they are all concerned with redefinitions of identity.

In art and literary theory the term has been used with increasing frequency to indicate a completely distinctive aesthetic, philosophical and political program. More simply, postmodernism is a fundamental questioning of the idea of history as progress, of history as the progress of reason. Dmitry Khanin (1991: 246), asks in a rhetorical question: "What is at stake after all in the current controversy over postmodernism if not the idea of progress?" He prefaces his remark with the following comment:

> Modernism can be formulated as simply this: it is the conviction that what is new is better than what is old just because it is a product of a later stage of development. What underlies this view is a particular conception of history as an evolving process whose further phases necessarily supersede the previous ones in every possible respect, using them as a platform for new breakthroughs. The debate of the ancients and the moderns in seventeenth-century France . . . might be taken as a watershed between the medieval type of consciousness which rested on the maxim, the older the better (the older being closer to the sacred truths of revelation) and the modern one, assured of the superiority of the present as more sophisticated and refined than what came before.

Postmodernism, then, is a questioning of the modern assumption that what is new is better; it is a questioning of the past as an ordered, linear and cumulative development which represents Western civilization as the apex of this process of cultural evolution. Leonard Meyer (1967: 98) addresses this notion directly in talking about developments in Western art which, since the first World War, has seen an end to the preceding 500 years of ordered, sequential change. We have now entered "a period of stylistic stasis, a period characterized not by a linear, cumulative development of a single style, but the co-existence of a multiplicity of quite different styles in a fluctuating and dynamic steady state."

Postmodernism, specifically in the arts and especially in architecture, is often described as a movement against modernism. Jencks (1987: 18) asserts that it was not

> until 1971 and Ihab Hassan's essay "POSTmodernISM: A Pancritical Bibliography" that the movement was actually christened and a pedigree provided even though the term, like its inconsistent capitalization, wasn't clearly defined.

One critic describes the American postmodern canon in terms of the novels of John Barth, Donald Barthelme, Robert Coover, Kurt Vonnegut, William Gass, Stanley Elkin, Thomas Pynchon (Stevick, 1985: 150). Another critic, taking the example of postmodern American fiction, with mock seriousness identifies November 22, 1963 (the day John Kennedy died) as the day postmodernism was officially inaugurated—"since that day was the day that symbolically signaled the end of a certain kind of optimism and naivete in our collective consciousness, the end of certain verities and assurances that had helped shape our notion of what fiction should be" (McCaffery, 1986: xii). McCaffery construes postmodernism by reference to the works of Thomas Pynchon, John Barth, Vladimir Nabokov, Robert Coover, William Gass, and

Richard Brautigan as a movement against modernist realistic fiction—which he links with the epistemological assurance and optimism of Western empiricism and rationalism. American postmodern fiction, by contrast, experiments with subjectivity, turned inward to the world of language and dream, to challenge the realist convention of a unified subject living in a world of stable essences. These experiments shared

> a general sense that fiction needed to acknowledge its own artificial, constructed nature, to focus the reader's attention on how the work was being articulated rather than merely on what was happening. Distrustful of all claims to truth and hypersensitive to the view that reality and objectivity were not givens but social or linguistic constructs, postmodern writers tended to lay bare the artifice of their work, to comment on the processes involved, to refuse to create the realist illusion that the work mimics operations outside itself (McCaffery, 1986: xxi).

Against this kind of backdrop, Trachtenberg (1985: 3) argues that the term "postmodern" suggests "a comparison with an era whose conventions no longer command general assent as a way of understanding an experience and making its values accessible." In postmodern literature, he adds, few novels describe the progress of a hero, leading to summary insights; "structure is assembled, additive rather than developed"; the "determining principle is adjacency"; "narrative movement is lateral rather than progressive." Here the autonomous subject of modernism is decentered and narrative modes more clearly embody the equivalence of collage and montage (from the visual arts) than they do the progressive unfolding of rationality or the subject's quest to give meaning to his/her life project. For example, Pynchon's novels "dramatize the difficulty of holding the self together in a world without meaning or coherent patterns, in which the search for patterns and connections turns back on itself in tightening solipsistic circles" (Lasch, 1985: 155). Postmodernism describes a "sensibility, a feeling for innovation, for experiment with conventional ways of framing experience." It is "performative rather than revelatory, superficial rather than imminent, aleatory rather than systematic, dispersed rather than focused . . ., fabulist rather than realist." In the postmodern novel, self-consciousness "is not concerned with its own artifice but with questioning its own premises" (Trachtenberg, 1985: 4–7).

Drawing on Huyssen's (1986) account, Hutcheon claims that "postmodern fiction has come to contest the modernist ideology of artistic autonomy, individual expression, and the deliberate separation of art from mass culture and everyday life" (1989: 15). The collapse of the modernist distinction between mass culture and "high art" is represented in the bronzed beer cans of Jasper Johns, the comic strip frames of Roy Lichtenstein and Andy Warhol's Coca Cola bottles—all of which parody consumer objects, in a similar way to that in which the novels of Manuel Puig and Carlos Fuentes transform the "vulgar" Hollywood images and objects of consumer-oriented mass culture into art.

18

It is interesting to note here that much recent Latin American literature has been seen in postmodern terms: the "canon" comprising works by Carlos Fuentes, Mario Vargas Llosa, Manuel Puig, Guillermo Cabrera Infante, Julio Cortazar and, not least, Jorge Luis Borges. MacAdam and Schiminovich (1985) argue that these Latin American writers became Western trendsetters by parodying European models. This parody, they claim, is more an inversion rather than a rejection of Western culture—"a declaration of cultural independence."

POSTMODERNISM AND THE MOVE TO CULTURE

The new problematics, the emergent outlines of which can be discerned in a variety of methodologies and approaches across the disciplines, operates on the basis of a radical decentering that denies an epistemic or historical privilege to either the traditional Cartesian notion of a "centered," transparent, individual subjectivity or the humanist ideal of a rational, autonomous and responsible self. These developments are clearly related to shifts in the centrality of both notions of language and culture in social science theorizing in recent years.

In sociology, for example, Mike Featherstone (1989: 148) has noted the way in which an interest in culture up until the mid-1970s was "considered eccentric, dilettantish, and, at best, marginal." He charts the huge rise of journals in the English-speaking world concerned with theorizations of culture, indicating how "feminism, Marxism, structuralism, poststructuralism semiology, critical theory, and psychoanalysis also helped to raise the profile of cultural questions."

More precisely, Eisenstadt (1989: 6) has detected a shift within recent sociological analysis away from conceiving "culture" as "fully structured according to clear principles, embedded in the very nature of the human mind, which, through the medium of a series of codes, regulate human behaviour." The emergent conception emphasizes, in a hermeneutical manner, the symbolic and expressive dimensions. Both structuralist-functionist and symbolic-expressive conceptions are motivated by underlying theories of language, giving the "cultural" a greater importance in social theory than was previously the case. The shift itself from strictly structuralist accounts (based, historically, on the work of Saussure and others) to interpretivist, symbolic and hermeneutical models, is directly related to developments in the theory of language: in particular, those developments attributable to the work of Saussure, Heidegger, Gadamer and Wittgenstein, among others.

Most recently, the growth of interest in poststructuralism, deconstruction and postmodernism, also motivated by changing conceptions and theories of language, have helped to push questions of cultural (and aesthetic) interest to centre stage (Featherstone, 1989:150).

It is clear that these developments across a range of disciplines immediately

19

focus on the interrelated concepts of language and culture. Certain views in philosophy of language, dating historically from different traditions—viz., those of Nietzsche, Heidegger, Wittgenstein and Saussure—have provided an orientation towards a more anthropologically differentiated notion of culture in the first instance which emphasizes at one and the same time its "linguisticality," historicity, dependence on a "politics of representation," and its role in socially constituting new inter-subjectivities.

In addition, these views of language and of representation have been used as grounds for a series of hypotheses drawing on semiological insights and understandings, concerning the emergence of a systemic "global culture." Within this, local differences and knowledges are increasingly submerged in the endless torrent of a global consumerism, circulated more effectively than at any time in the past by technological advances in telecommunications and world media, and finding its way into even the most remote corners of the earth.

In a strong sense it seems pointless to argue for a more differentiated notion of culture over a notion which, under the form of late capitalism, is driven by the market imperative to ever more global dimensions. These notions are probably best seen as competing tendencies and counter-tendencies within the culture of advanced industrialism or late capitalism, reflecting the ambiguous nature of postmodernism. To that extent these forces of homogeneity and difference—of rationalization and modernization on the one hand and cultural difference and diversity on the other—represent the continuation of historical tendencies already evident within modernity and modernism.

Linda Hutcheon (1989: 27), strongly influenced by poststructuralist developments, has indicated how representation "can no longer be considered a politically neutral and innocent activity." She depicts "culture" as the *effect* of representations (as opposed to their *source*), claiming that the primary agenda of postmodernism is "the investigation of the social and ideological production of meaning." Under the influence of new developments in semiotics, structuralist Marxism, feminism, psychoanalytic theory, and poststructuralism, traditional concerns with language as an innocent representing activity have given way to an interest in the production and reproduction of *meanings* more generally, which are seen to be embodied, and situated socially and economically. Hence, the politics of postmodern representation is concerned with "the ideological values and interests that inform any representation" (Hutcheon 1989: 7).

In this respect it is interesting to view Jean Baudrillard's work and its dramatic effect on cultural studies in the English-speaking world as a reworking of earlier themes of the politico-philosophical tradition of situationalism. Collins (1987: 3) indicates that by the late 1960s Guy Debord and Raoul Vaneigem had each

20

PETERS AND LANKSHEAR

elaborated a theory of the decline of "organic" social relations in contemporary Western culture brought about by the development of a particularly concentrated form of advanced capitalism which in turn resulted in an intensification of cultural commodification and a resultant "society of the spectacle."

The early work of Baudrillard is exemplary here. In the essay "Political Economy of the Sign" (1981: 147), he builds on a line of reasoning developed in *La Société de Consommation* (1970) where "consumption" is construed as an active labor involving the manipulation of signs. Baudrillard writes:

> Today consumption—if this term has a meaning other than that given it by vulgar economics—defines precisely *the stage where the commodity is immediately produced as a sign, as sign value, and where signs (culture) are produced as commodities.*

In this early text Baudrillard clearly has made use of Saussurean insights to interpret consumer society as a semiological system of signs where commodities, differentially related to each other, comprise a signifying system and the consumer consumes not the object itself, but the whole system. As Levin (1981: 5) notes, "it is this very condition of semiosis, engendered by the universalization of commodity relations, which privatizes experience in the first place. As we 'consume' the code, in effect, we 'reproduce' the system." Baudrillard's interpretation brings into focus the relations of "language" and "culture" since consumer society is understood in terms of a linguistic system. It also reminds us of its theoretical debt to Saussurean linguistics, which first problematized referential theories of meaning. On the model of structural linguistics, semiology taught us to regard meanings not in terms of relations between language and the world but rather as a differential system where nothing is regarded as meaningful in and of itself but only as it differs from other elements in the system.

Andrew Ross (1988: vii), surveying a collection of essays devoted to examining the politics of postmodernism, notes that for some theorists a politics of difference and a politics of the local and particular "are not only symptoms of, but also essential strategies for coping with a postmodernist culture that advertises itself as decentered, transnational, and pluralistic . . ." He sees postmodernism as "a belated response to the vanguardist innovations of high modernism . . . the continuation of modernism by other means" (ix). From a related standpoint, Chantal Mouffe (1988) describes the reformulation of the socialist project attempted in an earlier work (Laclau and Mouffe 1985), and indicates how such a project demands a nonessentialist epistemological perspective. Whilst acknowledging the role that the epistemological perspective of the Enlightenment played in the emergence of democracy, theorists like Laclau and Mouffe see it as now an obstacle to understanding the new form of politics characteristic of our times. According to Mouffe, an appropriate understanding calls for using "the theoretical tools established by different

21

currents of what can be called *the postmodern in philosophy* and of appropriating their critique of rationalism and subjectivism" (Mouffe, 1988:33. Our emphasis). By "the postmodern in philosophy," Mouffe clearly means poststructuralism, the philosophy of language of the later Wittgenstein and post-Heideggerian hermeneutics.

> To be capable of thinking politics today, and understanding the nature of these new struggles and the diversity of social relations that the democratic revolution has yet to encompass, it is indispensable to develop a theory of the subject as a decentered, detotalized agent, a subject constructed at the point of intersection of a multiplicity of subject-positions between which there exists no a priori or necessary relation . . . (Mouffe, 1988: 35).

This reappraisal represents, of course, a revision of the characteristically Marxist concepts of class and class struggle. To a large degree these notions were important in helping to inspire and to formulate the philosophies of feminism and de-colonialization, in elevating them to *universal* concerns. With the continued growth and fragmentation of the new social movements, which have taken place largely outside organized class interests and institutions, traditional Marxist notions have increasingly appeared reductionistic. The emergence of social and cultural difference seemingly cannot be captured theoretically or explained adequately in terms of simple "class interests." In one sense this juncture represents a conceptual shift from "class" to a more anthropologically differentiated notion of "culture." This, of course, is not to deny the importance of Marxism itself in influencing the "cultural turn." One has only to think here of the seminal works of Raymond Williams or E.P. Thompson, and their combined effect in devising new approaches to the study of cultural history and helping to initiate and delineate cultural studies as a field of legitimate academic interest (see Johnson: 1986).

Indeed, it was Raymond Williams who first took a "democratic" approach to the definition of culture and emphasized the modern diversity of cultural experience in which "working-class culture" could no longer be denied its own existence. In a later work Williams (1983: 87–93) maps the range and overlap of meanings of the word "culture": its early use as a noun of process; its metaphorical extension to human development until the late eighteenth century; and its status as an independent noun for an abstract process which marks the history of its use in modern times. His analysis is comprehensive. Williams maintains that the use of "culture" in French and German as a synonym for "civilization" underwent a marked change of use in the work of Herder, who challenged the assumption of (a) universal history which pictured "civilization" or "culture" as a unilinear process "leading to the high and dominant point" of eighteen century European culture. This was first and foremost a reassertion of the idea of the *Volksgeist*—an emphasis on national and traditional cultures—which later became the basis for attacking the ab-

stract rationalism and "inhumanity" of emerging industrial "civilization." After Herder, it became possible to speak of "cultures" in the plural: "the specific and variable cultures of nations and periods, but also the specific and variable cultures of social and economic groups within a nation" (Williams 1983:
89). The dominant sense of the word as it prevails in modern social science is
to be traced first to Klemm's "decisive innovation" and, subsequently, to Ty-
lor's usage.

In addition to these uses, Williams (1983: 90–91) also identifies a third and
relatively late use of "culture" as an "independent and abstract noun which
describes the works and practices of intellectual and especially artistic activity." He indicates that the opposition between the "material" and the "spiritual" that bedevilled its earlier usage, is repeated later in the disciplines. Archaeology and cultural anthropology refer to *material* production, whereas history
and cultural studies make reference, rather, to signifying or *symbolic* systems. In
Williams' view, this confuses and conceals the central question of the relations
between "material" and "symbolic" production, which he develops in providing a socialist theory of culture (1981).

Williams' observations are important, not only for their theoretical contributions, but also because they offer a standpoint for recognising the complexity of actual usage, the problems which arise from the conflation of different
senses, and the way in which the history of the word "culture" is still active,
still in the making. Thus, he notes the coining of *culchah* (a class mime-word),
and *culture-vulture* (American), as signs of hostility to the notion when it has
been used as a basis for making claims to superior knowledge, refinement and
"high" art. At the same time he indicates how this hostility has diminished as
the sociological and anthropological uses of the term (eg. in *subculture*) have
been steadily extended.

Many additions can be preferred to these specifically modern developments: e.g., "the cultural industry" (Max Horkheimer and Theodor Adorno);
"mass culture" (Irving Howe); "consumer culture"; "the culture of narcissism"
(Christopher Lasch); and even more recently "information culture," "popular
culture," and most recently, "global culture." These terms variously attempt to
describe culture in its ambiguous relationship to late capitalism or advanced
industrial society. In a word these epithets attempt to characterize what we
will call "postmodernism": a word, incidentally, to which Williams (1989: 48)
himself, takes exception. He regards postmodernism as "a strictly ideological
compound from an enemy formation." He is not alone in taking this position. As noted above, in his now classic formulation, Jameson (1983) theorizes
postmodernism as the cultural logic of late capitalism. Significantly, however,
he leaves open the possibility that it may have the double capacity to also resist that logic.

Hal Foster (1985) was, perhaps, the first to name this ambiguity by an-
nouncing a "postmodernism of reaction" and its antithesis in a "postmod-

23

PETERS AND LANKSHEAR

ernism of resistance." Others like Hutcheon (1989: 21) have followed him, emphasizing the complicity of postmodernism with late capitalism while, at the same time, seeking an agenda for resistance. As already indicated, they recognize that since the advent of "postmodernism" representation can "no longer be considered a politically and theoretically innocent activity."

Jameson (1989a; 1989b; 1990) has seen cause to modify the starkness and purity of his original position. He recommends that his ideas be understood "as an attempt to theorise the specific logic of the cultural reproduction of [the] third stage of capitalism" named by Mandel, and not as "yet another disembodied cultural critique." He calls for "the renewal of historical analysis itself," and confronts the paradox of asserting a totalizing, unified theory of differentiation by challenging the levels of abstraction: "a system that constitutively produces differences remains a system" (Jameson, 1989a: 34). The logic of capital, he insists, is "a dispersive and atomistic, 'individualistic' one" which, contradictorily, stems from its own systemic structure. That is, "the very concept of differentiation . . . is itself a systemic one" (ibid, 35). Even so, he argues, the mode of production is not a "total system" in the forboding sense alluded to by Foucault and Weber. Rather, it

> includes a variety of counterforces and new tendencies within itself, of "residual" as well as "emergent" forces, which it must attempt to manage or control (Gramsci's conception of hegemony): were those heterogeneous forces not endowed with an effectivity of their own, the hegemonic project would be unnecessary (ibid).

24

Jameson argues that in the current transitional period, during which earlier economic forms are being restructured on a global scale, a new international proletariat will eventually emerge. This hints at a pluralism which admits of a distinctively postmodern politics of resistance. Elsewhere (Jameson, 1989b: 11), he claims that the idea of a cultural dominant does not exclude forms of resistance, and emphasizes that postmodernism has both positive and negative factors: the democratization of culture "cannot be altogether bad"; "even heterogeneity is a positive thing." For Jameson the point is that "many of these seemingly negative features can be looked at positively if they are seen historically" (1989b: 13). He stresses the fact that "these developments have to be confronted as a historical situation rather than as something to be morally deplored or simply celebrated" (ibid: 12), elaborating his analysis in an interview with Stuart Hall (Jameson 1990: 28). Within a "relatively anonymous systemic culture," says Jameson, it becomes "problematic to talk about ruling classes in the old way." One sign of postmodernism as a "tendentially complete modernization" is the "plebianization of culture":

> the way in which much larger sections of the public now consume culture on a regular basis and live within culture in ways that they didn't have the occasion to

do before. That's a crucial part of post-modernism, which underscores its ambiguity. One cannot object to the democratization of culture, but one must object to other features of it. These mixed feelings have to be preserved in any analysis of the postmodern (Jameson, 1990:29).

It seems that the notion of "class culture" becomes less applicable in new circumstances emphasizing a systemicity. Rather, looked at from the outside, from the perspective of the non-West, the old term "cultural imperialism" seems to be more relevant. In this sense the real object is *North American culture* as an expression of corporate capitalism "which is exported and implanted by way of media technology." The crucial point is that such "consumer culture" is now more systemic, more regulated and rationalized, than ever before. Cultural production has reached a stage where reflexive, critical distance from it is both less obvious and less possible. Even oppositional and critical forms have become fully enmeshed or integrated into the system of cultural production, to the point where there is no public space left for critical reflection on the system or its relation to the economic and political systems. Stuart Hall advances the central problem neatly. The question, says Hall, is

> whether what is going on in the postmodern is simply a dominant system producing marked differentiation as part of its own logic of domination: or whether there really has been a shift, representing the power of the marginalised or subordinated cultures and people to make what you called, earlier, a real difference (Hall 1990: 30).

If it is the case that the system is producing its own differentiation "then the 'logic of history' in a classical marxist sense is still operating, while going through one of its many epochal changes." If, on the other hand, the second scenario holds, these changes may in fact represent the suspension of the "logic of history" and the end of the metanarrative of classical Marxism.

Certainly Jameson (1990: 30) is clear on its being a political "plus" that subgroups and subcultures have been able to attain "a certain collective existence that they didn't have before." At the same time, however, he observes how these developments fit into "a kind of cultural commodification on the part of the industries that now have a new submarket and produce new things for it." He is pessimistic about a purely cultural politics, agreeing with Hall that the sense of totality, collective action and solidarity has been undermined by the new logic of "difference." Nevertheless, he is adamant that the new phase of global capitalism also carries with it a new class logic which "has not yet completely emerged because labor has not yet reconstituted itself on a global scale" (Jameson 1990: 31).

Others have recognized the tension (contradiction?) between forces of cultural homogenization and those of cultural heterogenization within "the

25

PETERS AND LANKSHEAR

global cultural economy" (Appadurai, 1990). In this context some theorists have stressed "a postmodernism of resistance." Featherstone (1990: 2), for one, adopts a positive and optimistic reading of postmodernism. He writes:

> Postmodernism is both a symptom and a powerful cultural image of the swing away from the conceptualization of global culture less in terms of alleged homogenising processes (theories which present cultural imperialism, Americanization and mass consumer culture as a proto-universal culture riding on the back of Western economic and political domination) and more in terms of the diversity, variety and richness of popular and local discourses, codes and practices which resist play-back systemicity and order. (ibid)

This implies that sociology must develop new modes of investigation which render problematic conceptions of society tied exclusively to the bounded nation-state, as well as assumptions inherent in models of rationalization, modernization and industrialization. "In effect," says Featherstone (1990: 3), "the assumption is that we have moved beyond the logic of the universal "iron cage" nationalization process." He advocates discarding the binary logic which seeks to understand culture in terms of mutually exclusive opposites: homogeneity/heterogeneity, integration/disintegration, unity/diversity.

Anthony Smith (1990) fleshes out further the argument proceeding from analyses of late capitalism and/or postindustrialism. He suggests that the main thrust of such analyses is to signal a move away from small-scale community towards a world of cultural imperialism which is technical and elitist in terms of its cultural base, promoted "from above," with little popular or public participation.

> A global culture, so the argument runs, will be eclectic like its Western or European progenitor, but will wear a uniformly streamlined packaging. Standardized, commercialized mass commodities will nevertheless draw for their content upon revivals of traditional, folk or national motifs and styles in fashion, furnishings, music and the arts, lifted out of their original contexts and anaesthetized. So that a global culture would operate at several levels simultaneously: as a cornucopia of standardized commodities, as a patchwork of denationalized ethnic or folk motifs, as a series of generalized "human values and interests," as a uniform "scientific" discourse of meaning, and finally as the interdependent system of communications which forms the material base for all other components and levels (Smith, 1990: 176).

Smith adds that today's emerging global culture is contextless, in the sense that it is tied to no place or period. It is likewise timeless, in that it is cut off from any past. Despite these claims, he nonetheless contends that the project of a global culture (as opposed to global communications) is somewhat premature. Collective identity is always historically specific and dependent upon shared memories and a sense of continuity between generations. He believes national cultures, "inspired by rediscovered ethno-histories, [will] continue to divide our world into discrete cultural blocks, which show little sign of harmonization, let alone amalgamation" (Smith 1990: 183).

While mindful of world cultural diversity and the power of unifying systems of non-Western national symbols, Smith may underplay the influence of market forces in global terms. Various studies (c.f., Sennett, Lasch, Richards and Rustin) have examined the process of identity formation in the West and, particularly, the way in which young people now grow up in the market rather than at home. Richards (1984: 134), for instance, writes:

> Finding one's identity means establishing oneself in a particular niche in the world of commodities; it means putting together, from the available elements, *an idiosyncratic style of consumption.* Selfhood is thus increasingly dependent on consumption and less so on secure intrapsychic identification with other persons (our emphasis).

Michael Rustin (1989: 121) plots parallels between postmodern thought and the evolution of post-Kleinian ideas. He suggests that the undermining of transcendental certainties is partly a cultural concomitant of consumer society: "a way of rationalising (and celebrating) the experience of an overload of meanings, cut off from their integral location in historical time and social space." He claims that identity is fragmented by "the multiplicity of choices," as well as being depleted in its sense of depth by "discontinuities"—that is, by the apparently "untenable and provincial quality of any definite cultural affiliation."

The observations of people like Richards and Rustin enrich our understanding of how young people growing up as *first generation* heirs to global telecommunications, and to an emerging global consumer culture, rapidly take on the characteristic behaviours of consumers, defining themselves in terms of the styles of clothing, food, music, and the host of available products in the market. This applies as much to young people from more "traditional" cultures as it does to white bourgeois and "working-class" youth—especially those living in modern metropolises which function as large but segmented niche markets for consumer products.

Sometimes the process is more one of fusion than fission. From here it is possible to gain insight into the incipient global processes. The fact that television "family sit-coms" in Latin America are delivered in Spanish, or that the "cult of celebrity" in Hong Kong movie-making ventures revolves around indigenous "stars" does not weaken the point of argument: the recipes, the format and the logic of the production of culture are the same. We must keep in mind the extent to which Western mass culture emphasizes global forms of postmodernism. The same popular television appears on screens all over the world.

27

PETERS AND LANKSHEAR

American "postmodern" television programs include include early starters like *Miami Vice, Moonlighting, The Max Headroom Show,* and *L.A. Law* (Grossberg, 1987: 8). To these we can add others, like *The Simpsons,* and more recent arrivals, including *Ren and Stimpy, Beavis and Butthead* and *Wayne's World*—not to mention the entire *MTV* phenomenon. UK programs include *Edge of Darkness, The Singing Detective* and *Rock Follies* (Hayward and Kerr, 1987:7), with latter day additions including *The Young Ones* and *Sticky Moments,* among others. Sit-coms and soaps emanating from Latin American producers in Mexico, Venezuela, and Brazil join forces with *The Simpsons* and reach deep into impoverished peasant neighbourhoods in countries as poor as Nicaragua.

In this context, Collins (1987: 26) reminds us that "the postmodern redefinition of mass culture does not necessitate an open acceptance of all popular texts or the end of 'dedicability of effect.'" The exercise and vigilance of aesthetic and ideological judgment are required at precisely those points where the products of an imported mass consumer culture threaten to overwhelm a local indigenous culture, in a way that displaces, substitutes local "authentic" images, and rides rough-shod over questions of self-definition and identity.

Arjun Appadurai (1990) speaks of "homogenization" arguments emanating from "the left end of the spectrum of media studies." These, he says, "subspeciate" into an argument about Americanization or about commodification; very often the two are closely linked. These arguments—including, specifically, Jameson's original essay—are problematic since they ignore the ways "metropolitan forces" are indigenized.

28

> [F]or the people of Irian Java, Indonesianization may be more worrisome than Americanization, as Japanization may be for Koreans, Indianization for Sri Lankans, Vietnamization for the Cambodians, Russianization for the people of Soviet Armenia and the Baltic Republics (Appadurai 1990: 295).

Appadurai (1990: 296) argues that the new global cultural economy cannot be understood in terms of existing center-periphery models, or even in terms of models postulating multiple centers and peripheries. Rather, it must be understood "as a complex, overlapping, disjunctive order," with "fundamental disjunctures" between the economic, cultural and political spheres. Appadurai characterizes his own work as an attempt to restructure the Marxist narrative in this way, taking care to avoid

> the dangers of obliterating difference within the "third world," of eliding the social referent . . . and of retaining the narrative authority of the Marxist tradition, in favour of greater attention to global fragmentation, uncertainty and difference (1990: 308).

To this end he advances a fruitful "elementary framework" for exploring such disjunctures. This employs relationships between five dimensions of

PETERS AND LANKSHEAR

global cultural "flows": namely, ethnoscapes; mediascapes; technoscapes; financapes and ideoscapes. Ethnoscapes are produced by flows of *people* including tourists, immigrants, refugees and exiles. Mediascapes involve flows of *images and ideas* in terms of telecommunications, magazines, films and newspapers. Technoscapes are *plant and machinery flows* through the conduits of multinational and national corporations as well as government organizations. Finanscapes refer to flows of money in the stock exchanges and currency markets. Ideoscapes are "linked to flows of images which are associated with state or counter-state movement ideologies . . . comprised of elements of the Western Enlightenment worldview—images of democracy, freedom, rights, welfare . . ." (Featherstone 1990: 5).

By means of such an analysis, Appadurai stresses the role of imagination as a social practice in the global cultural process. He consciously draws together the old idea of images (as mechanical reproduction, from the Frankfurt school), with the notion of the "imagined community" (in Benedict Anderson's sense), and with the French "structuralist" idea of the "imaginary," as a constructed landscape of collective aspirations. The complexity of the current global economy hypothesized in terms of fundamental disjunctures (between the economic, the political and the cultural) comprises an area "we have barely begun to theorize." (Appadurai, 1990: 296) Nonetheless, the contours along which it will be theorized in the near future are reasonably clear.

Having traced in general theoretical ways some key developments in recent attempts to theorize "culture" we should note that they have impacted strongly on educational inquiry. There is now a vast literature in education which refers explicitly to "cultural studies." Indeed, educational theorists were instrumental in launching British cultural studies, especially in its second generation, where the work of Paul Willis and Angela McRobbie was prominent. From a different perspective, the work of Pierre Bourdieu and Claude Passeron has had a profound impact on educational research and, in particular, sociology of education. The recent influence of poststructuralism is making its influence felt in education, providing a distinctively new perspective on cultural questions, especially when it comes to questions of language and representation.

Cultural studies in education necessarily takes account of what might broadly be called "indigenous theory." It is diverse in that it draws on a number of theoretical strands. These include the early work in the sociology of education of Michael Young, focused on questions of knowledge and control; Paulo Freire's writings on critical literacy and empowerment; the "philosophy of decolonization" based around Aimé Césaire, Frantz Fanon and, more recently, theorists like Edward Said and Homi Bhabha who set the contemporary agenda for the contested fields of the "neocolonial" and the "postcolonial." This work has a distinctive practical focus centering on struggle for control over indigenous knowledge, and its praxis is defined by the project of indigenous schooling movements. Within this general project, which embodies a commitment to indigenous epistemologies, concepts, values and practices, we find numerous other elements concerning critical literacy and the schooling of indigenous children, and the contesting of colonial histories.

The work of feminist educationists provides a further and particularly influential example of key assumptions and constructs of "cultural studies" finding embodiment in critical ethnographies of gender differences in the area of cultural reproduction. Feminist theory and approaches are diverse, and include neo-Marxist and "poststructuralist" variants drawing on intellectual work by feminist scholars of many stripes. At a more "orthodox" level new approaches in the established tradition of political sociology of education centered around education policy and the state have adopted aspects of a cultural studies perspective, combining insights from poststructuralism and psychoanalysis.

Lawrence Grossberg (1993: 89) suggests that cultural studies "encompasses a set of approaches that attempt to understand and intervene into the relations of culture and power." He identifies three commitments of cultural studies as an emerging critical practice. First, reality is made through human action and, consequently, contestation is a basic category. Second, the "popular" is regarded as the "terrain on which people live and political struggle must be carried out in the contemporary world" (ibid: 90). Finally, cultural studies is committed to a radical contextualism which means that cultural practices cannot be reduced to or simply treated as texts. Grossberg argues that to engage the politics of culture in current times involves "placing particular practices into particular relations or contexts, and . . . transforming one set of relations, one context, into another" (ibid). This is the kind of work we attempt in the chapters which follow, where we theorize a range of situated contemporary cultural practices and productions around the theme of counternarratives of official culture.

COUNTERNARRATIVES OF OFFICIAL CULTURE: THE PLAN OF THE BOOK

The distinctively postmodern stance of *incredulity* evident in global responses to metanarratives infects contemporary politics surrounding "official" cultural productions generally. These politics are often played out on more "localized" and "contingent" terrain than the transcendent, universalist, ahistoric turf of metanarratives. Having explored at length the larger theoretically prior sense of "counternarratives" identified above, and situated it broadly within the complex currents of postmodernism as theories and lived experiences, we turn in subsequent chapters to specific examples of postmodern counternarratives in the second, derivative and more highly contextualized sense: a sense we understand in richer and deeper ways in light of the larger and prior sense of the term.

In Chapter 2, ("Is there a Place for Cultural Studies in Colleges of Education?") Henry Giroux explores the potential of cultural studies as a political and ethical project grounded in understanding and addressing pressing challenges of "the contemporary." As a praxis of theory and practice, cultural studies provides opportunities for teachers to confront the dominant official narrative of classroom education. According to this official view, teaching is an ideologically and institutionally innocent engagement, and pedagogy can essentially be reduced to possessing a set of neutral skills and tools. As counternarrative, cultural studies informs the pursuit of a transformative pedagogies which reject technocratic rationality in general and technicist conceptions of teaching and learning in particular—searching, instead, for practices which enact democratic uses of knowledge, texts and cultural productions. These proceed from assumptions that traditional disciplinary demarcations simply cannot account for contemporary diversity; that learning must provide opportunities for students to cross different public spaces to experience forms of practical politics and active citizenship, and to address issues at the intersections of language, work, social responsibility, cultural production and identity formation; that learning must enable students to understand political, economic and cultural forces, so that they can act on them with effect rather than merely be victims of them.

Giroux pushes deeper into this terrain in Chapter 3, "Slacking Off: Border Youth and Postmodern Education." He develops in critical fashion the relationship between postmodern discourses and the promise of pedagogy with respect to "border youth." The counternarration in this chapter is complex. At one level we are introduced to a sample of "little (postmodern) narratives of border youth," as framed against official narratives of how young people are/ought to be. At a second level the chapter comprises a counternarrative to those intellectuals who refuse to recognize the potential inherent in postmodern discourses for grasping experiences of contemporary youth, and for appreciating the rapidly escalating diversity associated with decline of traditional authority, economic uncertainty, the proliferation of electronically mediated technologies, and the extension of consumer pedagogy to all aspects of youth culture. Third, postmodernism as *theory* makes available elements of an oppositional discourse for understanding and responding to cultural and educational shifts impacting on youth in North America and elsewhere. Finally, postmodernism—whether in the form of counternarratives of border youth, or of postmodern discourses as more or less systematic theories of "new times"—must be interrogated and brought into productive dialogue with other narratives, such as progressive elements of "critical modernism." In the final analysis, Chapter 3 presents a counternarrative of pedagogy as critical cultural practice which draws on progressive aspects of extant narratives and critiques their counterproductive tendencies, in pursuit of narratives of democratic pedagogy in opposition to official normalizing conceptions and practices of "instruction and measurement."

31

Chapters 4 and 5 build on the groundwork laid out by Giroux in the previous chapters. In Chapter 4, ("Media Knowledges, Warrior Citizenry, and Postmodern Literacies") Peter McLaren and Rhonda Hammer mine some of the now-extensive cultural studies literature to develop a transdisciplinary framework for analyzing media literacies and, particularly, for analyzing television spectacles created by the news media. While the specific case at issue here is the Gulf War and the theme of globalized and localized violence, the analysis is timely in the fallout after the nine month O.J. Simpson trial as "TV Spectacular." The argument in Chapter 4 complements some of Giroux's insights in his analysis of films dealing with the predicaments of postmodern "border youth" inhabiting slacker culture—living in liminal spaces between the modern world of certainty and order and the postmodern world of hybridized identities. The authors share Giroux's concern with the ways (new) technologies service capital, as they effectively appropriate difference for the expressed purpose of mobilizing the desires and dreams of youth and creating dream economies of affective investment. "Media Knowledges" narrates opposition to characteristically current forms and practices of violence. It counters "official" media narratives of violence, exemplified by CNN's media production of the war against Iraq (the "Gulf War") and its valorization of viewers as "phallomilitary warrior citizens." The chapter also articulates an oppositional discourse to narratives that objectively do violence to people in their everyday lives: for example, the relations and practices of (late) capitalism which effectively produce violence (and counter violence) as seemingly meaningful responses to the conditions of everyday life experienced by marginalized persons; and the signifying practices of mass communication media which are heralding an age of unprecedented painful loss of everyday history and shared popular memory. The authors further weave into the thread of the argument a more localized and poignant counter statement to violence as actual flesh and blood "narrated lives", and critique a well-intentioned but ultimately unsuccessful "anti-violence narrative": arguing that it lacks the necessary analytic, theoretical and therapeutic depth to meet the challenge of "monumentalized violence" within the US which it seeks to address. McLaren and Hammer's substantive contribution is a counternarrative of critical media literacy in pursuit of a democratic and emancipatory social vision. Their resounding message is that the present historical conjuncture desperately needs a pedagogy that is "not simply a condition of the heart" but also "an exercise of historical will [which is] tempered by forms of critical social theory and informed by a praxis of hope." In this they follow Giroux's lead in attempting to rethink uncertainty and indeterminacy in ways informed by projects of social justice. The argument also resonates with themes addressed in the final chapter where possibilities for critical literacy are projected into cyberspace.

Chapter 5, by Peter McLaren, takes up the theme of "Liberatory Politics and Higher Education" from a Freirean perspective. It moves the book back into the contested arena of the university, linking with Giroux's earlier concern for aspects of curriculum and pedagogy within colleges of education. McLaren maintains the focus on critical literacy developed in Chapter 4. This time, however, the argument develops its pedagogical praxis at the level of the university. It is a praxis grounded in Freirean perspectives, but which is deepened and extended through a dialogue with North American critical theorists like bell hooks, Cornell West, and Sande Cohen. The chapter asks: Can such a Freirean pedagogy, linked to progressive political change in the direction of socialism, be viable in the context of the hegemonic articulations that surround North American university teaching? Reading Freire against the grain, the chapter aims to sketch a tentative framework for ideological intervention into the practice of university teaching as it relates to the role of the educator as a cultural worker. The educator is conceptualized as a decentering, displacing, and transforming force in a project aimed at pursuing social justice: not only in the classroom, but also at the level of the larger society in which the educator finds herself. The argument spells out a pedagogical praxis that goes beyond merely unsettling the imperializing discourses of received ("official") pedagogical traditions and their discursive embeddedness and forms of ideological address. It suggests ways in which pedagogy can be conceptualized as a way of life: in Freirean terms, as a way of critically reading both word and world. McLaren argues that in a climate of global economic shift to the market, and the triumph of neoliberalism in political life and neoconservatism in (higher) education, Freire's work needs to be directed toward deeper understandings of the strategic and tactical relationships between the role of hegemony in the formation of public intellectuals and the function of academe itself in the context of wider social and political formations. McLaren maintains a dynamic interconnection of "worlds" and "cultures" throughout the chapter: notably, those of the North American and Latin American academies, minorities within and without the respective academies, and the contending interests and forces that are mobilized and engaged by "initiatives" like California's Proposition 187. Drawing extensively on the work of scholars from diverse backgrounds, held together thematically by their broad commitment to a project "premised on the construction of an emancipatory cultural imaginary," McLaren explores ways in which Freirean perspectives can help deepen the debate over the role of the university in contemporary North American culture. Framed as it is within a global perspective, the Freirean counternarrative developed here also helps situate the struggle of Latin American educators within the concerns of postmodern, post-colonial and insurgent criticisms of the academy.

A book concerned with postmodern counternarratives would be incomplete if it did not deal with computer and electronically mediated communications, which are close to the very heart of postmodernity as lived experience. In the final chapter, "Critical Pedagogy in Cyberspace," Colin Lankshear, Michael Peters, and Michele Knobel address possibilities for reshaping the project of critical pedagogy in ways that take account of digital texts and electronically mediated communications within various sites available on the Internet and other networks which, collectively, make up "cyberspace." They define a range of contemporary concepts and themes—e.g., "enclosures of the text," "decoupling body and Subject"—and investigate the nature of information, knowledge, and understanding within "cyber contexts" which radically refigure subjectivities and social relations. Besides treating pedagogy in the context of cyberspace, the argument makes links to earlier chapters dealing with modern media—particularly, new "high tech" elements of youth culture ("Slacking Off") and representations of global media events like the Gulf War. The chapter addresses the theme of counternarratives at two levels. In its various forms, critical pedagogy has always emerged as a counternarrative against official methods of instruction and ways of approaching texts: particularly, technicist approaches, whether behaviorist, cognitivist, therapeutic, or whatever. To date, however, the generic project of critical pedagogy has drawn very largely on available critical traditions in ways that are characteristically modernist. The argument essays a "double counternarrative" by moving beyond both official narratives of pedagogy and characteristically modernist accounts of critical pedagogy. Furthermore, there exists a predominant technological narrative which purveys a distinctively North American optimism and hype about possibilities inherent in new communications technologies. This is reflected in the ways terms like "cyberspace," "hypermedia," and "hypertext" have become self-referential, and have already spawned a legacy of magical faith in technological quick fixes and the inevitability of educational progress contingent upon wiring teaching and learning to high technology "gadgets." The early result of this reification has been to largely domesticate computer mediated communications, by incorporating them as an integral part of the American Dream. This, of course, is educationally disastrous in times when official media constructions of events like the Gulf War present concrete instances of how selecting and editing images may produce a simulated foreign policy success by employing a typically modernist strategy of "totalizing" and "demonizing" an entire country and its culture(s) in order to negate this Other. A critical pedagogy in cyberspace would begin to deconstruct such official accounts by making use of a vast range of resources and facilities available on and via "the Net." The authors advance a conceptual and methodological framework for developing such a pedagogy.

NOTES

1. See here Peters, M. (1993), Postmodernism, language and culture, *Access* 12, 1 & 2, pp. 1–16, and Intellectuals, poststructuralism and postmodern culture, in his *Poststructuralism, Politics and Education,* New York: Bergin and Garvey (forthcoming).

Hudson (1989) considers a series of characterizations of postmodernism as: a myth; a periodization; a condition or situation; an experience; an historical consciousness; a sensibility; a climate; a crisis; an episteme; a discourse; a poetics; a retreat; a topos; a task or project. He argues that in most cases accounts of postmodernism fail to observe clearly the differences between the post-modern, modernism-postmodernism, and modernity-postmodernity distinctions, and do not alert us to the basis and the importance of such distinctions. These differences should be respected, although current usage tends to collapse them. This is signified in the use of "postmodernism" and "postmodern theory," which tends to reflect, linguistically, a changing assessment of postmodernism.

2. Journals include: *New Literary History* 3, 1 (1971); *Tri Quarterly* 26, 30, 32, 33 (1973, 1974, 1975); *Modern Literature* 3 (1974); *Drama Review* 19, 1 (1975); *New German Critique* 22, 33 (1981, 1984); *Salmagundi* 63 (1985); *Cuadernos del Norte* 8, 42 (1987); *Genre* 20, 3 & 4 (1987); *Cultural Critique* 5 (1987); *Screen* 28, 2 (1987); *Theory, Culture and Society* 2, 3 and 5, 2 & 3 (1985, 1988). See Connor (1989) for a bibliography up to the late 1980s.

3. Wellbery (1985: 232) emphasizes the lecture was a "politico-symbolic ceremony involving homage to an honoured father figure (Adorno) and celebration of the continuity and vitality of *'a tradition of thought'*" (our emphasis). He further claims that French poststructuralist thought problematizes Habermas' ideal of a transparent communication, where immanent discursive validity claims are redeemable at the level of discourse—in the realm of pure argumentation. For their part, against Habermas' view, the French poststructuralists "investigate the opacities inherent in speech itself", and hold that "consensus can only be established on the basis of acts of exclusion" (ibid). Wellbery does not consider, however, the way in which Lyotard's *La Condition Postmoderne* (1979)—published a year before Habermas' lecture—was an attack on Habermas' concept of a "legitimation crisis" and vision of a "noisefree," transparent, fully communicational society.

4. This transformation may be conceptualized in terms of the play of a series of forces and resistances: for example, the homogenizing forces of late consumer capitalism which threatens to replace a genuine cultural diversity with a uniform consumer hyper-reality, on the one hand, as against the defensive resistances of the heterogeneous new social movements and the struggles of ethnic groups, under philosophies of decolonialization, to consolidate or seek for new identities. This is evident within the realm of social theory in debates between celebrants of the new order—e.g., the technological optimists of post-industrial society—and those who emphasize the darker side of such developments. Hal Foster (1985), among the first to recognize this ambivalence, distinguishes a "postmodernism of reaction" from a "postmodernism of resistance." Might it be that this reaction and resistance expresses by other means a continuation and final exhaustion of the *modern* age—the legacy of the struggle between high modernism and its counter-culture?

5. It is interesting here that in spite of the lesson deconstruction teaches—to deconstruct implicit hierarchies or binary oppositions which privilege one term over another—much of the literature of postmodernism remains framed in terms of binary oppositions. This is surely the case with Habermas' (1981) essay, "Modernism versus Postmodernism."

REFERENCES

Adorno, Theodor and Max Horkheimer. (1972). *Dialectic of Enlightenment*. New York: Seabury Press.

Appadurai, A. (1990). Disjuncture and Difference in the Global Culture Economy. *Theory, Culture and Society*, 7, 2–3, June, 295–310.

Baudrillard, Jean. (1970). *La Société de Consommation*. Paris: Gallimard.

Baudrillard, Jean. (1981). *For a Critique of the Political Economy of the Sign*. St. Louis: Telos Press.

Bertens, Hans. (1986). The Postmodern *Weltanschauung* and its Relation with Modernism: An Introductory Survey. In D. Fokkema and H Bertens (eds.), *Approaching Postmodernism*. Amsterdam, John Benjamins.

Bürger, Peter. (1985). The Decline of the Modern Age. *Telos*, 62:117–130.

Collins, James. (1987). Postmodernism and Cultural Practice: Defining the Parameters, *Screen*, 28(2):11– 26.

Conner, Steven. (1989). *Postmodernist Culture: An Introduction to Theories of the Contemporary*. Oxford: Blackwell.

Eisenstadt, S. (1989). Introduction: Culture and Social Structure in Recent Sociological Analysis. In H. Haferkamp (ed.) *Social Structure and Culture*. Berlin & New York: de Gruyter.

Featherstone, Mike. (1989). Towards a Sociology of Postmodern Culture. In H. Haferkamp (ed.) *Social Structure and Culture*. Berlin & New York: de Gruyter.

Featherstone, Mike. (1990). Global Culture: An Introduction. *Theory, Culture and Society* 7, 2–3, June, 1–14.

Flax, Jane. (1990). Post-modernism and Gender Relations in Feminist Theory. In L. Nicholson (ed.) *Post-modernism/Feminism*. London: Routledge: 39–62.

Foster, Hal. (1985). Postmodernism: A Preface. In H. Foster (ed.), *Postmodern Culture*. London: Pluto Press.

Foucault, Michel. (1984). What is Enlightenment? In P. Rabinow (ed.) *Foucault Reader*. New York: Pantheon.

Frampton, K. (1985). Towards a critical regionalism: Six points for an architecture of resistance. In H. Foster (ed.) *Postmodern Culture*. London: Pluto Press.

Frankel, Boris. (1987). *Post-Industrial Utopians*. Cambridge: Polity Press/Blackwell.

Fraser, Nancy. (1981). Foucault on Modern Power: Empirical Insights and Normative Confusions. *Praxis International* 1: 272–87.

Fraser, Nancy. (1983). Foucault's Body-Language: A Post-Humanist Political Rhetoric?. *Salmagundi* 61: 55–70.

Grossberg, Lawrence. (1993). Can Cultural Studies Find True Happiness in Communication? *Journal of Communication* 43, 4, Autumn, 89–97.

Habermas, Jürgen. (1971). *Knowledge and Human Interests*, trans. J. Shapiro, Boston: Beacon Press.

Habermas, Jürgen. (1981). Modernity Versus Postmodernity. *New German Critique* 22, 3–22.

Habermas, Jürgen. (1987a). *The Philosophical Discourse of Modernity*, trans. F. Lawrence. Cambridge, Mass.: the MIT Press.

Habermas, Jürgen. (1990). Remarks on the Discussion. *Theory, Culture and Society* 7: 127–132.

Hall, Stuart. (1990). Clinging to the Wreckage: A Conversation. *Marxism Today* September, 28–31.

Harvey, David. (1989). *The Condition of Postmodernity: An Enquiry into the Origins of Cultural Change*. Oxford, Blackwell.

Hassan, Ihab. (1971). POSTmodernISM: A Pancritical Bibliography. *New Literary History* 3(1):5–30.

Hayward Philip and Paul Kerr. (1987). Introduction to issue on postmodernism. *Screen* 28, (2): 2–10.

Howe, Irving. (1959). Mass Society and Postmodern Fiction. *Partisan Review* 26:430–36.

Hudson, Wayne. (1989). Postmodernity and Contemporary Social Thought. In P. Cassman (ed.) *Politics and Social Theory*. London, Routledge and Kegan Paul.

Hutcheon, Linda. (1989). *The Politics of Postmodernism*. London & New York: Routledge.

Huyssen, Andreas. (1986). *After the Great Divide: Modernism, Mass Culture, Postmodernism*. Bloomington, Ind.: Indiana University Press.

Jameson, Fredric. (1983). Postmodernism or the Cultural Logic of Late Capitalism. *New Ldft Review* 146:53–93.

Jameson, Fredric. (1984a). Foreword. In J-F. Lyotard, *The Postmodern Condition*, Minneapolis: University of Minnesota Press.

Jameson, Fredric. (1984b). The Politics of Theory: Ideological Positions in the Postmodernism Debate. *New German Critique* 33:53–66.

Jameson, Fredric. (1985). Postmodernism and Consumer Society. In H. Foster (ed.) *Postmodern Culture*. London & Sydney: Pluto Press, 111–125.

Jameson, Fredric. (1989a). Marxism and Postmodernism. *New Left Review* 176, 31–43.

Jameson, Fredric. (1989b). Regarding Postmodernism: A Conversation with Frederic Jameson, by Anders Stephanson. In A. Ross (ed.) *Universal Abandon?: The Politics of Postmodernism*. Edinburgh: Edinburgh University Press.

Jameson, Fredric. (1990). Clinging to the Wreckage: A Conversation. *Marxism Today* September, 28–31.

Jencks, Charles. (1987). *Post-Modernism: The New Classicism in Art and Architecture*. London, Academy Editions.

Johnson, R. (1986). The Story So Far: and Further Transformations. In D. Punter (ed.) *Introduction to Contemporary Cultural Studies*. Harlow: Longman, 277–313.

Klotz, H. (1988). *History of Postmodern Architecture*, trans. Radka Donnell. Cambridge, MA: MIT Press.

Kumar, Krishan. (1978). *Prophecy and Progress*. Harmondsworth: Penguin.

Laclau, Ernesto. & Mouffe, Chantal. (1985). *Hegemony and Socialist Strategy: Towards a Radical Democratic Politics*. London: Verso.

Lasch, Christopher. (1985). *The Minimal Self: Psychic Survival in Troubled Times*. London, Picador.

Lash, Scott with Roy Boyne. (1990). Communicative Rationality and Desire. In S. Lash, *Sociology of Postmodernism*, London: Routledge.

Levin, C. (1981). Translator's Introduction. In J. Baudrillard, *For a Critique of the Political Economy of the Sign*. St. Louis: Telos Press, 5–28.

Levin, Harry. (1966). What Was Modernism? In: *Refractions.* New York, Oxford University Press.

Lovibond, Sabina. (1989). Feminism and Postmodernism. *New Left Review* 178: 5–28.

Lyotard, Jean-François. (1984). *The Postmodern Condition: A Report on Knowledge,* trans. G. Bennington & B. Massumi. Manchester: Manchester University Press.

Lyotard, Jean-François. (1989) Defining the postmodern. In Lisa Appignanesi (ed.) *Postmodernism: ICA Documents,* London, Free Association Books: 7–10.

Lyotard, Jean-François. (1993). A Svelte Appendix to the Postmodern Question. In *Political Writings,* trans. Bill Readings and Kevin Paul Geiman, Foreword by Bill Readings. Minneapolis: University of Minnesota Press.

MacAdam, Alfred and Flora Schiminovich. (1985). Latin American Literature in the Postmodern Era. In: S. Trachtenberg (ed.) *The Postmodern Moment.* Westport and London, Greenwood Press: 251–262.

McCaffery, Larry ed. (1986). *Postmodern Fiction: A Bio-Bibliographical Guide.* New York and London: Greenwood Press.

Mandel, E. (1975). *Late Capitalism,* trans. Joris de Bres. London: Humanities Press.

Mascia-Lees, Frances, Patricia Sharpe and Colleen Cohen. (1989). The Postmodern Turn in Anthropology: Cautions From a Feminist Perspective. *Signs: Journal of Women in Culture and Society* 15, (1): 7–33.

Meyer, L. (1967). *Music, the Arts and Ideas: Patterns and Predictions in Twentieth-Century Culture.* Chicago: Chicago University Press.

Mouffe, Chantal. (1988). Radical democracy: Modern or postmodern? In A. Ross (ed.) *Universal Abandon? The Politics of Postmodernism.* Minneapolis: University of Minnesota Press.

Nicholson, Linda ed. (1990). *Post-Modernism/Feminism.* London: Routledge.

Portoghesi, Paolo. (1982). *After Modern Architecture,* New York: Rizzoli.

Poster, Mark. (1981). The future according to Foucault: The archaeology of knowledge and intellectual history. In D. Lacapra and S. Kaplan (eds.) *Modern European Intellectual History: The Appraisal and New Perpectives,* Ithaca, NY: Cornell University Press: 137–52.

Raulet, Gérard. (1983). Structuralism and Post-Structuralism: An Interview with Michel Foucault. *Telos,* 53:119–206.

Readings, Bill. (1993). Foreword: The end of the political. In: *Political Writings,* trans. Bill Readings and Kevin Paul Geiman, Foreword by Bill Readings. Minneapolis: University of Minnesota Press:xiii-xxvi.

Richards, Barry. (1984). Schizoid states and the market. In B. Richards (ed.), *Capitalism and Infancy.* London: Free Association Press, 122–166.

Rorty, Richard. (1985). Habermas and Lyotard on Postmodernity. In R. Bernstein (ed.) *Habermas and Modernity,* Cambridge: Polity Press.

Ross, Andrew. (1988). Introduction. In A. Ross (ed.) *Universal Abandon? The Politics of Postmodernism.* Minneapolis. University of Minnesota Press, vii–xviii.

Rustin, Michael. (1989). Post-Kleinian Psychoanalysis and the Postmodern. *New Left Review* 173, 109–126.

Ryan, Michael. (1988). Postmodern politics. *Theory, Culture and Society* 5:559–576.

Slemon, Stephen. (1989). Modernism's Last Post. *Ariel* 20(4):3–17.

Smith, Anthony. (1990). Towards a Global Culture. *Theory, Culture and Society* 7, 2–3, June: 171–192.

Stephanson, A. (1989). Regarding Postmodernism: A Conversation with Fredric Jameson. In A. Ross, *Universal Abandon? The Politics of Postmodernism*. Edinburgh: Edinburgh University Press.

Sugimoto, Yoshio. (1990). A Post-Modern Japan? *Arena* 91:48–59.

Trachtenberg, Stanley. (1985). Introduction. In his (ed.) *The Postmodern Moment: A Handbook of Contemporary Innovation in the Arts*. Westport, Connecticut; London, Greenwood Press.

van Reijen, Willem. (1990). Philosophical-political polytheism: Habermas versus Lyotard. *Theory, Culture and Society* 7: 95–103.

van Reijen, Willem and Veerman, Dick. (1988). An interview with Jean-François Lyotard. *Theory, Culture and Society* 5 : 302.

Wellbery, David. (1985). Postmodernism in Europe: On Recent German Writing. In S. Trachtenberg (ed.) *The Postmodern Moment*, London, Greenwood Press: 229–250.

White, Stephen. (1988). *The Recent Work of Jürgen Habermas: Reason, Justice and Modernity*, Cambridge: Cambridge University Press.

Williams, Raymond. (1981). *Culture*. London: Fontana.

Williams, Raymond. (1983). *Keywords: A Vocabulary of Culture and Society*. London: Fontana.

Williams, Raymond. (1989). When Was Modernism?. *New Left Review* 175.

Wittgenstein, Ludwig. (1953). *Philosophical Investigations*. Oxford: Blackwell.

39

IS THERE A PLACE FOR CULTURAL STUDIES IN COLLEGES OF EDUCATION?[1]

Henry A. Giroux

chapter 2

INTRODUCTION

SINCE THE late 1980s cultural studies has become something of a boom industry. Book stores scurry to set up cultural studies displays housing the growing lists of texts now being published under its theoretical banner. Within universities and colleges, cultural studies programs are appearing with growing frequency in both traditional disciplinary departments and new interdisciplinary units. Large crowds are attending cultural studies symposia at academic conferences. Moreover, as its locus of activity has shifted from England to Australia, Canada, Africa, Latin America and the United States, cultural studies has emerged as one of the few fields to have travelled across multiple borders and spaces loosely uniting diverse intellectuals who are challenging conventional understandings of the relationship between culture, power, and politics. Far from residing in the margins of a specialized discourse, cultural studies has more recently attracted the interests of both the popular media and established press.

Given the lavish attention cultural studies has received, many critics have dismissed it as simply another academic fashion. More serious criticism has focused on its eurocentric tendencies, its narrow academic presence, and what some have called its political fuzziness. I believe that in spite of its popularity and the danger of commodification and appropriation that haunts its growing influence and appeal, cultural studies is a field that holds enormous promise for progressives who are willing to address some of the fundamental dilemmas of our times. The promise of cultural studies will, however, depend on more than just the relevance of the challenges, contexts, and problems it addresses. It will depend also in part on the willingness of cultural studies practitioners to enter into its interdisciplinary discourses less as a journey into sacred theoretical ground than as ongoing critical interrogation of its own formation and practice as a political and ethical project. This raises as many questions for those who practice cultural studies as it does for educators who might be interested in applying its insights to educational theory and practice, especially with respect to reforming colleges of education.

Given the popularity of cultural studies for a growing number of scholars, I have often wondered why so few academics have incorporated cultural studies into the language of educational reform, particularly as it applies to colleges and schools of education. In part, this indifference may be explained by the narrow technocratic models that dominate mainstream reform efforts and structure many education programs. Other considerations would include a history of educational reform overly indebted to practical considerations that often support a long tradition of anti-intellectualism. Within such a tradition, management issues become more important than understanding and furthering schools as democratic public spheres. Hence, the regulation, certification, and standardization of teacher behavior is emphasized over creating conditions for teachers to undertake the sensitive political and ethical roles they might assume as public intellectuals educating students for responsible, critical citizenship. Moreover, the dominant tradition favors containing and assimilating cultural differences rather than treating students as bearers of diverse social memories with a right to speak and represent themselves in the quest for learning and self-determination. While other disciplines have appropriated, engaged, and produced new theoretical languages in keeping with changing historical conditions, colleges of education have maintained a deep suspicion of theory and intellectual dialogue.[2]

Cultural studies is largely concerned with the relationship among culture, knowledge and power. Consequently, it is not surprising that mainstream educators rarely engage it except to dismiss it as another theoretical fashion. The refusal on the part of such educators can partly be understood against their claim to being professional, scientific, and objective.

In opposition to this alleged "view from nowhere," cultural studies challenges the alleged ideological and institutional innocence of mainstream edu-

42

GIROUX

cators by arguing that teachers always work and speak within historically and socially constructed relations of power. Shaped in the intersection between social and cultural reproduction, on the one hand, and the disruptions produced through competing, resisting, and unsettling practices and discourses on the other, education is an ongoing site of struggle and contestation. As institutions actively engaged in forms of moral and social regulation, schools presuppose fixed notions of cultural and national identity. As educators who act as agents in the production, circulation, and use of particular forms of cultural and symbolic capital, teachers occupy an inescapable political role.[3]

By virtue of its refusal to decouple the dynamics of politics and power from schooling, cultural studies is often charged with being "too ideological," or else is simply ignored on account of its criticisms regarding how education generates a privileged narrative space for some students and a space that fosters inequality and subordination for others. Embodying dominant forms of cultural capital, schooling often functions to affirm the eurocentric, patriarchal histories, social identities, and cultural experiences of middle-class students while either marginalizing or erasing the voices, experiences, and cultural memories of so-called "minority" students. For many students, schooling means either experiencing daily forms of classroom interaction that are irrelevant to their lives, or else bearing the harsh reality of discrimination and oppression expressed through tracking, policing, harassment, and expulsion.[4]

Traditionally, schools and colleges of education in the United States have been organized around either conventional subject based studies (i.e., math education) or disciplinary/administrative categories (curriculum and instruction). Within this type of intellectual division of labor, students generally have few opportunities to study larger social issues through multidisciplinary perspectives. This slavish adherence to structuring the curriculum around disciplines is at odds with the field of cultural studies whose theoretical energies are largely focused on issues regarding gender, class, sexuality, national identity, colonialism, race, ethnicity, cultural popularism, textuality, and critical pedagogy.[5] The considerable resistance to cultural studies may also be due to the fact that it reasserts the importance of comprehending schooling as a mechanism of politics embedded in relations of power, negotiation, and contestation.[6] By enabling educators to construct and access a critical language through which to examine the ideological and political interests that structure conservative reform efforts such as nationalized testing, standardized curriculum, and efficiency models, cultural studies incurs the wrath of mainstream and conservative educators who often are silent about the political interests underlying their discursive practices and reform agendas.

Cultural studies also rejects the notion of pedagogy as a technique or set of neutral skills, arguing instead that pedagogy is a cultural practice understandable only through considerations of history, politics, power, and culture. Given its concern with everyday life, its pluralization of cultural communities, and

43

GIROUX

its emphasis on knowledge that is "between or among the disciplines without being reducible to any or all of them,"[7] cultural studies is less concerned with issues of certification and testing than with how knowledge, texts, and cultural products are used. Pedagogy becomes in this instance the terrain through which students critically engage and challenge the diverse cultural discourses, practices, and popular media they experience in their everyday existence. Indeed, such a pedagogy would examine the historical, social, economic, and political factors that impel the concern with issues of certification at the present time. From this perspective, culture is the ground "on which analysis proceeds, the object of study, and the site of political critique and intervention."[8] This partly explains why some advocates of cultural studies are increasingly interested in "how and where knowledge needs to surface and emerge in order to be consequential" with respect to expanding the possibilities for a radical democracy.[9]

During the next century, educators will not be able to ignore the hard questions that schools will have to face regarding issues of multiculturalism, race, identity, power, knowledge, ethics, and work. These issues will play a major role in defining the meanings and purposes of schooling, what it means to teach, and how students should be taught to live in a world that will be vastly more globalized, high tech, and racially diverse than at any other time in history. As capitalist globalization integrates financial systems, mobilizes world wide communication and consumption networks, and increasingly divides a post-Fordist labor force between "core" and "periphery"/"knowledge" and "service" workers, cultural studies will need to recognise that the political space of globalization is one of struggle and contestation, and not merely a space of domination.[10]

Cultural studies offers some possibilities for educators to rethink the nature of educational theory and practice as well as what it means to educate future teachers for the twenty-first century.[11] This chapter will chart some of the diverse assumptions and practices defined loosely under the theoretical banner of cultural studies that must inform any transformative pedagogical project. It will conclude by attempting to suggest how this field might have important consequences for those of us who are concerned about reforming schools and colleges of education. It will also address how progressive educators might contribute to inserting a notion of the political into cultural studies that would allow the field to be taken up as part of a larger discourse of social reconstruction.

THE SPACE OF CULTURAL STUDIES

Within the past decade, the field of cultural studies has developed a broad following in the United States.[12] In the most general sense, cultural studies signifies a massive shift away from Eurocentric master narratives, disciplinary knowledge, high culture, scientism, and other legacies informed by the diverse heritage of modernism. The parameters and cartography of this shift include but are not limited to three important assumptions.

First, cultural studies is premised on the belief that we have entered a period in which the traditional distinctions that separate and frame established academic disciplines cannot account for the great diversity of cultural and social phenomena that has come to characterize an increasingly hybridized, postindustrial world. The university has long been linked to a notion of national identity that is largely defined by and committed to transmitting traditional, Western culture.[13] Typically, this has been a culture of exclusion, one which has ignored the multiple narratives histories and voices of culturally and politically subordinated groups. Challenging this legacy, diverse social movements have emerged arguing for a genuinely multicultural and multiracial society. These movements have contested schools that use academic knowledge to make students voiceless. That is, such movements have contested how the cultural differences of subordinate groups are often regulated and licensed so as to prevent students from drawing upon their own histories and cultural experiences in order to narrate themselves within the context of a supposedly liberal education. Moreover, the spread of electronically mediated culture to all spheres of everyday intellectual and artistic life has shifted the ground of scholarship away from the traditional disciplines designed to preserve a "common culture" to the more hybridized fields of comparative and world literature, media studies, ecology, society and technology, and popular culture.

Second, advocates of cultural studies have argued strongly that the role of media culture, including the power of the mass media with its massive apparatuses of representation and its mediation of knowledge is central to understanding how the dynamics of power, privilege, and social desire structure the daily life of a society. This concern with culture and its connection to power has necessitated a critical interrogation of the relationship between knowledge and authority, and the historical and social contexts that deliberately shape students' understanding of representations of the past, present and future. But if a sea change in the development and reception of what counts as knowledge has taken place, it has been accompanied by an understanding of how we define and apprehend the multitude of electronic, aural, and visual texts that have become a determining feature of media culture and everyday life in the United States. By analyzing the full range of diverse and densely layered sites of learning such as the media, popular culture, film, advertising, mass communications, and religious organizations, among others, cultural studies expands our understanding of the pedagogical and its role outside of school as the traditional site of learning.

At stake here is the attempt to produce new theoretical models and methodologies for addressing the production, structure and exchange of knowledge. This approach to inter/post disciplinary studies is invaluable be-

45

cause it addresses the pedagogical issue of organizing dialogue across and outside of the disciplines. It does so in order to promote alternative approaches to research and teaching about culture and the newly emerging technologies and forms of knowledge. For instance, rather than organize courses around strictly disciplinary concerns arising out of English and social studies courses, it might be more useful and relevant for colleges of education to organize courses that broaden students' understandings of themselves and others by examining events that evoke a sense of social responsibility and moral accountability. Such courses might focus on scholarship that addresses a multiplicity of contexts in which issues concerning identity formation, language, work, cultural production, and social responsibility intersect. For instance the politics and pedagogy of health care could be linked to analyzing public attitudes toward schooling, or the question of national identity and education could be analyzed through filmic narratives shaped against the "othering" of diasporic groups who have helped shape the United States but have always been on its margins in terms of the politics of representation. Equally important is the need to link the imperatives of cultural studies to pedagogical projects in which students traverse different public spaces in order to learn the dynamics of practical politics and active citizenship. Whether through historical inquiry, public service, or analyses of larger public events, educators can provide students with the opportunity both to engage problem-solving projects that teach the lessons of civic education and provide students with opportunities to interact with diverse groups that engage social issues within specific public arenas. For example, the relationship between racism and schooling can be analyzed through forms of antiracist education conducted by diverse groups in the larger community. Students can both meet with such groups in order to understand how different views of racial justice are brought to bear on the issue of racism and reflect on how such views might inform their historical and social formation as teachers, along with the pedagogies they use in their classrooms.

Third, in addition to broadening the terms and parameters of learning, cultural studies rejects the professionalization of educators and the alienating and often elitist discourse of professionalism and sanitized expertise. Instead, it argues for educators who self-consciously produce knowledge and power related discourses that must be examined in relation to both "the conditions of their construction and their social effects."[14] In this view, teachers must be accountable in their teaching to the ways in which they take up and respond to the problems of history, human agency, and the renewal of democratic public life. Cultural studies strongly rejects the assumption that teachers are simply transmitters of existing configurations of knowledge. Academics are always implicated in the dynamics of social power and knowledge that they produce, mediate, and legitimate in their classrooms. In this perspective, intellectual work is incomplete unless it self-consciously assumes responsibility for its effects in the larger public culture. Hence, cultural studies raises questions about what knowledges are produced in the university and how these might extend and deepen democratic public life. Equally important is the issue of how to democratize schools, so as to enable those groups largely divorced from—or simply not represented in—the curriculum to be able to produce their own self-images, tell their own stories, and engage in respectful dialogue with others.

DOING CULTURAL STUDIES: AN AGENDA FOR COLLEGES OF EDUCATION

The current drive in the United States toward the vocationalization of colleges of education is evident from the ascendancy of reforms emphasizing efficiency and applied learning. Lost from this reductionistic emphasis on the practical is any broader sense of vision, meaning, or motivation regarding the role that colleges of education might play in expanding the "scope of democracy and democratic institutions."[15] The moral bankruptcy of the new vocationalization is increasingly matched by the predilections of state legislatures and others to further mandate the current emphasis on the technical training of prospective teachers. The rhetoric of cost efficiency, restructuring, and downsizing have become code words to tie education more closely to the ideological and economic imperatives of the labor market. This is evident, for instance, in the current conservative assessment of liberal arts programs as ideologically expendable and economically unfeasible. In many universities, including Yale and the University of Minnesota, critical programs within the humanities focusing on ethnicity, feminism, and literary studies have been either eliminated or drastically reduced in size.

47

Corporate influence in the university can be seen in the funding of endowed chairs, research projects, and policy institutes organized around conservative ideological interests and training programs that promise future employment in the new global order. Whereas higher education might once have applauded educating students for occupations that revitalize public life, such as health care, teaching, and social work, the new emphasis is on educating students for work in technical and managerial fields, such as computer and financial services. The MBA has become the degree of choice in higher education, and the ideological considerations that legitimate it have become the model for evaluating other college and university programs.[16]

In opposition to this view, I believe cultural studies offers possibilities for defining and providing institutional spaces and practices for educating teachers and administrators to play vital roles in renewing civic life. Former CUNY chancellor, Joe Murphy, has captured the spirit of what it means for teachers to address such a project. He argues that teachers should "give students sensibility to understand economic, political, and historical forces so they're not just victims of these forces but can **act on them with effect.**

GIROUX

Giving [students, especially the poor] this power is a threatening idea to many. But it is essential to the health of a democratic society."[17]

Broadly conceived, cultural studies can become the theoretical matrix for producing teachers at the forefront of interdisciplinary, critically engaged work. Central to such an approach would be a number of identifying themes that would organize lectures, seminars, research projects, academic programs, and collaborative work among both faculty and students. While there are any number of theoretical elements that could give shape to the context and content of a cultural studies approach that would address reforming schools and colleges of education, there is space here only to suggest a partial list of considerations.

First, by making culture a central construct in our classrooms and curricula, cultural studies focuses the terms of learning around issues relating to cultural differences, power, and history. In order to make a difference, cultural studies needs to analyze these issues as part of a wider struggle to extend the possibility for dialogue and debate about the quality of democratic public life. In this perspective, both the construction of curriculum knowledge and pedagogy provide narrative space for the understanding and critical analysis of multiple histories, experiences, and cultures. Cultural studies offers educational theorists a transnational approach to literacy and learning. By pluralizing the concept of literacy, cultural studies provides fertile theoretical ground for taking up pedagogy as an act of decentering, a form of transit and border crossing, a way of constructing an intercultural politics in which dialogue, exchange, and translation take place across different communities, national boundaries, and regional borders. Cultural studies has traditionally been concerned with culture as something that is unfinished, incomplete, and always in process. In this approach, the study of culture is grounded in a continual analysis of local, national, and global conditions of existence, as they enable or prevent the possibilities for human dignity and critical agency in others. In this perspective, knowledge and beliefs are not rendered legitimate or useful by virtue of their production within specific disciplines, or by their indebtedness to what is alleged to be Western culture. Rather, they mix and merge with different cultural histories and environments both within and outside of the United States.

Second, cultural studies places a major emphasis on the study of language and power, particularly in terms of how language is used to fashion social identities and secure specific forms of authority. In this instance, language is studied not as a technical and expressive device, but as historical and contingent practices actively engaged in the production, organization, and circulation of texts and institutional powers. The implication here is that educators can address the diverse ways in which different discursive practices constitute a formative rather than merely expressive force. That is, the pedagogical challenge for cultural studies is to analyze how language functions to include or

GIROUX

exclude certain meanings, secure or marginalize particular ways of behaving, and produce or prevent certain pleasures and desires. Language in this sense is analyzed through the various ways in which it actively produces and mediates the context and content of students' lives within and across numerous public arenas and sites of learning. The link between language and the construction of individual and social identities is evident, for instance, in the way in which language is used to privilege representations that exclude subordinate groups. It is evident in the ways in which discourses of testing, assessment, and management are given priority over the language of politics and ethics when dealing with the purposes and meanings of schooling at all levels. And, of course, it is evident in the assumption that standard English rather than, for example, an African-American idiom, is the proper way to speak and write in schools. Historical analysis of the relationship between power and language can be addressed by analyzing how different discourses have been privileged over time to legitimate and regulate institutional sites such as schools, the justice system, the work place, unions, media culture, and other sites of learning. But the study of language must not fall prey to what Stuart Hall has called an overwhelming textualization. Cultural studies cannot run the risk of constituting "power and politics as exclusively matters of language and textuality."[18] Material forces and institutions have a social gravity that can only be understood through language but cannot be reduced simply to a representational practice. Students can learn that the critical value of language is not based merely on its possibilities for expanding the range of textual literacy, but on understanding how language is actually used by people and social groups as a way of mobilizing resistance, cultural authority, and empowering social relationships.

The relationship between language and literacy must extend beyond its pedagogical importance as vehicle of interpretation; it should also be understood as a site of social contestation. As part of a broader struggle over signs and social practices, language cannot be abstracted from the power of those institutional forces that use it as part of a systematic effort to silence, exclude, and dictate the voices of subordinate groups. As a discourse of possibility, language must be understood as both a politics of representation and a social practice through which identities are refigured, struggles produced, and hopes mobilized. Hence, the study of language becomes crucial for understanding how structures of inequality and oppression work in schools and through the larger society. For educators, the study of language becomes essential for revealing how power functions as a condition for and a form of representation. Educational politics and pedagogical practices are impossible to grasp critically without focusing on how language works in deploying the machinery of power, discipline, and regulation.

For many cultural studies advocates, the study of language is also important for redefining the relationship between theory and practice. The language of

49

GIROUX

theory is crucial to the degree that it is grounded in real life experiences, issues, and practices. Theory must address both complex issues and events that give meaning to everyday life. Theory needs to be translated into practice that makes a difference, that ensures that people live out their lives with dignity and hope. At the same time, considerations of the practical cannot take place without a detour through theory. The practice of everyday life does not privilege the pragmatic in opposition to theory, but views it as being both informed by and transformative of reflective theoretical considerations. As a pedagogical issue, theory is not only a matter of students learning other people's discourses. It is also about students doing their own theorizing around historical undertakings and contemporary issues. Theory has to be done, it has to become a form of cultural production, and not merely a storehouse of insights drawn from the books of the "great theorists."

Third, cultural studies places a strong emphasis on linking the curriculum to the experiences that students bring to their encounter with institutionally legitimated knowledge. For cultural studies advocates, texts cannot be understood outside of the context of their historical and social production. Nor can such texts be removed from the experiences and narratives of the students who engage them. The pedagogical implication here is that schools and colleges of education should take the lead in refiguring curriculum boundaries. In part, this suggests reformulating the value and implications of established disciplines and those areas of study that constitute mass culture, popular culture, youth culture, and other aspects of student knowledge and the contested terrain of common sense. This is not a matter of abandoning high culture, or simply substituting it for popular culture. It is, rather, an attempt to refigure the boundaries of what constitutes culture and really useful knowledge in order to study it in new and critical ways.

Future and existing teachers need to be educated about the viability of developing context-dependent learning that takes account of student experiences and their relationships to popular culture and to the terrain of pleasure. Despite the growing diversity of students in both public schools and higher education, there are few examples of curriculum sensitivity to the multiplicity of economic, social, and cultural factors bearing on a student's educational life. Even where there is a proliferation of programs such as ethnic and black studies in higher education, these are marginalized in small programs far removed from the courses organized around history, science, and the humanities majors. Cultural studies at least provides the theoretical tools for allowing schools and colleges of education to recognize that the crucial culture war today is between education institutions which do not meet the needs of a massively shifting student population and students and their families for whom schools are perceived as merely one more instrument of repression.[19]

Fourth, cultural studies is committed to studying the production, reception, and situated use of varied texts, and how they structure social relations, values, particular notions of community, the future, and diverse definitions of the self. Texts in this sense do not merely refer to the culture of print or the technology of the book, but to all those audio, visual, and electronically mediated forms of knowledge that have prompted a radical shift in the construction of knowledge and the ways in which knowledge is produced, received, and consumed. It is worth noting that contemporary youth do not simply rely on the technology and culture of the book to construct and affirm their identities; instead, they are faced with the task of finding their way through a decentered cultural landscape no longer caught in the grip of a technology of print, closed narrative structures, or the certitude of a secure economic future. The new emerging technologies which construct and position youth represent interactive terrains that cut across "language and culture, without narrative requirements, without character complexities. . . . Narrative complexity [has given] way to design complexity; story [has given] way to a sensory environment."[20] It seems unlikely that educators and schools of education can address the shifting attitudes, representations, and desires of this new generation of youth within the dominant disciplinary configurations of knowledge and practice. On the contrary, youth are constituted within languages and cultural practices that intersect differently across and within issues of race, class, gender, and sexual differences. Consequently, the conditions through which youth attempt to narrate themselves must be understood within the context of their struggles and the shared language of agency that points to a project of hope and possibility. It is precisely this language of difference, specificity, and possibility that is lacking in most attempts at educational reform.

51

Fifth, cultural studies also rightly argues for the importance of analyzing history not as a unilinear narrative unproblematically linked to progress, but as a series of ruptures and displacements. History in this sense becomes decentered, more complex, and diffuse. Rather than taking up history within the confines of a rigid and narrowly defined tradition, teachers can name and address the multiple traditions and narratives that constitute the complex and multilayered constructions, deployments, and uses of national identity. The pedagogical benefit of such an approach is that it makes available to students those narratives, local histories, and subjugated memories that have been excluded and marginalized in dominant renditions of history. Through the lens of cultural studies, history can be read from a transnational and intercultural perspective.[21] In part, history becomes a critical focused reading of the local and global relations that the United States and other imperial powers have constructed over time with other countries. Historical learning in this sense is not about constructing a linear narrative but about blasting history open, rupturing its silences, highlighting its detours, and organizing its limits within an open and honest concern for human suffering, values, and the legacy of the often unrepresentable or misrepresented.

History is not an artifact, but a struggle over the relationship between rep-

GIROUX

resentation and agency. James Clifford is insightful in arguing that history should "force a sense of location on those who engage with it."[22] In other words, history is not merely about looking at facts, dates, and events. It is also about critically examining one's own historical location amid relations of power, privilege, or subordination. Similarly, cultural studies strongly supports the notion that the work of theory, research, and practice must, in part, be approached through historical undertakings and struggles around nationhood, ethnicity, race, gender, class, youth cultures, and other contestations over culture and politics.

Sixth, the issue of pedagogy is increasingly becoming one of the defining principles of cultural studies.[23] Teachers must expand the definition of pedagogy in order to move beyond a limited emphasis on the mastery of techniques and methodologies. This should enable students to understand pedagogy as a configuration of textual, verbal and visual practices that seek to engage the processes through which people understand themselves and the possible ways in which they engage others and their environment. Pedagogy represents a form of cultural production implicated in and critically attentive to how power and meaning are employed in the construction and organization of knowledge, desires, values and identities. Pedagogy in this sense is not reduced merely to promoting mastery of skills or techniques. Rather, it is defined as a cultural practice that must be accountable ethically and politically for the stories it produces, the claims it makes on social memories, and the images of the future it deems legitimate. As both an object of critique and a method of cultural production, pedagogy refuses to hide behind claims of objectivity, and works vigilantly to link theory and practice in the service of expanding the possibilities for democratic life.

While this list is both schematic and incomplete, it points to a core of theoretical considerations that offer a beginning for advancing a more public vision for schools and colleges of education. Hopefully, it also suggests theoretical tools for constructing new forms of collaboration among faculty, a broadening of the terms of learning for teachers, and new approaches toward interdisciplinary research that address local, national, and international concerns. The potential that cultural studies has for developing forms of collaboration that cut across national boundaries is enormous. Some of the possibilities indicated here are taken up in later chapters.

Of course cultural studies needs also to be interrogated so as to expand its theoretical reach and pedagogical possibilities. Given the interdisciplinary nature of educational work, the space it provides for linking theory and practice, and the important role that teachers play as public intellectuals, educational theorists can make a major contribution to how cultural studies is taken up by deepening and expanding some important considerations central to the intersection of pedagogy, cultural studies and a project for political change. Three examples may suffice here.

First, while cultural studies has multiple languages, histories, and founding moments, its underlying commitment to political work has not been adequately developed as part of a wider project for social reconstruction and progressive change. As cultural studies has moved from its earlier emphasis on adult literacy, class analysis, and youth subcultures to its later concern with feminism, racism, popular culture, and identity politics, it has failed to unite its different historical undertakings under a comprehensive democratic politics and shared notion of public struggle and social justice. While issues of racism, class, gender, textuality, national identity, subjectivity, and media culture must remain central elements in any cultural studies discourse, the issue of radical democracy must be located at the center of its politics.

Progressive educators can both amplify and build upon the various ways in which cultural studies has broadened our understanding of how politics and power work through institutions, language, representations, culture, and across diverse economies of desire, time, and space. But in enabling this vast reconceptualization of power and resistance, cultural studies has failed to provide a clear sense of what these sites have in common. Educators can address this issue by emphasizing the importance of radical democracy as a political, social, and ethical referent for rethinking how citizens can be educated to deal with a world made up of different, multiple, and fractured public cultures. Cultural studies confronts the need for constructing a new ethical and political language to map the problems and challenges of a newly constituted global public. It is within this postmodern politics of difference and the increasingly dominant influence of globalization that cultural studies and the field of education need to become more sufficiently attentive to restoring the language of ethics, agency, power, and identity as part of the wider revitalization of democratic public life.

At stake here is the necessity for progressive educators' studies to provide some common ground in which traditional binarisms of margin/center, unity/difference, local/national, public/private can be reconstituted through more complex representations of identification, belonging, and community. Critical educators must address how cultural studies can continue to develop new theoretical frameworks for challenging the way we think about the dynamics and effects of cultural and institutional power. This suggests the need for a discourse of ruptures, shifts, flows, and unsettlement, one that functions less as a politics of transgression than as part of a concerted effort to construct a broader vision of political commitment and democratic struggle. Cultural studies in combination with progressive educational theory can further expand its theoretical horizons by addressing the issue of radical democracy as part of a wider discourse of rights and economic equality. In this context, cultural studies as a pedagogical discourse offers the possibility for extending the democratic principles of justice, liberty, and equality to the widest possible set of social relations and institutional practices that constitute everyday life. Un-

GIROUX

53

der the project of radical democracy, critical educators can rewrite the possibilities for cultural studies to forcefully assert its own politics by affirming the
importance of the particular and contingent while acknowledging the centrality of the shared political values and ends of a democratic society.

Second, cultural studies both reinvigorates intellectual work through its
transdisciplinary and transcultural scholarship and echoes Walter Benjamin's
call for intellectuals to assume responsibility with regard to the task of trans-
lating theory back into a constructive practice that transforms the everyday
terrain of cultural and political power. Unlike traditional vanguardist or elitist
notions of the intellectual, cultural studies advocates that the vocation of intellectuals be rooted in pedagogical and political work tempered by humility,
a moral focus on suffering, and the need to produce alternative visions and
policies that go beyond a language of critique. On one level this means that
cultural studies is important because it takes on the task of establishing, and
struggling over, institutional spaces and practices that might produce public
intellectuals. Critical educators must stress the need for cultural workers to
struggle for the institutional space necessary for public intellectuals to have a
voice. In addition, however, they should urge a cautious pedagogical regard
for striking a critical balance between producing rigorous intellectual work,
on the one hand, and exercising authority that is firm rather than rigid, self-
critical and concretely utopian rather than repressive and doctrinaire, on the
other. Rather than denouncing authority, those who engage in cultural studies must use it to organize their cultural work and at the same time avoid
committing pedagogical terrorism by allowing their own forms of authority
to be held up to critical scrutiny.

This suggests rejecting the notion of the educator who speaks as the "universal intellectual" as well as the specific intellectual who speaks exclusively
within the often essentializing claims of identity politics. Cultural studies
needs to rethink the role of educators as both public and border intellectuals.
If the universal intellectual speaks for everyone, and the specific intellectual is
wedded to serving the narrow interests of specific cultural and social formations, the border intellectual travels within and across communities of difference working in collaboration with diverse groups and occupying many sites
of resistance while simultaneously defying the specialized, parochial knowledge of the individual specialist, sage, or master ideologue. By connecting the
role of the intellectual to the formation of democratic public cultures, critical
educators can argue for a version of cultural studies that provides an ethical
referent for cultural workers inhabiting sites as diverse as the arts, religious institutions, schools, media, the work place, and other spheres. As border intellectuals, educators can articulate and negotiate their differences as part of a
broader struggle to secure social justice, economic equality, and human rights
within and across regional, national, and global spheres.

Third, cultural studies has played an important role in providing theoretical

54

GIROUX

frameworks for analyzing how power works through the popular and every-day to produce knowledge, social identities, and maps of desire. Crucial here is the ongoing pedagogical work of understanding how social practices which deploy images, sounds and other representational practices are redefining the production of knowledge, reason, and new forms of global culture. While cultural studies has been enormously successful in making the objects of every-day life legitimate sources of social analysis, it now faces the task of interrogating how technology and science are combining to produce new information systems that transcend high/low culture dichotomies. Virtual reality systems and the new digital technologies that are revolutionizing media culture will increasingly come under the influence of an instrumental rationality that relegates their use to the forces of the market and passive consumption. Critical educators can make it clear that popular culture must be addressed not merely for the opportunities it provides to revolutionize how people learn or how to become cultural producers, but for the role it will play in guaranteeing human rights and social justice. This suggests the need for a new debate around reason, Enlightenment rationality, technology, and authority.

Colleges of education are uniquely suited to developing a language for re-thinking the complex dynamics of cultural and material power within expanded notions of the public, of solidarity, and of democratic struggle. What cultural studies offers educators is a conception of the political that is open yet committed, respects specificity without erasing global considerations, and provides new spaces for collaborative work engaged in productive social change. What critical education offers cultural studies is the centrality of de-veloping a political project in which power, history, and human agency can play an active role in constructing the multiple and shifting political relations and cultural practices necessary for connecting the construction of diverse political subjects to the revitalization of democratic public life.

NOTES

1. This chapter draws on two earlier essays on cultural studies by Henry Giroux: Doing cultural studies: Youth and the challenge of pedagogy, *Harvard Educational Review* (Fall 1994); Doing cultural studies in colleges of education, in Joyce Canaan and Debbie Epstein, Eds. *Teaching Cultural Studies* (Boulder, CO.: Westview Press, forth-coming). The present chapter is a slightly modified version of an article published in *Review of Education/Pedagogy/Critical Studies.*

2. This issue is taken up in detail in Henry A. Giroux, *Schooling and the Struggle for Public Life* (Minneapolis: University of Minnesota Press, 1988), and in *Living Danger-ously* (New York: Peter Lang, 1993).

3. This is taken up in Paul Smith, The political responsibility of the teaching of lit-eratures, in *Margins in the Classroom*, Kostas Myrsiades and Linda S. Myrsiades: Univer-sity of Minnesota Press, 1994), pp. 64–73.

4. The literature on this issue is too abundant to repeat here, but examples can be found in Lilia Bartolome, Beyond the methods fetish: Towards a humanizing peda-

55

gogy, *Harvard Educational Review* 64:2 (Summer 1994), pp. 173–194; Michelle Fine, *Framing Dropouts* (Albany: SUNY Press, 1991); Stanley Aronowitz and Henry A. Giroux, *Education Still Under Siege* (Westport, Ct.: Bergin and Garvey Press, 1993); Donaldo Macedo, *Literacies of Power* (Boulder, CO.: Westview Press, 1994); Jeanne Brady, *Schooling Young Girls* (Albany: SUNY Press, 1995).

5. For representative examples of the diverse issues taken up in the field of cultural studies, see Cary Nelson, Paula Treichler, and Larry Grossberg (eds.), *Cultural Studies* (New York: Routledge, 1992); Simon During, Ed. *The Cultural Studies Reader* (New York: Routledge, 1993).

6. The relationship between cultural studies and relations of government are taken up in Tony Bennett, Putting policy into cultural studies, *Cultural Studies,* ibid., pp. 23–34.

7. Peter Hitchcock, The othering of cultural studies, *Third Text,* No. 25 (Winter 1993–1994), p. 12.

8. Cary Nelson, Paula Treichler, and Lawrence Grossberg (1992), Cultural studies: An introduction, in their (ed.) *Cultural Studies*, New York: Routledge, p. 5.

9. Tony Bennett, Putting policy into cultural studies. In *ibid.*, p. 32.

10. The notion of globalization as a space of struggle is taken from Lawrence Grossberg (forthcoming), The space of culture, the power of space: Cultural studies and globalization, in Iain Chambers and Lydia Curti, Eds. *The Question of the Post Colonial*, New York: Routledge. See also, Stuart Hall, Culture, community, nation, *Cultural Studies* 7:3 (October 1993), pp. 349–363.

11. These issues are taken up in more detail in Henry A. Giroux, *Border Crossings* (New York: Routledge, 1992) and in *Disturbing Pleasures: Learning Popular Cultures* (New York: Routledge, 1994).

12. For a history of cultural studies in the United States and England, see: Stanley Aronowitz (1993), *Roll Over Beethoven: The Return of Cultural Strife,* Hanover: Wesleyan University Press; also see, Lawrence Grossberg (1993), The formations of cultural studies: An American in Birmingham, in Valda Blundell, John Shepard, and Ian Taylor (eds.) *Cultural Studies: Developments in Theory and Research,* New York: Routledge, pp. 21–66. For a shorter analysis, see the Introduction to *Cultural Studies* by Nelson, Treichler, and Grossberg, and Stuart Hall's, Cultural studies and its theoretical legacies, in *Cultural Studies*, op. cit, pp. 277 286.

13. Anyone who has been following the culture wars of the last ten years is well aware of the conservative agenda for reordering public and higher education around the commercial goal of promoting economic growth for the nation while simultaneously supporting the values of Western civilization as a common culture designed to undermine the ravages of calls for equity and multiculturalism. For a brilliant analysis of the conservative attack on higher education, see Ellen Messer-Davidow, Manufacturing the attack on liberalized higher education, *Social Text* No. 36 (Fall 1993), pp.40–80.

14. Douglas Crimp (1992), Portraits of people with Aids. In Cary Nelson, Paula Treichler and Larry Grossberg (eds.), *Cultural Studies,* New York: Routledge, p. 126.

15. Cornel West, America's three-fold crisis, *Tikkun* 9:2 (1994), p. 41.

16. For an example of this, see Alisa Solomon, Lower education: Is CUNY abandoning its mission to educate the poor? *The Village Voice* (December 14, 1993), pp. 11–18.

17. Joe Murphy quoted in Alisa Solomon, Lower education, *ibid.*, p. 18.

18. Stuart Hall, Cultural studies and its theoretical legacies, *op. cit.*

19. This issue is taken up in Stanley Aronowitz and Henry A. Giroux, *Education Still Under Siege* (Westport, Ct.: Bergin and Garvey Press, 1993), especially in the Introduction: Beyond the melting pot—Schooling in the twenty-first century.

20. Walter Parkes, Random access, remote control: The evolution of story telling. *Omni* (January 1994), p. 50.

21. Paul Gilroy is very instructive on this point. He writes: "There is a plea here that further enquiries should be made into precisely how discussions of "race," beauty, ethnicity, and culture have contributed to the critical thinking that eventually gave rise to cultural studies. . . . The emphatically national character ascribed to the concept of modes of production (cultural and otherwise) is another fundamental question which demonstrates the ethnohistorical specificity of dominant approaches to cultural politics, social movements, and oppositional consciousness. . . . I want to develop the suggestion that cultural historians could take the Atlantic as one single, complex unity of analysis in their discussions of the modern world and use it to produce an explicitly transnational and intercultural perspective." See Paul Gilroy (1993), *The Black Atlantic: Modernity and Double Consciousness*, Cambridge: Harvard University Press, pp. 9, 15.

22. James Clifford (1992), Museums in the borderlands. In Carol Becker, et. al. (eds.) *Different Voices*, New York: Association of Art Museum Directors, p. 129.

23. See Henry A. Giroux and Peter McLaren, Eds. *Between Borders: Pedagogy and the Politics of Cultural Studies* (New York: Routledge, 1993).

REFERENCES

Aronowitz, S. (1993). *Roll Over Beethoven: The Return of Cultural Strife*. Hanover: Wesleyan University Press.

Aronowitz, S. and Giroux, H. (1993). *Education Still Under Siege*. Westport, CT.: Bergin and Garvey Press.

Bartolome, L. (1994). Beyond the methods fetish: Towards a humanizing pedagogy. *Harvard Educational Review* 64, 2.

Bennett, T. (1992). Putting policy into cultural studies. In L. Grossberg, C. Nelson, and P. Treichler (eds.) *Cultural Studies*. New York: Routledge.

Brady, J. (1995). *Schooling Young Girls*. Albany, NY: SUNY Press.

Clifford, J. (1992). Museums in the borderlands. In C. Becker et al (eds.), *Different Voices*. New York: Association of Museum Art Directors.

Crimp, D. (1992). Portrait of people with aids. In L. Grossberg et al (eds.), *op. cit.*

During, S. ed. (1992). *The Cultural Studies Reader*. New York: Routledge.

Fine, M. (1991). *Framing Dropouts*. Albany, NY.: SUNY Press.

Gilroy, P. (1993). *The Black Atlantic: Modernity and Double Consciousness*. Cambridge, MA.: Harvard University Press.

Giroux, H. (1988). *Schooling and the Struggle for Public Life*. Minneapolis: University of Minnesota Press.

Giroux, H. (1992). *Border Crossings*. New York: Routledge.

Giroux, H. (1993). *Living Dangerously*. New York: Peter Lang.

Giroux, H. (1994a). Doing cultural studies: Youth and the challenge of pedagogy. *Harvard Educational Review* 64, 3.

GIROUX

Giroux, H. (1994b). *Disturbing Pleasures: Learning Popular Cultures*. New York: Rout-ledge.

Giroux, H. (1994c). Is there a place for cultural studies in colleges of education? *Review of Education/Pedagogy/Critical Studies*.

Giroux, H. (forthcoming). Doing cultural studies in colleges of education. In J. Canaan and D. Epsein (eds.), *Teaching Cultural Studies*, Boulder, CO.: Westview Press.

Giroux, H. and McLaren, P. (1993). *Between Borders: Pedagogy and the Politics of Cultural Studies*. New York: Routledge.

Grossberg, L. (1993). The formations of cultural studies: An American in Birmingham. In V. Blundell, J. Shepard, and I. Taylor (eds.), *Cultural Studies: Developments in Theory and Research*, New York: Routledge.

Grossberg, L. (forthcoming). The space of culture, the power of space: Cultural studies and globalization. In I. Chambers and L. Curti (eds.), *The Question of the Post Colonial* New York: Routledge.

Hall, S. (1992a). Cultural studies and its theoretical legacies. In L. Grossberg et al (eds.), *op. cit*.

Hall, S. (1992b). Culture, community, nation. *Cultural Studies*, 7, 3.

Macedo, D. (1994). *Literacies of Power*. Boulder, CO.: Westview Press.

Messer-Davidow, E. (1993). Manufacturing the attack on liberalized higher eduction. *Social Text* 36, Fall.

Nelson, C., Treichler, P. and Grossberg, L. eds. (1992). *Cultural Studies*. New York: Routledge.

Nelson, C., Treichler, P., and Grossberg, L. (1992). Cultural studies: An introduction. In *ibid*.

Parkes, W. (1994). Random access, remote control: The evolution of story telling. *Omni* January.

Smith, P. (1994). The political responsibility of the teaching of literatures. In K. Myrsiades and L. Myrsiades (eds.), *Margins in the Classroom,* Minneapolis: University of Minnesota Press.

Solomon, A. (1993). Lower education: Is CUNY abandoning its mission to educate the poor? *Village Voice* December 14.

West, C. (1994). America's three-fold crisis. *Tikkun* 9, 2.

SLACKING OFF: BORDER YOUTH AND POSTMODERN EDUCATION

Henry A. Giroux

The task is to get to grips with the "passage to post-modernity," which has opened up since the late 1960s and the end of the post-war boom in the global capitalist economy, to achieve an understanding of the emerging new culture of time and space, and related transformations in forms of knowledge and experience in the (post)-modern world. (Smart, *Modern Conditions* 202)

chapter 3

INTRODUCTION

FOR MANY theorists occupying various positions on the political spectrum, the current historical moment signals less a need to come to grips with the new forms of knowledge, experiences, and conditions that constitute post-modernism than the necessity to write its obituary. The signs of exhaustion are in part measured by the fact that postmodernism has gripped two genera-tions of intellectuals who have pondered endlessly over its meaning and im-plications as a "social condition and cultural movement" (Jencks 1992: 10). The "postmodern debate" has spawned little consensus and a great deal of confusion and animosity. The themes are, by now, well-known: master narra-tives and traditions of knowledge grounded in first principles are spurned; philosophical principles of canonicity and the notion of the sacred have be-come suspect; epistemic certainty and the fixed boundaries of academic knowledge have been challenged by a "war on totality" and disavowal of all encompassing, single, world views; the rigid distinctions between high and low culture have been rejected by the insistence that the products of the so-called mass culture, popular, and folk art forms are proper objects of study; the Enlightenment correspondence between history and progress and the modernist faith in rationality, science, and freedom have incurred a deep-rooted skepticism; the fixed and unified identity of the humanist subject has been replaced by a call for narrative space that is pluralized and fluid; and, finally—although by no means completely—the view of history as a unilinear process that moves the West progressively toward a final realization of freedom has been roundly rejected.[1]

These and other issues have become central to the postmodern debate. They are connected through the challenges and provocations they provide to modernity's conception of history, agency, representation, culture, and the responsibility of intellectuals. The postmodern challenge comprises more than a diverse body of cultural criticism alone. It must also be seen as a contextual discourse that has challenged specific disciplinary boundaries in such fields as literary studies, geography, education, architecture, feminism, performance art, anthropology, sociology, and many other areas.[2] Given its broad theoretical reach, its political anarchism, and its challenge to "legislating" intellectuals, it is not surprising that there has been a growing movement on the part of diverse critics to distance themselves from postmodernism.

While postmodernism may have been elevated to the height of fashion hype in both academic journals and the popular press in North America during the last twenty years, it is clear that a more sinister and reactionary mood has emerged which constitutes a veritable backlash. Of course, postmodernism did become something of a fashion trend, but such events are short lived and rarely take any subject seriously. But the power of fashion and commodification should not be underestimated in terms of how such practices bestow on an issue a cloudy residue of irrelevance and misunderstanding. But there is more at stake in the recent debates on postmodernism than just the effects of fashion and commodification; in fact, the often essentialized terms in which critiques of postmodernism have been framed suggest something more onerous. In the excessive rhetorical flourishes that dismiss postmodernism as reactionary nihilism, or as simply a new form of consumerism, there appears a deep-seated anti–intellectualism, one that lends credence to the notion that theory is an academic luxury and has little to do with concrete political practice. Anti–intellectualism aside, the backlash against postmodernism also points to a crisis in the way in which the project of modernity attempts to appropriate, prescribe, and accommodate issues of difference and indeterminacy.

Much of the criticism that now so blithely dismisses postmodernism appears trapped in what Zygmunt Bauman (1992: xi) refers to as modernist "utopias that served as beacons for the long march to the rule of reason [which] visualized a world without margins, leftovers—the unaccounted for—without dissidents and rebels." Against the indeterminacy, fragmentation, and skepticism of the postmodern era, the master narratives of modernism, particularly Marxism and liberalism, have been undermined as oppositional discourses. One consequence is that "a whole generation of postwar intellectuals have experienced an identity crisis . . . What results is a mood of mourning and melancholia" (Mercer 1992: 424).

The legacy of essentialism and orthodoxy seems to be reasserting itself on the part of intellectuals who reject postmodernism as a style of cultural criticism and knowledge production. It can also be seen in the refusal on the part of intellectuals to acknowledge the wide ranging processes of social and cultural transformation taken up in postmodern discourses that are appropriate to grasping the contemporary experiences of youth and the wide ranging proliferation of forms of diversity within an age of declining authority, economic uncertainty, the proliferation of electronic mediated technologies, and the extension of what I call consumer pedagogy into almost every aspect of youth culture.

This chapter seeks to shift the terms of the debate in which postmodernism is usually engaged, especially by its more recent critics. In doing so, it will argue that postmodernism as a site of "conflicting forces and divergent tendencies" (Patton 1988: 89) becomes useful pedagogically when it provides elements of an oppositional discourse for understanding and responding to the changing cultural and educational shift affecting youth in North America, and elsewhere. A resistant or political postmodernism seems invaluable for helping educators and others address the changing conditions of knowledge production in the context of emerging mass electronic media and the role these new technologies are playing as critical socializing agencies in redefining both the locations and the meaning of pedagogy.

The concern of this chapter with expanding the way educators and cultural workers understand the political reach and power of pedagogy as it positions youth within a postmodern culture suggests that postmodernism is to be neither romanticized nor casually dismissed. On the contrary, postmodernism is acknowledged as a fundamentally important discourse that needs to be mined critically in order to assist educators in understanding the modernist nature of public schooling in societies like our own.[3] It is also useful for educators to comprehend the changing conditions of identity formation within electronically mediated cultures and to appreciate how they are producing a new generation of youth which exists between the borders of a modernist world of certainty and order, informed by the culture of the West and its technology of print, and a postmodern world of hybridized identities, electronic technologies, local cultural practices, and pluralized public spaces. Before the task of developing the critical relationship between postmodern discourse and the promise of pedagogy and its relationship to border youth is

GIROUX

taken up, however, some further comment on the recent backlash against postmodernism, and why this reproduces rather than constructively addresses some of the pedagogical and political problems affecting contemporary schools and youth, is in order.

WELCOME TO THE POSTMODERN BACKLASH

Whereas conservatives such as Daniel Bell (1976) and his ilk may see in postmodernism the worst expression of the radical legacy of the 1960s, an increasing number of radical critics view postmodernism as the cause of a wide-range of theoretical excesses and political injustices. For example, recent criticism from the British cultural critic, John Clarke (1991), argues that the hyperreality of postmodernism wrongly celebrates and depoliticizes the new informational technologies and encourages metropolitan intellectuals to proclaim the end of everything in order to commit themselves to nothing (especially the materialist problems of the masses).[4] Dean MacCannell (1992: 187) goes further and argues that "postmodern writing [is] an expression of soft fascism." Feminist theorist, Susan Bordo (1993: 291), dismisses postmodernism as just another form of "stylish nihilism," and castigates its supporters for constructing a "world in which language swallows up everything." The nature of the backlash has become so prevalent in North America that the status of popular criticism and reporting seems to necessitate proclaiming that postmodernism is "dead." Hence, comments ranging from the editorial pages of *The New York Times* to popular texts such as *13th Gen* to popular academic magazines such as *The Chronicle of Higher Education* admonish the general public in no uncertain terms that it is no longer fashionable to utter the "p" word.

Of course, more serious critiques have appeared from the likes of Jürgen Habermas (1978), Perry Anderson (1984), David Harvey (1989), and Terry Eagleton (1985), but the current backlash has a different intellectual quality to it, a kind of reductionism that is both disturbing and irresponsible in its refusal to engage postmodernism in any kind of dialogical, theoretical debate.[5] Many of these left critics often assume the moral high ground and muster their theoretical machinery within binary divisions that create postmodern fictions, on the one side, and politically correct, materialist freedom fighters on the other. One consequence is that any attempt to engage the value and importance of postmodern discourses critically is sacrificed to the cold winter winds of orthodoxy and intellectual parochialism. This is not to suggest that all critics of postmodernism fall prey to such a position, nor that concerns about the relationship between modernity and postmodernity, the status of ethics, the crisis of representation and subjectivity, or the political relevance of postmodern discourses should not be problematized. But viewing postmodernism as a terrain to be contested suggests theoretical caution rather than reckless abandonment or casual dismissal.

GIROUX

What is often missing from these contentious critiques is the recognition that since postmodernism does not operate under any absolute sign, it might be more productive to reject arguments that position postmodernism within an essentialized politics, an either/or set of strategies. A more productive encounter would attempt, instead, to understand how postmodernism's more central insights illuminate how power is produced and circulated through cultural practices that mobilize multiple relations of subordination.

Rather than proclaiming the end of reason, postmodernism can be analyzed critically for how successfully it interrogates the limits of the project of modernist rationality and its universal claims to progress, happiness, and freedom. Instead of assuming that postmodernism has vacated the terrain of values, it seems more useful to address the ways in which it accounts for how values are constructed historically and relationally, and how they might be addressed as the basis or "precondition of a politically engaged critique" (Butler 1991: 6–7). Similarly, instead of claiming that postmodernism's critique of the essentialist subject denies a theory of subjectivity, it seems more productive to examine how its claims about the contingent character of identity, constructed in a multiplicity of social relations and discourses, redefine the notion of agency. One example of this type of inquiry comes from Judith Butler (ibid: 13), who argues that acknowledging that "the subject is constituted is not [the same as claiming] that it is determined; on the contrary, the constituted character of the subject is the very precondition of its agency." The now familiar argument that postmodernism substitutes representations for reality indicates less an insight than a reductionism that refuses to engage critically with how postmodern theories of representation work to give meaning to reality.

A postmodern politics of representation might be better served through an attempt to understand how power is mobilized in cultural terms, how images are used on a national and local scale to create a representational politics that is reorienting traditional notions of space and time. A postmodern discourse could also be evaluated through the pedagogical consequences of its call to expand the meaning of literacy by broadening "the range of texts we read, and . . . the ways in which we read them" (Berube 1992–93: 75). The fact of the matter is that mass media plays a decisive role in the lives of young people, and the issue is not whether such media perpetuates dominant power relations but, rather, how youth and others experience the culture of the media differently, or the ways media is "experienced differently by different individuals" (Tomlinson 1991: 40). Postmodernism pluralizes the meaning of culture, while modernism firmly situates it theoretically in apparatuses of power. It is precisely in this dialectical interplay between difference and power that postmodernism and modernism inform each other rather than cancel each other out. The dialectical nature of the relationship that postmodernism has to modernism warrants a theoretical moratorium on critiques that affirm or

63

GIROUX

negate postmodernism on the basis of whether it represents a break from modernism. The value of postmodernism lies elsewhere.

Acknowledging both the reactionary and progressive moments in post-modernism, antiessentialist cultural work might take up the challenge of "writing the political back into the postmodern" (Ebert 1991: 291), while simultaneously radicalizing the political legacy of modernism in order to promote a new vision of radical democracy in a postmodern world. One challenge in the debate over postmodernism is whether its more progressive elements can further our understanding of how power works, how social identities are formed, and how the changing conditions of the global economy and the new informational technologies can be articulated to meet the challenges posed by progressive cultural workers and the new social movements.

More specifically, the issue for critical educators lies in appropriating postmodernism as part of a broader pedagogical project which reasserts the primacy of the political while simultaneously engaging the most progressive aspects of modernism. Postmodernism becomes relevant to the extent that it becomes part of a broader political project in which the relationship between modernism and postmodernism becomes dialectical, dialogic, and critical.

What follows seeks to illuminate and then analyze some of the tensions between schools as modernist institutions and the fractured conditions facing a postmodern culture of youth along with the problems they pose for critical educators. First, there is the challenge of understanding the modernist nature of existing schooling and its refusal to relinquish a view of knowledge, culture, and order that undermines the possibility for constructing a radical democratic project in which a shared conception of citizenship simultaneously challenges growing regimes of oppression and struggles for the conditions needed to construct a multiracial and multicultural democracy. Second, there is a need for cultural workers to address the emergence of a new generation of youth who are increasingly constructed within postmodern economic and cultural conditions that are almost entirely ignored by the schools. Third, there is the challenge to critically appropriate those elements of a postmodern pedagogy that might be useful in educating youth to be the subjects of history in a world that is increasingly diminishing the possibilities for radical democracy and global peace.

MODERNIST SCHOOLS AND POSTMODERN CONDITIONS

A clip from [the film] *War Games*: David Lightman (Matthew Broderick) sees a brochure of a computer company promising a quantum leap in game technology coming this Christmas . . . breaks into a system and, thinking it's the game company computer, asks to play global thermonuclear war . . . Sees on TV that for three minutes Strategic Air Command went on full alert thinking there had been a Soviet sneak attack . . . is arrested and interrogated . . . breaks back into the system and asks the computer, "Is this a game or is it real?" The computer answers: "What's the difference?" (Parkes 1991: 48).

64

GIROUX

Wedded to the language of order, certainty, and mastery, public schools are facing a veritable sea change in the demographic, social, and cultural composition of the United States for which they are radically unprepared. As thoroughly modernist institutions, public schools have long relied upon moral, political, and social technologies that legitimate an abiding faith in the Cartesian tradition of rationality, progress, and history. The consequences are well known. Knowledge and authority in school curricula are organized not to eliminate differences but to regulate them through cultural and social divisions of labor. Class, racial, and gender differences are either ignored in school curricula or are subordinated to the imperatives of a history and culture that is linear and uniform.

Within the discourse of modernism, knowledge draws its boundaries almost exclusively from a European model of culture and civilization and connects learning to the mastery of autonomous and specialized bodies of knowledge. Informed by modernist traditions, schooling becomes an agent of those political and intellectual technologies associated with what Ian Hunter (1988) terms the "governmentalizing" of the social order. The result is a pedagogical apparatus regulated by a practice of ordering that views "contingency as an enemy and order as a task" (Bauman 1992: xi). The practice of ordering, licensing, and regulating that structures public schooling is predicated on a fear of difference and indeterminacy. The effects reach deep into the structure of public schooling and include: an epistemic arrogance and faith in certainty that sanctions pedagogical practices and public spheres in which cultural differences are viewed as threatening; knowledge becomes positioned in curricula as an object of mastery and control; the individual student is privileged as a unique source of agency irrespective of iniquitous relations of power; the technology and culture of the book is treated as the embodiment of modernist high learning and the only legitimate object of pedagogy.

While the logic of public schooling may be utterly modernist, it is neither monolithic nor homogeneous. At the same time, however, the dominant features of public schooling are characterized by a modernist project that has increasingly come to rely upon instrumental reason and the standardization of curricula. In part, this can be seen in the regulation of class, racial, and gender differences through rigid forms of testing, sorting, and tracking. The rule of reason reveals its Western cultural legacy in highly centered curricula that more often than not privilege the histories, experiences, and cultural capital of largely white, middle-class students. Moreover, the modernist nature of public schooling is evident in the refusal of educators to incorporate popular culture into the curriculum or to take account of the new electronically mediated, informational systems in the postmodern age that are generating massively new socializing contexts for contemporary youth.

The emerging conditions of indeterminacy and hybridity that the public schools face but continue to ignore can be seen in a number of elements that characterize what might loosely be called postmodern culture. First, the United States is experiencing a new wave of immigration which, by the end of this century, may exceed in volume and importance, the last wave at the turn of the 20th century. In key geographic areas within the country—chiefly large metropolitan regions of the Northeast and Southwest, including California—major public institutions, especially those of social welfare and education, are grappling with entirely new populations that bring with them new needs. In 1940, 70 percent of immigrants came from Europe, but in 1992 only 15 percent came from Europe, while 44 percent came from Latin America and 37 percent from Asia. National identity can no longer be written through the lens of cultural uniformity or enforced through the discourse of assimilation. A new postmodern culture has emerged marked by specificity, difference, plurality, and multiple narratives.

Second, the sense of possibility that has informed the American Dream of material well-being and social mobility is no longer matched by an economy that can sustain such dreams. In the last two decades, the American economy has entered a prolonged era of stagnation, punctuated by short term growth spurts. In the midst of an ongoing recession and declining real incomes for low- and middle-income groups, the prospects for economic growth over the next period of US history appear extremely limited. The result has been the expansion of service economy jobs and an increase in the number of companies that are downsizing and cutting labor costs in order to meet global competition. Not only are full time jobs drying up, but there has also been an surge in the "number of Americans—perhaps as many as 37 million—[who] are employed in something other than full-time permanent positions" (Jost 1993: 633). These so called "contingent workers" are "paid less than full-time workers and often get no health benefits, no pensions and no paid holidays, sick days or vacations" (ibid: 628). Massive unemployment and diminishing expectations have become a way of life for youth all over North America. *Maclean's Magazine* reports that in Canada "People aged 15 to 24 are currently facing unemployment rates of more than 20 percent, well above the national average of 10.8 percent" (Blythe 1993: 35). For most contemporary youth, the promise of economic and social mobility no longer warrants the legitimating claims it held for earlier generations of young people. The signs of despair among this generation are elsewhere. Surveys strongly suggest that contemporary youth from diverse classes, races, ethnicities, and cultures "believe it will be much harder for them to get ahead than it was for their parents—and are overwhelmingly pessimistic about the long-term fate of their generation and nation" (Howe and Strauss 1993: 16).

Clinging to the modernist script that technological growth necessitates progress, educators refuse to give up the long-held assumption that school credentials provide the best route to economic security and class mobility. While such a truth may have been relevant to the industrializing era, it is no

66

GIROUX

longer sustainable within the post–Fordist economy of the West. New economic conditions call into question the efficacy of mass schooling in providing the "well-trained" labor force that employers required in the past. In light of these shifts, it seems imperative that educators and other cultural workers reexamine the mission of the schools.

Rather than accepting the modernist assumption that schools should train students for specific labor tasks, it makes more sense in the present historical moment to educate students to theorize differently about the meaning of work in a postmodern world. Indeterminacy, and not order, should become the guiding principle of a pedagogy in which multiple views, possibilities, and differences are opened up as part of an attempt to read the future contingently instead of from the perspective of a master narrative that assumes rather than problematizes specific notions of work, progress, and agency. Under such circumstances, schools need to redefine curricula within a postmodern conception of culture linked to the diverse and changing global conditions that necessitate new forms of literacy, a vastly expanded understanding of how power works within cultural apparatuses, and keener sense of how the existing generation of youth are being produced within a society in which mass media plays a decisive, if not unparalleled, role in constructing multiple and diverse social identities.

As Aronowitz and Giroux (1993: 6) point out:

> Few efforts are being made to rethink the *entire* curriculum in the light of the new migration and immigration, much less develop entirely different pedagogies. In secondary schools and community colleges for example, students still study "subjects"—social studies, math, science, English and "foreign" languages. Some schools have "added" courses in the history and culture of Asian, Latin American and Caribbean societies, but have little thought of transforming the entire humanities and social studies curricula in the light of the cultural transformations of the school. Nor are serious efforts being made to integrate the sciences with social studies and the humanities; hence, science and math are still being deployed as sorting devices in most schools rather than seen as crucial markers of a genuinely innovative approach to learning.

As modernist institutions, public schools have been unable to open up the possibility of thinking through the indeterminate character of the economy, knowledge, culture, and identity. Hence, it has become difficult, if not impossible, for schools to understand how social identities are fashioned and struggled over within political and technological conditions that have produced a crisis in the ways in which culture is organized in the West.

BORDER YOUTH AND POSTMODERN CULTURE

The programmed instability and transitoriness characteristically widespread among a generation of 18 to 25 year old border youth is inextricably rooted in a larger set of postmodern cultural conditions informed by the following assumptions: a general loss of faith in the modernist narratives of work and emancipation; the recognition that the indeterminacy of the future warrants confronting and living in the immediacy of experience; an acknowledgment that homelessness as a condition of randomness has replaced the security, if not misrepresentation, of home as a source of comfort and security; an experience of time and space as compressed and fragmented within a world of images that increasingly undermine the dialectic of authenticity and universalism. For border youth, plurality and contingency, whether mediated through the media or through the dislocations spawned by the economic system, the rise of new social movements, or the crisis of representation have resulted in a world with few secure psychological, economic, or intellectual markers. This is a world in which one is condemned to wander across, within, and between multiple borders and spaces marked by excess, otherness, difference, and a dislocating notion of meaning and attention. The modernist world of certainty and order has given way to a planet in which hip-hop and rap condense time and space into what Paul Virilio (1991) calls "speed space." No longer belonging to any one place or location, youth increasingly inhabit shifting cultural and social spheres marked by a plurality of languages and cultures.

Communities have been refigured as space and time mutate into multiple and overlapping cyberspace networks. Youth talk to each other over electronic bulletin boards in coffee houses in North Beach, California. Cafes and other public salons, once the refuge of beatniks, hippies, and other cultural radicals have given way to members of the hacker culture. They reorder their imaginations through connections to virtual reality technologies, and lose themselves in images that wage a war on traditional meaning by reducing all forms of understanding to random access spectacles.

This is not meant to endorse a Frankfurt School dismissal of mass or popular culture in the postmodern age. On the contrary, it seems likely that the new electronic technologies with their proliferation of multiple stories and open ended forms of interaction have altered not only the context for the production of subjectivities, but also how people "take in information and entertainment" (Parkes 1994: 54). Values no longer emerge from the modernist pedagogy of foundationalism and universal truths, or from traditional narratives based on fixed identities and a requisite structure of closure. For many youth, meaning is in rout, media has become a substitute for experience, and what constitutes understanding is grounded in a decentered and diasporic world of difference, displacement, and exchanges.

The concept of border youth will be taken up through a general analysis of some recent films that have attempted to portray the plight of young people within the conditions of a postmodern culture. This will focus on three films: *A River's Edge* (1986), *My Own Private Idaho* (1991) and *Slacker* (1991). Each of these films points not only to some of the economic and social conditions at

68

GIROUX

work in the formation of youth, but they often do so within a narrative that combines a politics of despair with a fairly sophisticated depiction of the sensibilities and moods of a generation of youth. The challenge for critical educators is to question how a critical pedagogy might be employed to cancel out the worst dimensions of postmodern cultural criticism while appropriating some of its more radical aspects. At the same time, there is the issue of how a politics and project of pedagogy might be constructed to create the conditions for social agency and institutionalized change among postmodern youth.

For many postmodern youth, showing up for adulthood at the fin-de-siècle means pulling back on hope and trying to put off the future rather than take up the modernist challenge of trying to shape it. Postmodern cultural criticism has captured much of the ennui among youth and has made clear that "What used to be the pessimism of a radical fringe is now the shared assumption of a generation" (Anshaw 1992: 27). Postmodern cultural criticism has helped to alert educators and others to the fault lines marking a generation, regardless of race or class, who seem neither motivated by nostalgia for some lost conservative vision of America nor at home in the New World Order paved with the promises of the expanding electronic information highway. For most commentators, youth have become "strange," "alien," and disconnected from the real world (Green and Bigum 1993). For instance, in Gus Van Sant's film, *My Own Private Idaho*, the main character Mike, who hustles his sexual wares for money, is a dreamer lost in fractured memories of a mother who deserted him as a child. Caught between flashbacks of Mom shown in 8mm colour, and the video world of motley, street hustlers and their clients, Mike moves through his existence by falling asleep in times of stress only to awake in different geographic and spatial locations. What holds Mike's psychic and geographic travels together is the metaphor of sleep, the dream of escape, and the ultimate realization that even memories cannot fuel hope for the future. Mike becomes a metaphor for an entire generation forced to sell themselves in a world with no hope, a generation that aspires to nothing, works at degrading McJobs, and lives in a world in which chance and randomness rather than struggle, community, and solidarity drives its fate.

A more disturbing picture of youth can be found in *A River's Edge*. Teenage anomie and drugged apathy are given painful expression in the depiction of a group of working class-youth who are casually told by John, one of their friends, that he has strangled his girlfriend, another of the group's members, and left her nude body on the riverbank. The group at different times visit the site to view and probe the dead body of the girl. Seemingly unable to grasp the significance of the event, the youths initially hold off in informing anyone of the murder and with different degrees of concern initially try to protect John, the teenage sociopath, from being caught by the police. The youths in *A River's Edge* drift through a world of broken families, blaring rock music, schooling marked by dead time, and a pervasive indifference to life in general. Decentered

69

GIROUX

and fragmented, they view death like life itself as merely a spectacle, a matter of style rather than substance. In one sense, these youth share the quality of being "asleep" that is depicted in *My Own Private Idaho*. But what is more disturbing in *A River's Edge* is that lost innocence gives way not merely to teenage myopia, but to a culture in which human life is experienced as a voyeuristic seduction, a video game, good for passing time and diverting oneself from the pain of the moment. Despair and indifference cancel out the language of ethical discriminations and social responsibility while elevating the immediacy of pleasure to the defining moment of agency. In *A River's Edge*, history as social memory is reassembled through vignettes of 1960s types portrayed as either burned out bikers or as the ex radical turned teacher whose moralizing relegates politics simply to cheap opportunism. Exchanges among the young people in *A River's Edge* appear like projections of a generation waiting either to fall asleep or to commit suicide. After talking about how he murdered his girlfriend, John blurts out "You do shit, it's done, and then you die." Pleasure, violence, and death, in this case, reasserts how a generation of youth takes seriously the dictum that life imitates art or how life is shaped within a violent culture of images in which, as another character states, "It might be easier being dead." To which her boyfriend, a Wayne's World type replies, "Bullshit you couldn't get stoned anymore." *A River's Edge* and *My Own Private Idaho* reveal the seamy and dark side of a youth culture while employing the Hollywood mixture of fascination and horror to titillate the audiences drawn to these films. Through the use of the postmodern aesthetic of revulsion, locality, randomness, and senselessness, youth in these films appear to be constructed outside of a broader cultural and economic landscape. Instead, they become visible only through visceral expressions of psychotic behavior or the brooding experience of a self-imposed comatose alienation.

One of the more celebrated youth films of the early 1990s has been Richard Linklater's *Slacker*. A decidedly low-budget film, *Slacker* attempts in both form and content to capture the sentiments of a twenty-something generation of White youth who reject most of the values of the Reagan/Bush era but have a difficult time imagining what an alternative might look like. Distinctly non-linear in its format, *Slacker* takes place, in a twenty-four hour time frame in the college town of Austin, Texas. Borrowing its antinarrative structure from films like Luis Bunuel's *Phantom of Liberty* and Max Ophlus' *La Rhonde*, *Slacker* is loosely organized around brief episodes in the lives of a variety of characters, none of whom are connected to each other except in that each provides the pretext to lead the audience to the next character in the film. Sweeping through bookstores, coffee shops, auto-parts yards, bedrooms, and nightclubs, *Slacker* focuses on a disparate group of young people who possess little hope in the future and drift from job to job speaking a hybrid argot of bohemian intensities and new age-pop cult babble. The film portrays a host of young people who randomly move from one place to the next, border crossers with no sense of where they have come from or where they are going. In this world of multiple realities, "schizophrenia emerges as the psychic norm of late capitalism" (Hebdige 1988: 88). Characters work in bands with names like "Ultimate Loser," and talk about being forcibly put in hospitals by their parents. One neo-punker attempts to sell a Madonna pap smear to two acquaintances she meets in the street. "Check it out, I know it's kind of disgusting, but it's like sort of getting down to the real Madonna." This is a world in which language is wedded to an odd mix of nostalgia, pop-corn philosophy, and MTV babble. Talk is organized around comments like: "I don't know . . . I've travelled . . . and when you get back you can't tell whether it really happened to you or if you just saw it on TV." Alienation is driven inward and emerges in comments like "I feel stuck." Irony slightly overshadows a refusal to imagine any kind of collective struggle. Reality seems too despairing to care about. This is humorously captured in one instance by a young man who suggests: "You know how the slogan goes, workers of the world, unite? We say workers of the world, relax." People talk, but appear disconnected from themselves and each other, lives traverse each other with no sense of community or connection. There is a pronounced sense in *Slacker* of youth caught in the throes of new information technologies that both contain their aspirations while at the same time holding out the promise of some sense of agency.

At rare moments in the films, the political paralysis of solipsistic refusal is offset by instances in which some characters recognize the importance of the image as a vehicle for cultural production, as a representational apparatus that can not only make certain experiences available but can also be used to produce alternative realities and social practices. The power of the image is present in the way the camera follows characters throughout the film, at once stalking them and confining them to a gaze that is both constraining and incidental. In one scene, a young man appears in a video apartment surrounded by television sets he claims he has had on for years. He points out that he has invented a game called a "Video Virus" in which, through the use of a special technology, he can push a button and insert himself onto any screen and perform any one of a number of actions. When asked by another character what this is about, he answers: "Well, we all know the psychic powers of the televised image. But we need to capitalize on it and make it work for us instead of working for it." This theme is taken up in two other scenes. In one short clip, a history graduate student shoots the video camera he is using to film himself, indicating a self-consciousness about the power of the image and the ability to control it at the same time. In another scene, with which the film concludes, a carload of people, each equipped with their Super 8 cameras, drive up to a large hill and throw their cameras into a canyon. The film ends with the images being recorded by the cameras as they cascade to the bottom of the cliff in what suggests a moment of release and liberation.

71

GIROUX

Within the postmodern culture depicted in these three films, there are no master narratives at work, no epic modernist dreams. Nor is there any element of social agency that accompanies the individualized sense of dropping out, of self-consciously courting chaos and uncertainty.

In many respects, these movies, along with more recent youth films such as *Metropolitan* (1990), *Bodies, Rest, and Motion* (1993), *Clerks* (1994), and *Barcelona* (1994), present a slacker culture of white youth who exist largely as consuming rather than social subjects. These white youth are both terrified and fascinated by the media, and appear overwhelmed by "the danger and wonder of future technologies, the banality of consumption, the thrill of brand names, [and] the difficulty of sex in alienated relationships" (Kopkind 1992: 183). The significance of these films rests, in part, in their attempts to capture the sense of powerlessness that increasingly cuts across race, class, and generations. What is missing from these films, however, along with the various books, articles, and reportage concerning what is often called the "Nowhere Generation," "Generation X," "13th Gen," or "Slacker" is any sense of the larger political and social conditions in which youth are being framed. What in fact should be seen as a social commentary about "dead-end capitalism" emerges simply as a celebration of refusal dressed up in a rhetoric of aesthetics, style, fashion, and solipsistic protests. Within this type of commentary, postmodern criticism is useful but limited because of its prevailing theoretical inability to take up the relationships between identity and power, biography and the commodification of everyday life, or the limits of agency in a post-Fordist economy as part of a broader project of possibility linked to issues of history, struggle, and transformation. The contours of this type of criticism are captured in a comment by Andrew Kopkind, a keen observer of slacker culture.

72

> The domestic and economic relationships that have created the new consciousness are not likely to improve in the few years left in this century, or in the years of the next, when the young slackers will be middle-agers. The choices for young people will be increasingly constricted. In a few years, a steady job at a mall outlet or a food chain may be all that's left for the majority of college graduates. Life is more and more like a lottery—is a lottery—with nothing but the luck of the draw determining whether you get a recording contract, get your screenplay produced, or get a job with your M.B.A. Slacking is thus a rational response to casino capitalism, the randomization of success, and the utter arbitrariness of power. If no talent is still enough, why bother to hone your skills? If it is impossible to find a good job, why not slack out and enjoy life? (1992: 187).

GIROUX

The pedagogical challenge represented by the emergence of a postmodern generation of youth has not been lost on advertisers and market research analysts. According to a 1992 Roper Organization, Inc. study, the current generation of 18–29 year olds have an annual buying power of 125 billion. Addressing the interests and tastes of this generation, "McDonald's, for instance, has introduced hip-hop music and images to promote burgers and fries, ditto Coca-Cola, with its frenetic commercials touting Coca-Cola Classic" (Hollingsworth 1993: 30). Benetton, Reebok, and other companies have followed suit in their attempts to mobilize the desires, identities, and buying patterns of a new generation of youth. What appears as a dire expression of the postmodern condition to some theorists, becomes for others a challenge to invent new market strategies for corporate interests. In this scenario, youth may be experiencing the conditions of postmodernism, but corporate advertisers are attempting to theorize a pedagogy of consumption as part of a new way of appropriating postmodern differences. What educators need to do is to make the pedagogical more political by addressing both the conditions through which they teach and what it means to learn from a generation that is experiencing life in a way that is vastly different from the representations offered in modernist versions of schooling. The emergence of the electronic media coupled with a diminishing faith in the power of human agency has undermined the traditional visions of schooling and the meaning of pedagogy. The language of lesson plans and upward mobility, and the forms of teacher authority on which it was based, have been radically delegitimated by the recognition that culture and power are central to the authority/knowledge relationship. Modernism's faith in the past has given way to a future for which traditional markers no longer make sense.

POSTMODERN EDUCATION

This section develops the thesis that postmodern discourses offer the promise, but not the solution, for alerting educators to a new generation of border youth. Indications of the conditions and characteristics that define such youth are far from uniform or agreed upon. But the daunting fear of essentializing the category of youth should not deter educators and cultural critics from addressing the effects on a current generation of young people who appear hostage to the vicissitudes of a changing economic order with its legacy of diminished hopes, on the one hand, and a world of schizoid images, proliferating public spaces and an increasing fragmentation, uncertainty, and randomness that structures postmodern daily life on the other. Central to this issue is whether educators are dealing with a new kind of student forged within organizing principles shaped by the intersection of the electronic image, popular culture, and a dire sense of indeterminacy. Differences aside, the concept of border youth represents less a distinct class, membership, or social group than a referent for naming and understanding the emergence of set of conditions, translations, border crossings, attitudes, and dystopian sensibilities among youth that cuts across race and class that represents a fairly new phenomenon. In this scenario, the experiences of contemporary Western youth in the late modern world are being ordered around coordinates that structure the experience of everyday life outside of the unified principles and maps of certainty

73

GIROUX

that offered up comfortable and secure representations to previous generations. Youth increasingly rely less on the maps of modernism to construct and
affirm their identities; instead, they are faced with the task of finding their
way through a decentered cultural landscape no longer caught in the grip of a
technology of print, closed narrative structures, or the certitude of a secure
economic future. The new emerging technologies which construct and position youth represent interactive terrains that cut across "language and culture,
without narrative requirements, without character complexities . . . Narrative
complexity [has given] way to design complexity; story [has given] way to a
sensory environment" (Parkes 1994: 50).

A postmodern pedagogy must address the shifting attitudes, representations, and desires of this new generation of youth being produced within the
current historical, economic, and cultural conjuncture. For example, the
terms of identity and the production of new maps of meaning must be understood within new hybridized cultural practices inscribed in relations of
power that intersect differently with race, class, gender, and sexual orientation. Such differences must be understood not only in terms of the context of
their struggles, but also through a shared language of resistance that points to
a project of hope and possibility. This is where the legacy of a critical modernism becomes valuable, in that it reminds us of the importance of the language of public life, democratic struggle, and the imperatives of liberty, equality, and justice.

Educators need to understand how different identities among youth are
being produced in spheres generally ignored by schools. Included here would
be an analysis of how pedagogy works to produce, circulate, and confirm particular forms of knowledge and desires in those diverse public and popular
spheres where sounds, images, print, and electronic culture attempt to harness
meaning for and against the possibility of expanding social justice and human
dignity. Shopping malls, street communities, video halls, coffee shops, television culture, and other elements of popular culture must become serious objects of school knowledge. More, however, is at stake here than just an
ethnography of those public spheres where individual and social identities
are constructed and struggled over. More important is the need to fashion a
language of ethics and politics that serves to discriminate between relations
that do violence and those that promote diverse and democratic public cultures through which youth and others can understand their problems and
concerns as part of a larger effort to interrogate and disrupt the dominant
narratives of national identity, economic privilege, and individual empowerment.

Pedagogy must redefine its relationship to modernist forms of culture,
privilege, and canonicity, and serve as a vehicle of translation and cross–fertil-
ization. Pedagogy as a critical cultural practice needs to open up new institutional spaces in which students can experience and define what it means to

be cultural producers capable of both reading different texts and producing them, of moving in and out of theoretical discourses but never losing sight of the need to theorize for themselves. Moreover if critical educators are to move beyond the postmodern prophets of hyper reality, politics must not be exclusively fashioned around plugging into the new electronically mediated community. The struggle for power is not merely about expanding the range of texts that constitute the politics of representation. It is also about struggling within and against those institutions that wield economic, cultural, and political power.

It is becoming increasingly fashionable to argue for a postmodern pedagogy in which it is important to recognize that "One chief effect of electronic hyper text lies in the way it challenges now conventional assumptions about teachers, learners, and the institutions they inhabit" (Landow 1992: 120). As important as this concern is for refiguring the nature of the relationship between authority and knowledge and the pedagogical conditions necessary for decentering the curriculum and opening up new pedagogical spaces, it does not go far enough, and runs the risk of degenerating into a another hyped up methodological fix.

Postmodern pedagogy must be more sensitive to how teachers and students negotiate both texts and identities, but it must do so through a political project that articulates its own authority within a critical understanding of how the self recognizes others as subjects rather than as objects of history. In other words, postmodern pedagogy must address how power is written on, within, and between different groups as part of a broader effort to reimagine schools as democratic public spheres. Authority in this instance is linked to auto-critique and becomes a political and ethical practice through which students become accountable to themselves and others. By making the political project of schooling primary, educators can define and debate the parameters through which communities of difference defined by relations of representation and reception within overlapping and transnational systems of information, exchange, and distribution can address what it means to be educated as a practice of empowerment. In this instance, schools can be rethought as public spheres, as "borderlands of crossing" (Clifford 1992: 134), actively engaged in producing new forms of democratic community organized as sites of translation, negotiation, and resistance.

What is also needed by postmodern educators is a more specific understanding of how affect and ideology mutually construct the knowledge, resistances, and sense of identity that students negotiate as they work through dominant and rupturing narratives attempting in different ways to secure particular forms of authority. Fabienne Worth is right in castigating postmodern educators for undervaluing the problematic nature of the relationship between "desire and the critical enterprise" (1993: 8). A postmodern pedagogy needs to address how the issue of authority can be linked to democratic

GIROUX

processes in the classroom that do not promote pedagogical terrorism and yet still offer representations, histories, and experiences that allow students to critically address the construction of their own subjectivities as they simultaneously engage in an ongoing "process of negotiation between the self and other" (ibid: 26).

The conditions and problems of contemporary border youth may be postmodern, but they will have to be engaged through a willingness to interrogate the world of public politics while at the same time recognizing the limits of postmodernism's more useful insights. In part, this means rendering postmodernism more political by appropriating modernity's call for a better world while abandoning its linear narratives of Western history, unified culture, disciplinary order, and technological progress. In this case, the pedagogical importance of uncertainty and indeterminacy can be rethought through a modernist notion of the dream-world in which youth and others can shape, without the benefit of master narratives, the conditions for producing new ways of learning, engaging, and positing the possibilities for social struggle and solidarity. Radical educators cannot subscribe to either an apocalyptic emptiness or to a politics of refusal that celebrates the immediacy of experience over the more profound dynamic of social memory and moral outrage forged within and against conditions of exploitation, oppression, and the abuse of power. Postmodern pedagogies need to confront history as more than simulacrum and ethics as something other than the casualty of incommensurable language games. Postmodern educators need to take a stand without standing still, to engage their own politics as public intellectuals without essentializing the ethical referents to address human suffering.

In addition, postmodern pedagogy needs to go beyond a call for refiguring the curriculum so as to include new informational technologies. Rather, it needs to assert a politics that makes the relationship among authority, ethics, and power central to practices of learning and teaching that expand rather than close down possibilities of a radical democratic society. Within this discourse, images do not dissolve reality into simply another text. On the contrary, representations become central to revealing the structures of power relations at work in the public schools, society, and the larger global order. Difference does not succumb to fashion in this logic (another touch of ethnicity); instead, difference becomes a marker of struggle in an ongoing movement towards a shared conception of justice and a radicalization of the social order.

NOTES

1. For a particularly succinct examination of postmodernism's challenge to a modernist conception of history, see Vattimo (1992) especially Chapter One.

2. A number of excellent anthologies have appeared that provide readings in postmodernism cutting across a variety of fields. Some of the more recent examples include: Jencks (1992); Natioli and Hutcheon (1993); Docherty (1993).

GIROUX

3. This issue has been taken up in greater detail by Giroux (1988; 1992).

4. John Clarke (1991), *New Times and Old Enemies: Essays on Cultural Studies and America* (New York: Harper Collins), especially Chapter Two. Clarke's analysis has little to offer a complex reading of postmodernism beyond a defensive reaction embedded in his own refusal to take seriously a postmodern critique of the modernist elements in Marxist theories.

5. Needless to say, one can find a great deal of theoretical material that refuses to dismiss postmodern discourses so easily and in doing so performs a theoretical service by unraveling its progressive from its reactionary tendencies. Early examples of this work can be found in Hal Foster (1985); Hebdige (1988); Vattimo (1988); Ross (1988); Hutcheon (1988); Collins (1989); and Connor, (1989). More recent examples, include Nicholson (1990); Lasch (1990); Chambers (1990); Aronowitz and Giroux (1991); Best and Kellner (1991); Denzin (1991); Owens (1992).

REFERENCES

Anderson, Perry. (1984). Modernity and revolution. *New Left Review* No. 144: 96–113.

Anshaw, Carol. (1992). Days of whine and poses. *Village Voice* 10 November: 25–27.

Aronowitz, Stanley and Henry A. Giroux. (1991). *Postmodern Education*. Minneapolis: University of Minnesota Press.

Aronowitz, Stanley and Henry A. Giroux. (1993). *Education Still Under Siege*. Westport: Bergin and Garvey. 2nd Edition.

Bauman, Zygmunt. (1992). *Intimations of Postmodernity*. New York: Routledge.

Berube, Michael. (1992–93). Exigencies of value. *The Minnesota Review* No. 39: 63–87.

Bell, Daniel. (1976). *The Cultural Contradictions of Capitalism*. New York: Basic Books.

Best, Stephen and Douglas Kellner. (1990). *Postmodern Theory*. New York: Guilford Press.

Bishop, Katherine. (1992). The electronic coffeehouse. *New York Times* 2 August, Section: The Street p. 3.

Blythe, Scott. (1993). Generation Xed. *Maclean's* 106, 31 (August): 35.

Bordo, Susan. (1993). *Unbearable Weight: Feminism Western Culture and the Body*. Berkeley: University of California Press.

Butler, Judith. (1991). Contingent foundations: Feminism and the question of postmodernism. In J. Butler and J. Scott (eds.), *Feminists Theorize the Political,* New York: Routledge, 3–21.

Chambers, Iain. (1990). *Border Dialogues*. New York: Routledge.

Clarke, John. (1991). *New Times and Old Enemies*. New York: Harper Collins.

Clifford, James (1992). Museums in the borderlands. In C. Becker et al (eds.), *Different Voices*. New York: Association of Museum Art Directors.

Collins, Jim. (1989). *Uncommon Cultures*. New York: Routledge.

Connor, Steven. (1989). *Postmodernist Culture*. Cambridge, MA: Blackwell.

Denzin, Norman. (1991). *Images of a Postmodern Society*. Newbury Park: Sage.

Docherty, Thomas. Ed. (1993). *Postmodernism: A Reader*. New York: Columbia University Press. 1993.

Eagleton, Terry. (1985). Capitalism, modernism, and postmodernism." *New Left Review* 185 (July): 60–73.

Ebert, Teresa. (1991). Writing in the political: Resistance (Post)modernism. *Legal Studies Forum*. 15, 4, 291–303.

Foster, Hal. Ed. (1985). *Postmodern Culture*. London: Pluto Press.

Giroux, Henry. (1988). *Schooling and the Struggle for Public Life*. Minneapolis: University of Minnesota Press.

Giroux, Henry. (1992). *Border Crossings*. New York: Routledge.

Giroux, Henry. (1994). *Disturbing Pleasures: Learning Popular Culture*. New York: Routledge.

Green, Bill and Chris Bigum. (1993). Aliens in the classroom. *Australian Journal of Education* 37,2.

Habermas, Jürgen. (1978). *The Philosophical Discourse of Modernity*. Cambridge: MIT Press.

Harvey, David. (1989). *The Condition of Postmodernity*. Cambridge: Basil Blackwell.

Hebdige, Dick. (1988). *Hiding in the Light*. New York: Routledge.

Hollingsworth, Pierce. (1993). The new generation gaps: Graying boomers, golden agers, and Generation X. *Food Technology*. 47, 10 (October): 30.

Howe, Neil and Bill Strauss. (1993). *13th Gen: Abort Retry Ignore Fail?* New York: Vantage Books.

Hunter, Ian. (1988). *Culture and Government: The Emergence of Literary Education*. London: Macmillan.

Hutcheon, Linda. (1988). *The Poetics of Postmodernism*. New York: Routledge.

Jencks, Charles. (1992). The postmodern agenda. In his (ed.) *The Postmodern Reader*, New York: St. Martin's Press.

Jost, Kenneth. (1993). Downward mobility. *Congressional Quarterly Researcher* 3:27 (July 23): 627–644.

Kopkind, Andrew. (1992). Slacking toward Bethlehem. *Grand Street* No. 44: 177–188.

Landow, George. (1992). *Hypertext: The Convergence of Contemporary Critical Theory and Technology*. Baltimore: The Johns Hopkins University Press.

Lasch, Scott (1990). *Sociology of Postmodernism*. New York: Routledge.

MacCannell, Dean. (1992). *Empty Meeting*. New York: Routledge.

Mercer, Kobena. (1992). '1968': Periodizing politics and identity. In C. Nelson, P. Treichler and L. Grossberg (eds.), *Cultural Studies*, New York: Routledge.

Natioli, Joseph and Linda Hutcheon, Eds. (1993). *A Postmodern Reader*. Albany: SUNY Press.

Nicholson, Linda, Ed. (1990). *Feminism/Postmodernism*. New York: Routledge.

Owens, Craig. (1992). *Beyond Recognition: Representation, Power, and Culture*. Eds. Scott Bryson, et. al. Berkeley: University of California Press.

Parkes, Walter. (1994). Random access, remote control: The evolution of story telling. *Omni* (January): 48–54, 90–91.

Patton, Paul. (1988). Giving up the ghost: Postmodernism and anti nihilism. In L. Grossberg (ed.) *It's a Sin*, Sydney: Power Publications, 88–95.

Ross, Andrew. Ed. (1988). *Universal Abandon? The Politics of Postmodernism*. Minneapolis: University of Minnesota Press.

Smart, Barry. (1991). Theory and analysis after Foucault. *Culture and Society*. 8: 144–145.

Smart, Barry. (1992). *Modern Conditions. Postmodern Controversies*. New York: Routledge.

Tomlinson, John. (1991). *Cultural Imperialism*. Baltimore: The Johns Hopkins University Press.

Vattimo, Gianni. (1992). *The Transparent Society*. Baltimore: The Johns Hopkins University Press.

Virilio, Paul. (1991). *Lost Dimension*. Trans. Daniel Moshenberg. New York: Semiotext(e).

Willinsky, John. (1991). Postmodern literacy: A primer. *Interchange*. 22, 4: 56–76.

Worth, Fabienne. (1993). Postmodern pedagogy in the multicultural classroom: For inappropriate teachers and imperfect strangers. *Cultural Critique*. No. 25 (Fall): 5–32.

GIROUX

MEDIA KNOWLEDGES, WARRIOR CITZENRY, AND POSTMODERN LITERACIES[1]

Peter McLaren and Rhonda Hammer

The actants, those structures of narrative action, had to sustain the drama of masculine words and deeds for the most ethereal and most lusted-after of goals—to be seen by all not to have backed down, to have drawn the line in the sand and made the inscription matter. The sands turn to concrete when the manly write in them. These are old, indeed old-fashioned, tendentious, unscrupulously generalizing feminist remarks. They need to be made again, as long as virtu, the quality of manliness, means the readiness to kill, that is, to be a replicant, of whatever biological or technological description, in the reproductive dramas of the Father, who forever structures the action in order to produce, again and again, the sacred image of the same. In saecula saeculorum. And, ageless, Bush and Saddam Hussein, those two secular figure heads of secular stages, each declaring holy war, figured in blinding mirror image as autocrat and democrat, are surely knowingly enmeshed in the brotherly salvation histories that have driven their two Peoples of the Book for centuries.

Donna Haraway, 1991, pp. 42–43

chapter 4

The subject is constructed through acts of differentiation that distinguish the subject from its constitutive outside, a domain of abjected alterity conveniently associated with the feminine, but clearly and not exclusively so. Precisely in this recent war we see the Arab as figured as the abjected Other, a site of homophobic fantasy well made clear in the abundance of bad jokes grounded in the linguistic sliding from Saddam to Sodom.

Judith Butler, 1991, p. 76

Postmodern wars are not fought for clearly defined goals. Combatants may well invoke pretexts, but these pretexts are subject to change. As goals change, these wars come to assume an anarchic aspect. Postmodern wars have opened up multiple discursive spaces in which individuals can find agency; women who have always been part of war can find in postmodern war a space to articulate this participation. This articulation threatens to undermine the Homeric war myth, yet it is itself always threatened by the entrenchedness of that archetype. The disenfranchised who before submitted to the distortions of dominant discourse are making their voices heard and their faces seen and thus exposing the mechanisms of power consolidation.

Miriam Cooke, 1991, p. 27

MEDIA KNOWLEDGES: A BRICOLAGE

WE HAVE for some time been chilled by the recognition that we are living in an age gone mad. Such madness is of an escalating variety, not unlike that characterized by Lewis Carroll's Mad Hatter's Tea Party, where Alice's recognition of the privileging discourses of Wonderland—as pathological—was essential for her survival and ultimate escape.

News events of recent years have greatly confirmed our suspicion that the madness surrounding us functions within wider discursive practices. We have referred to the outcome of such practices as "media knowledges." As we followed the media coverage related to the Iran/Contra hearings, the expulsion of the televangelist Jim Bakker, and the ignominious fall from political grace of the Democratic Party's "great white hope," Gary Hart (coverage that was referred to as the three "gates"—"Contra," "Holy," and "Forni"—that followed in the wake of Watergate), we became convinced that our liberation from Wonderland (were it possible) would in no way be comparable to the conditions surrounding Alice's escape. For unlike Alice, who never doubted the lunacy of Wonderland, the majority of North Americans give some semblance of credibility to the mythical landscape of representations and literacies constructed by contemporary media.

We are interested in providing conditions for educators to approach the issue of literacy critically, by recognizing that we live in a world of multiple literacies—you could call them "postmodern literacies"—in which knowledge can be understood as a form of meaning-making. Such knowledge production consists of both our cognitive engagement with and affective investment in various cultural forms (print, film, television, and radio). In this essay we want to draw on Walter Benjamin's figure of the *flâneur* to discuss the role of media commentators as popular intellectuals. More specifically, we want to draw attention to the way media knowledges constitute possibilities for human agency as well as textual restraints placed on teachers as cultural workers—who deal in codes, social texts, and the semiotic circuitry of classrooms and everyday life, and who act as cultural cartographers, mapping cultural life in terms of understanding whose stories are visible and whose memories lie buried in the established archives of history.

THE *FLÂNEUR* IN POSTMODERN CULTURE

Our analysis of the media production by CNN of the war against Iraq and its valorization of the viewer as "phallomilitary warrior-citizen" (Cooke, 1991; Butler, 1991) follows the observation by Susan Buck-Morss (1989) that the role of the news reporter as "*flâneur*-become detective [who] covers the beat", or "photojournalist [who] hangs about like a hunter ready to shoot" has changed as capitalism has expanded into hitherto uncommodified social and cultural realms and has further implicated itself in the signifying practices

82

McLAREN AND HAMMER

of mass communication media. We have followed Buck-Morss in tracing the views of Walter Benjamin towards Baudelaire's figure of the *flâneur*, the "street reader," who strolls ambiguously and ambivalently through the city streets, projecting a "distaste for the industrial labor through which he glides" (Eagleton, 1981, p. 26) and abandoning himself to the crowd like a commodity.

According to Buck-Morss (1989: 306), Benjamin saw the *flâneur* in shifting roles, from "person of leisure (*Musse*)" to someone engaged in "loitering (*Mussigang*)" to the "prototype of the new form of salaried employee who produces news/literature/advertisements for the purpose of information entertainment/persuasion." Buck-Morss paints a final portrait of the *flâneur* as someone whom Benjamin felt advertised not simply commodities but ideological propaganda. Like a "sandwichman" who is "paid to advertise the attractions of mass culture" (pp. 306–307), the *flâneur* as "journalist-in-uniform" advertises the state and "profits by peddling the ideological fashion" (p. 307).

Benjamin's early depiction of the *flâneur*, who "moves majestically against that historical grain that would decompose his body into an alien meaning, reduce his numinous presence to an allegory of loss" (Eagleton, p. 154) was, as a socially rebellious cultural worker, the bohemian prototype—or "urform"—of the modern intellectual (Buck-Morss, p. 304). His method of literary production rejected the mandarin status of the metropolitan intellectual and consisted in strolling the city streets and reflecting on the everyday production of cultural life.

Our understanding of contemporary forms of electronically produced media knowledges has been informed by what we perceive as the changing role of the *flâneur* in the age of late capitalism—one that is as ominous and drastic as the changes that Benjamin perceived. We suggest that the *flâneur* no longer provides the service of teaching his or her generation about "their own objective circumstances"; rather, we suggest that the *flâneur*, as global newscaster, has transmogrified into the afterimage of fascism.

Today we are living in a precarious historical moment in which the *flâneur*—as signifying agent—is undergoing even further metamorphosis. The postmodern *flâneurs* of today are corporate individuals cunningly managing and shaping the world of mass-produced images, superannuated servants of the state whose forms of knowledge production are mediated by and fastened securely to the logic of consumption. They still stroll the city streets, as in Benjamin's era, but this time they are accompanied by a video-production crew and, in wartimes, a military censor. Often the products of salaried employees of transnational corporations and other standard bearers of Imperialism, the insights served up by the global, postmodern *flâneur* (to audiences exceeding millions at one viewing) more often than not mystify and further camouflage race, class, and gender antagonisms, and thereby hinder rather than help viewers understand the conditions of everyday existence.

As reality increasingly becomes confused with the image, and the mediascape becomes the driving force of our time, the image of the postmodern *flâneur* becomes embodied not in human presence but in human immanence transmuted through an electronic signal, a satellite beam roaming the earth in search of new spectacles through which to present and contain reality. We are entering an age of painful loss of everyday history and shared popular memory that has followed the development of media technology since the beginning of the century (Schwoch, White, and Reilly, 1992).

Media knowledges produced by the postmodern *flâneur* serve as a discourse about action that teleologically fulfills itself in the sense that it recounts an event, that is, it emplots an event. Yet, paradoxically, it is an emplotment of a history—an event—that is manufactured not simply as narrative but also as mood, as a "structure of feeling." Often it has no real beginning (*arche*) or end (*telos*) other than the illusion created by the context of its production. The Gordian knot of history is cleaved as history is declared dead in the frozen moment of the image.

Media knowledges offered up by the postmodern *flâneur*—what we refer to as "perpetual pedagogy"—constitute a moving, circulating signword that possesses a valorising and legitimating function in the way that it marks off the territory of the real. In the case of the Persian Gulf War, it was able to situate the mobile self of postmodernity in a synecdochal relation to a hyperreal, apocalyptic event, one that came ideologically unannounced yet was able to "cue" both our sign membership and our "affective investment" (Grossberg, 1988) into the political economy of patriotism and global citizenry.

COLONIZATION OF THE INTERIOR

Today's cultural and historical events bombard our sensibilities with such exponential speed and frequency and through such a variety of media forms that our critical comprehension skills have fallen into rapid deterioration. This collective loss of reasoning and of history appears to be reaching epidemic proportions with little hope of abatement. The etiology of this "plague," many scholars argue, stems from the expanding sophistication and complexity of networks of social relations that we call "television" (Gitlin, 1986).

It is indeed a paradox that a piece of videotape has no visible image inscribed upon it since, like audiotape, it holds nothing but electrical impulses. Television works by electronic scanning in which tiny dots of light on the screen are lit up, one at a time, by the firing of cathode ray guns across alternate lines on the front of the picture tube. Joyce Nelson describes the process as follows:

> The succession of glowing dots moves rapidly across and down, along alternate lines, in a sweep that lights up the first series of phosphors. In all there are 525 such lines of minuscule dots on North American TV sets. During each one-thirtieth of a second, the scanning process completes two full sweeps of the screen,

one on each alternative set of lines, to create, by electrical impulse, the whole mosaic of an instant's image. In terms of micro-seconds, however, there is actually never more than a single dot of light glowing on the screen. Our eyes receive each dot of light, sending its impulse to the brain. The brain records this bit of information, recalls previous impulses, and expects future ones. We "see" an entire image because the brain fills in or completes 99.999 percent of the scanned pattern each fraction of a second, below our conscious awareness. The only picture that ever exists is the one we complete in our brain (1987: 71).

Whereas in film viewing, the viewer fills in the motion between the frames, which change twenty-four times a second, in watching television the viewer fills in the motion and the picture (pp. 71–72). Researchers such as Krugman (cited in Nelson, p. 71) report that watching television shuts down the left hemisphere of the neo-cortex of the brain (which deals with part-by-part analytical thinking and logical analysis) and disengages information processing. This shutdown occurs either because of habituation to the scanning dot or "overloading" during the scanning process. Whatever the case, direct access to the right hemisphere is unquestionably enabled (since it goes into an alpha-rhythm state) and this promotes "evoked-recall" rather than "learned-recall" as well as free associations and unconscious connections.

In effect, this process opens up the private space of the individual viewer to feelings and associations that are ripe for colonization by the advertising industry. Messages designed by advertisers seek to match the coded expectations of viewers rhythm, melody, rhyme, harmony, pictorial triggers, etc. (ibid: 77). This technique provides optimal conditions for advertisers to label our feelings for us: With the help of advertisements and their products, we can purchase "feeling 7–Up" and "Oh what a feeling—Toyota" or Bell Telephone's "long distance feeling" (p. 78).

As a form of knowing, which we refer to as "perpetual pedagogy," mainstream television programming is decidedly anti-dialogical and rarely evokes acts of political refusal. Unreflective television viewing has a homogenizing, unifying force by unfixing the space of cultural enunciation through the right brain hemisphere and simultaneously recolonizing it through the left hemisphere—a form of double-encoding that rehistoricizes and translates heterogeneity and the instability of deep memories and associations into a mimetic correspondence with the real—like Coke, it becomes "the real thing." In effect, the television viewer becomes constructed within the pulsations of electronically mediated desire. Read against this televisually constructed and radically decentered subjectivity, we are able to conceive of the Kantian and Cartesian tradition of viewing the self as rational, unified, and autonomous as little more than a monstrosity. Within the dominant logocentric tradition, viewers are taught to misrecognize in the private space of their phantom selves the deep memories and associations that are evoked below the threshold of conscious awareness as self-conscious, autonomous, and willed desire—

that is, from the perspective of the rational subject as a detached, disembodied, and sovereign (patriarchal) observer of a transparent reality. Furthermore, the illusion that televisual desire can be controlled by an autonomous, self-effulgent ego occludes from viewers the way television works as a corporate mobilization of desire for objects that are constantly misrecognized as real in that liminal space between consciousness and repression.

In fact, the television images that we see are never really there. They exist as furtive shadows that we capture as viewers through forms of televisual address that are variously shaped by our "viewing formations," that is, through our deep cultural memories, our fears, our repressions, and our anxieties. Watching television is not so much having the self decentered or turned nomad against a totalizing regime of logocentric representation: Rather, it is to have one's sense of self-contained identity de-situated and deformed into concatenated levels of desire. We are not so much dealing here with regimes of signification as we are with what Larry Grossberg (1988) calls "mattering maps'—with investments of desire and pleasure.

Television viewing is like watching the world not through the rose-colored glasses of naive hope, but through a glass coffin inside memory's prison house. It offers us a new means of constituting subjectivity, a new "assemblage" formed within capitalism that "reterritorializes" the relation of human and the machine (Poster 1990: 136). As Deleuze and Guattari put it:

> With automation comes . . . a new kind of enslavement . . . One is enslaved by TV as a human machine insofar as the television viewers are no longer consumers or users, nor even subjects who supposedly "make" it, but intrinsic component pieces, "input" and "output" feedback or recurrences that are no longer connected to the machine in such a way as to produce or use it. In machine enslavement, there is nothing but transformations and exchanges of information (cited in Poster 1990: 136).

But the subjectivity constructed through machine enslavement is more than the subject's positioning within the circuit of information flows or the "schizoid pulsations of the unconscious." According to Poster, there occurs a radicalization of anti-logocentric bearings of the self brought on by electronically mediated communication, and the undermining of the space/time coordinates that hold together the Cartesian view of the subject as autonomous and rational. In Poster's view, this "reterritorialization" of subjectivity offers the possibility for radically new and potentially emancipatory forms of community. Since for Poster electronically mediated communication both supplements and substitutes for existing forms of sociability (Poster 1990: 154), there always exists a space for the construction of "new and unrecognizable modes of community." Yet, as we shall argue in the final section, whether or not these new modes of sociality and community will be emancipatory will depend to a large extent on what types of media literacy are permitted.

George Gerbner (1989, 1990) has made a good case for the development of critical media literacy. His research has revealed that U.S. television viewers accept a distorted picture of the real world "more readily than reality itself." According to Gerbner, television reality is one in which men outnumber women three to one, where women are usually portrayed as either mothers or lovers, rarely work outside the home, and are natural victims of violence. It is a reality in which less than ten percent of the population hold blue-collar jobs, where few elderly people exist, where Black youth learn to accept their minority status as inevitable and are trained to anticipate their own victimization (they are usually cast as the white hero's comic sidekick or as drug addicts, gang members, or killers). It is a world in which 18 acts of violence an hour occur in children's prime-time programs. Violence in television, Gerbner insists, demonstrates the social power of adult white males who are most likely to get involved with violence but most likely to get away with it. Television also serves as a mass spectacle reflecting and legitimating the allocative power of the state. That such an unreality could be rendered natural and commonsensical in a country that in 1990 reported the largest number of rapes against women in its history and a prison incarceration rate of Blacks that exceeded that of the former apartheid South Africa, where rich Angelenos are hiring private police, where wealthy neighborhoods display signs warning "Armed Response!" and where security systems and the militarization of urban life are refiguring social space along the lines of the postmodern film *Bladerunner*, is symptomatic of a moral and epistemological crisis of astonishing proportions.

We witnessed with alarm the CNN coverage of the aftermath of the Rodney King trial in Los Angeles, where viewers were presented with sweeping footage shot from helicopters of burning buildings, accompanied by voice-over denunciations by politicians of the looting and violence, and questions raised by news commentators that suggest that the social turmoil and rioting may only be tenuously connected to the outcome of the trial. Much of the coverage implied that the riots were simply fueled by "hoodlums" who were mostly black and Latino gang members taking advantage of the situation. Again and again the CNN coverage occulted the relationship among racism, economic injustice, and urban violence and crime. Most frightening of all were comments from viewers and some of the jurors who claimed that Rodney King actually controlled the circumstances surrounding his own beating by not assuming the correct arrest-ready posture. It is this same psychology of denial that allows a war against people of color to continue in our cities so that it is rarely ever seen for what it is. It is the same psychology of denial that frames the news coverage of social issues. It is the same ideological denial that permits a president to carry out a policy of race and class warfare under the cover of democracy and decency. Few treatments of the Los Angeles uprising cared to mention that Los Angeles is facing its worst recession since World War II and that many of the jobs that have been lost were semiskilled unionized positions.

McLAREN AND HAMMER

In the treatment by the national media of the O.J. Simpson verdict, the "racial thinking" of African-Americans was attacked while the historical victimization of African-Americans by the white judicial system was all but ignored. The media acts as if the American Dream were still possible for all segments of the society and that a paramilitary-style police force is the only reasonable option to protect those who still believe in the American Way. Most repugnant of all was George Bush's attempt to make the social policies of the 1970s the scapegoat for his own (and Reagan's) war on the underclass.

DEATH AS ENTERTAINMENT: FOR PATRIOTS ONLY

A highly precipitous occasion for our reflection on these themes has been the coverage of the three seemingly unrelated historical events known as the "gates." What struck us as most disconcerting was the conflation of these diverse and unrelated newsworthy events into a single representative category of public consumption—namely, entertainment—and thus of being (at least in the public eye) of equal import. To reduce the complex interactions of these events to the noun "gates" transforms these events into soap opera spectacles of individual transgression while ignoring their national, cultural, and geopolitical situatedness as social practices occurring in specific contexts at particular historical moments. What reduces these events to the same level of importance is their entertainment value: the sexual and political intrigue, the attempted cover-ups, the image value elicited by the personalities of the offenders, etc. This type of reductionism is what Wilden (1987) refers to as "symmetrization." Symmetrization involves the ideological and epistemological process of making hierarchically distinct levels of relationship seem "equal" or on the same level when one class of relationship is in reality a different logical type than another.

In *Amusing Ourselves to Death,* Neil Postman assures us that what we have been describing is neither hallucination nor historical accident. The culprit, as Postman sees it, is the complex, multileveled system of communication known as the television industry. As he puts it:

> Our politics, religion, news, athletics, education, and commerce have been transformed into congenial adjuncts of show business, largely without protest or even much popular notice. The result is that we are people on the verge of *amusing ourselves to death* (1985: 3–4: emphasis ours).

Within this context, we view these three news events as a representative metaphor for the state of news reporting in the age of the "postmodern *flâneur*," and an apt indicator of the shape of things to come in the state of 1990s broadcast news. Regardless of the relationships that both constrain and enable the construction of content, television's politics of representation and mode of information reduces everything from commercials, to comedy, to local, national, or international events to the same meta-form: entertainment.

McLAREN AND HAMMER

The media culture of the United States had already prepared the citizenry to delight in the human destruction of war-at-a-distance. In a recent book, Barry Sanders writes that "the handgun is the writing instrument of illiteracy" (1994, p. 163). Sanders links the growth of guns and the escalating violence in the United States to, among other things, a loss of print and oral literacy due to the proliferation of electronic media. For Sanders, technological innovation is linked more to commodity production than vernacular values such as self-reliance and self-awareness. Language has, Sanders contends, degraded through the electronic media into communication. The collapse of alphabetized narrative space—i.e., the collapse of that internalized text that constitutes our psychosocial frame of reference—has created people with little, if any, remorse or self-reflexivity. Since 1990, sixty thousand people in the United States have been killed by handguns, more than the number of Americans who lost their lives in Vietnam. There are two hundred and fifty thousand federally licensed gunshops in the United States compared to twenty-three thousand public high schools. In wealthy enclaves like Beverly Hills, California, alcohol and fine food is served at shooting ranges, while gun boutiques carry 357 Magnums, Colt Pythons, Smith & Wesson 29s, Sphinx AT-2,000's, and SIG-Sauer P-226s. There you can watch Hollywood actors, CEOs, and agents in Gaultier jackets and Armani suits and raw silk shirts fire at pop-up targets (Sanders, 1994). The structural unconscious of the United States has been fashioned out of gun mythologies, and the Cobray M11/9, the AK47 and the Uzi assault rifle are playing a formative part in constructing the moral agency of the country.

89

PROFANE ILLUMINATION: ENTERTAINMENT AS THE STRUCTURE OF COLONIALIST MODES OF SUBJECTIVITY

America: heroic, phallic America is dead. Great God America proclaimed itself the paramount power, the vital cultural center, and all the other gods died laughing.

(McKenzie Wark, 1991, p. 48)

Our previous investigations of the media (Hammer and Wilden, 1987: Giroux and McLaren, 1992: Hammer and McLaren, 1993; McLaren and Hammer, 1991) did little to prepare us for the violent semiotics of the media spectacle surrounding the coverage of the Persian Gulf War, especially the way it was able to meld the apocalyptic genre of catastrophe with the nonsense genre of carnival. More specifically, we were struck by the ability of the media to transform the military campaigns in Kuwait and Iraq into a twenty-four-hour advertising spectacle in which the newscaster as postmodern *flâneur* was (with the few notable exceptions of reporters who chose not to cooperate with military censors) reduced to a carnival huckster for patriotic zeal and a salesperson for machineries of destruction and death.

The propagandistic construction of the Gulf War is an extreme example of how the media serves up death for surplus consumption in a politics that centers primarily around the lifestyle industry and what Stuart Ewen (1988: 264) terms "info-tainment." As Ewen (p. 265) notes, "in the ratings game, the news—out of economic necessity—must be transformed into a drama, a thriller, entertainment. Within such a context, the *truth* is defined as *that which sells*" (emphasis original). Especially with reference to the CNN coverage of the war, a kindred range of film and videos dealing with war at a distance (*Top Gun, Iron Eagle*, etc.) tacitly coordinated the reception of many viewers to the aerial shots of "precision" hits through a superimposition of images and forms of emplotment—memories from postmodern war's electronic and celluloid Hollywood archive—transforming war coverage into a type of palimpsest blending the discontinuity of war with the continuity of Western narratives about it. Mark Poster remarks that there existed a "deja vu" effect with aerial shots that provoked memories of computer games of flight simulations: "Just when you are taken to the place of impact, the intensifying rhetoric of realism implodes into the hyperrealism of computer games" (1991, p. 221).

War in the age of video creates its own aesthetic images. The ghostly green images produced by night vision technology created a new wartime aesthetic—what James Der Derian calls "video verte"—which is "a powerful combination of the latest technology and the lowest-quality image" (1994, p. 271).

The mass production of patriotic sentiment and the mobilization of consent that allowed such a disproportionate and excessive use of force literally to disintegrate thousands of Iraqi soldiers fleeing north out of Kuwait (described as "one of the most terrible harassments of a retreating army in the history of warfare"; (Ellis, Saeeda, and Plott 1991: 21) was, in our minds, unquestionably designed as a mass advertisement: the hidden payoff was not the construction of a more critically informed public but rather an electronic display for showcasing weapons of mass destruction in a way that benefitted arms dealers, the war industry, and a phallic warfare state deploying identities politically and strategically by preparing its citizenry to assume a leadership role in a "new world order."

Douglas Kellner's impressive study of the Persian Gulf War (1992) has made it clear that the war was structured around common interests between the media and the military. For instance, General Electric (which owns NBC) received approximately nine billion dollars in military contracts in 1989. Also clear to us is the production of neo-imperialistic sentiment through the media, as evident, Said (1993) notes, in the U.S. feelings of ownership of the war and the way in which the American public felt it controlled the decision of whether or not force would be used.

According to Derian, the Gulf War is a preeminent manifestation of what he calls a simulation syndrome. War games computer-simulated by private

McLAREN AND HAMMER

contractors played a role not just on the battlefield in the Persian Gulf, but also in the very decision to go to war. Iraq purchased a wargame from the Washington military-consulting firm BDM International in its war with Iran. The software for its invasion of Kuwait was also purchased from the same firm. Operation Internal Look '90 was a simulated command-post exercise sponsored by General Schwartzkopf in July 1990 and, as it turned out, helped to set the stage for Operation Desert Storm. In fact, the U.S. victory in the Gulf War was a victory of wargame against wargame, a cyberwar of simulations. Derian acknowledges a number of successive victories by the U.S. in its cyberwar:

> First, the prewar simulation, Operation Internal Look '90, which defeated the Iraqi simulation for the invasion of Kuwait; second, the wargame of Air-Land battle, which defeated an Iraqi army that resembled the game's intended enemy, the Warsaw Pact, in hyperreality only; third, the war of spectacle, which defeated the spectacle of war on the battlefield of videographic reproduction; and finally, the postwar after-simulation of Vietnam, which defeated an earlier defeat by assimilating Vietnam's history and lessons into the victory of the Gulf War. (1994, p. 274).

Given the current tripolar global economy (the United States, Germany, Japan), the Gulf War could be seen as a shrewd market move to liquidate overstocked ammunitions warehouses and unused supplies of armaments. Can we tell the difference between actual and simulated war? It is difficult when the investigative gaze of the viewer is replaced by a giddy acquiescence to the accredited expertise of visiting military experts and politicians. This is not to suggest that there exist no readings among viewers that aggravate the techno-ideological thrust of the programming, but that the static and retrospective character of news shows is often enough to smudge the boundary between *doxa* and *episteme*. Spectacles do not invite situating information into a context. This was most evident in CNN's use of dazzling optical effects as exploding bombs and tracer bullets became luminously pockmarked against darkened skies while the Iraqi soldiers remained largely invisible except perhaps as oneiric battlefield abstractions that resembled the oval forms of Oliver Wascow photographs.

Derian remarks that "At some moments—the most powerful ones—the link between sign and signifier went into Möbius-strip contortions, as when we saw what the nose of a smart bomb saw as it rode a laser beam to its target, making its fundamental truth-claim not in a flash of illumination but in the emptiness of a dark screen" (1994, p. 272).

As Jochen and Linda Schulte-Sasse point out, we are speaking here of an event that is potentially more dangerous than what Walter Benjamin referred to as the "aestheticization of politics," since we are witnessing the very process of politics being constructed symbolically through the imaginary of media

91

McLAREN AND HAMMER

images (1991: 70). Not only was the media war in the Gulf "at least in part propelled by [its] power to unify the body politic and to instill in the state's subjects the illusion of being masterful agents of history," the war itself also became an epiphenomenon of the media's production of the war—what could be called "an appendix of image production, an inconvenient though unfortunately still necessary anchor in reality of media simulations" (pp. 70–71). The danger of media-produced wars turning spectators into narrator/agents of history is that it carries with it both the illusion of and addiction to omnipotence. Jochen and Linda Schulte-Sasse remark:

While experiencing ourselves, collectively and individually, as a unified body, we simultaneously fall prey to the illusion that we can decipher and master the world, we cover up our actual impotence as agents, which in turn worsens the nation's material situation (economy, infrastructure, educational system, etc.) and increases its dependence on images of superiority (p. 71).

The "totally administered stylistic environment" of the newscast is one of the best entertainment formats for promulgating "cognitive confusion" and geopolitical misunderstanding. Ewen remarks:

The highly stylized signature of the news program offers the only overarching principle of cohesion and meaning. Again, surface makes more sense than substance. The assembled facts, as joined together by the familiar, formulaic, and authoritative personality of "The News," becomes the most accessible version of the larger reality that most Americans have at their disposal. Consciousness about the world is continually drawn away from a geopolitical understanding of events as they take place in the world. As nations and people are daily sorted out into boxes marked "good guys," "villains," "victims," and "lucky ones," style becomes the essence, reality becomes appearance (1988: 265).

Investment in imperialism is important for the United States to retain its superpower status since it cannot compete successfully with Japan and Germany's demilitarized economies. We view the war coverage on CNN and other stations as a global media advertising campaign for sophisticated weapons technology—technology now being sold to countries in the Gulf region and elsewhere (e.g. Israel and Turkey). The Gulf War spectacle, in this sense, reflected the global push of transnational capital in the information-cultural sphere primarily through the transformation of the "theater" of battle into an international market economy. It was an advertisement for the "new world order" of Western-structured development and incorporation into the dominant world business order. Yet the new world order to which the Gulf War pointed was framed by a gaudy sideshow of flags, emblems, and military hardware—a counterfeit democracy produced through media knowledges able to harness the affective currency of popular culture such that the average

92

American's investment in being "American" reached an unparalleled high not approximated since the years around the post–World–War–II McCarthy hearings.

DOUBLESPEAK: THE NEW LANGUAGE OF DEMOCRACY

The destructiveness of war furnishes proof that society has not been mature enough to incorporate technology as its organ, that technology has not been sufficiently developed to cope with the elemental forces of society. The horrible features of imperialistic warfare are attributable to the discrepancy between the tremendous means of production and their inadequate utilization in the process of production—in other words to unemployment and the lack of markets. Imperialistic war is a rebellion of technology which collects, in the form of human material, the claims to which society directs a stream into a bed of trenches; instead of dropping seeds from airplanes it drops incendiary bombs over cities; and through gas warfare the aura is abolished in a new way.

(Walter Benjamin 1969: 242).

The success of the advertising campaign surrounding both the "selling" and the "displaying" of the Gulf War was largely due to the strategic use of doublespeak to disguise from television viewers the extent of the real terror and carnage of the military campaign against Iraq. When a euphemism is used to mislead or deceive, it becomes doublespeak. William Lutz writes that "doublespeak is a language that avoids or shifts responsibillty, language that is at variance with its real or purported meaning. It is a language that conceals or prevents thought; rather than extending thought, doublespeak limits it" (1981: 1).

For instance, Lutz reports that in 1984 the U.S. State Department announced it would no longer use the word "killing" in its annual report on the status of human rights in countries around the world. Instead, it chose the term "unlawful or arbitrary deprivation of life." While the State Department claimed that this term was a more accurate description of the condition, the term actually functioned to direct attention away from the embarrassing situation of government-sanctioned killings in countries supported by the United States and that have been certified by the United States as respecting the human rights of their citizens (p. 3). "Radiation enhancement device" is a term used by Pentagon officials to describe nuclear bombs. The neutron bomb was called a "cookie cutter" because it could kill people inside less than a three-quarter-mile radius without harming allied soldiers and civilians nearby.

Doublespeak occurs through the use of terms that are to a large extent technically true but that function as lies. For instance, a profit may be described as a "negative deficit;" firing staff may be described by such euphemisms as "staff reduction," "non-retention," "dehiring," or "rationalizing of resources."

McLAREN AND HAMMER

During the media's production of the Gulf War, there existed, in the words of Carol E. Cohn (1991: 88), a "reversal of metaphors between sentient beings and insentient things." For example, the term "air support" overlooks the devastation and loss of life from bombing raids; "collateral damage" refers to civilian deaths; "incontinent ordinances" are bombs or missiles that hit allied troops under conditions of "friendly fire"; a "party" is a battle; "bags of tools" refers to weapons; "theater of operations" to a battle field; "surgical strike" refers to precision bombing; and "delivering a package" to dropping bombs.

Cohn describes a radio news briefing on the Persian Gulf as "Madison Avenue's idea of a housewife's dream": General Colin Powell talks about fighting in a "sanitary fashion." The air force launches "surgically clean strikes." Instead of bombing the Iraqi troops, U.S. forces are "flying sorties," "engaging" the enemy, "taking out" Iraqi "assets," "servicing" targets, and "softening up" the Republican Guard. Iraqi soldiers do not blow up when they are hit by bombs or missiles. Instead, their "emplacements absorb the munitions" (p. 88). Human beings become insentient things while weapons become the living actors of war. "Smart" weapons that have eyes and computer "brains" make the decision when and where to drop seven-and-a-half tons of bombs, taking away the moral responsibility of the combatants themselves (p. 88). Margot Norris has noted the Pentagon's consistent strategy of juxtaposing "excessively specific information on the deployment and destruction of weaponry, machines, and "hard" targets with refusal to stipulate the soft "targets or Iraqi bodies"—a move that "has shaped both the fiction and the ideology" of the "technological utopianism" that became the central defense narrative in President Bush's "new world order" (1991: 224). Perhaps the full weight of the moral absurdity of doublespeak can be grasped in the *Newsweek* cover (1/18/91) that read "The New Science of War/High-Tech Hardware: How Many Lives Can It Save?"

CNN's spectacularization of the Gulf War managed to position the viewer so that to be against the war was to be "biased" and to be in favor of it was to be "objective." Its narrative apparatus with its apparent realism not only restructured our feelings surrounding the historical conditions being played out but through strategies of indirection and disinformation was also able to mobilize particular economies of affect. Again, our argument is that the war could be read as one large advertisement that served as unquestionably the "best show in town." Just as sure as U.S. bombs obliterated Iraqi soldiers and civilians, the media's war obliterated the particular historical and political background of Western imperialism that served as the context for the actual fighting. In words reminiscent of an advertisement, Richard Blystone of CNN (1/2/91) described a "Scud" missile as "a quarter-ton of concentrated hatred," while the Patriot missile was described by *USA Today* (1/22/91) as "three inches longer than a Cadillac Sedan de Ville" (Naureckas, 1991).

Adjectives used to describe the assault on Iraq were part of the lexicon of

94

corporate product assessment. The Pentagon's reaction to the war effort was reported by NBC's Robert Bazell as "spectacular news." CBS's Charles Osgood and Jim Stewart described bombing raids as "a marvel" and "picture-perfect" respectively. CBS's Dan Rather was witnessed by viewers exclaiming to a general, "Congratulations on a job wonderfully done!" (*Fairness and Accuracy in Reporting*, July/August, 1991).

It is ironic if not profoundly disturbing that the substanceless unreality of the Gulf War—its hyperreality—has become the metanarrative for a renewed U.S. patriotism and the meaning of citizenship. The construction of patriotism through the production of media unreality works—has meaning—as long as the viewer does not know his or her desire is being mobilized and structured through the advertisement mode of information. According to Mark Poster:

> As ad after ad is viewed, the representational critic gradually loses interest, becomes lulled into a noncritical stance, is bored, and gradually receives the communication differently . . . the ad only works to the extent that it is not understood to be an ad, not understood instrumentally. Through its linguistic structure the TV ad communicates at a level other than the instrumental which is placed in brackets. Floating signifiers, which have no relation to the product, are set in play; images and words that convey desirable or undesirable states of being are portrayed in a manner that optimizes the viewer's attention without arousing critical awareness.
>
> A communication is enacted, in the TV ad, which is not found in any context of daily life. An unreal is made real, a set or meanings is communicated which is more real than reality (1990: 63).

THE MASS SPECTACLE AS TOTEMIC ADVERTISEMENT

Perhaps the most important point to be made about the construction of subjectivity through media as a form of advertisement is its religious function. As Sut Jhally (1990: 202) notes in his historical tracing of the person-object relation in advertisements, advertisements now function as a form of *totemism* in which "utility symbolization and personalization are mixed and remixed under the sign of the group." Products no longer become venerated for their utility, their value as icons, or their power as fetishes: rather, they now function in the post-Fordist service economy as a badge of a group—*a form of shared lifestyle*. New world order patriots are now held together by lifestyle rather than particular political commitments. For example, Arnold Schwarzenegger purchased a special jeep (nicknamed the "Hummer") used in the Gulf War by U.S. troops for his own personal use. In New York City, manufacturers of bulletproof vests started *special fashion lines* for toddlers and elementary school children who might accidentally absorb stray bullets from homeboy dealers in "pumps," with ten-dollar gold tooth caps and who carry customized AK 47 assault rifles. The guns are not lifestyle accessories—yet. But gas masks are. New York celebrity fashion designer Andre Van Pier announced a spring fashion line based on the theme of "Desert Storm." It attempted to capture the "Gulf War look." Fashion accessories included neon-colored gas masks slung renegade-chic over the shoulder. To add insult to injury, a major New York baseball card manufacturer revealed a line of Gulf War cards that were supposed to be "educational." Of course, the cards included photos of all the major U.S. war hardware and portraits of the American generals, but the only item represented from Iraq in this "educational" collection was a Scud missile.

The Gulf War was packaged for U.S. viewers in the form of the lifestyle politics of watching football spectacles. According to Emest Larsen (1991: 5), following the Gulf War Superbowl in January 1991, "General Schwartzkopf explain[ed] the fine points of bombing runs, with the same delivery style and the same instant replay as the network football commentators have just used." Further, he notes that the idiom used on television to describe the war

> also evoked the jingoist jocksniffery of football announcers. The emphasis on number, names, and stats, on graphics, plays, and kicking ass, and later, on "cutting it off and killing it," in Colin Powell's unstudied phrase, are all derived from the sports world, that sweaty utopia of repressed homoerotic ritual combat made up of grown-up males in uniforms whose entire livelihood is concentrated on their ability to use their fetishized bodies with the forceful precision of high-tech weapons. At one point Bush even called the war his Superbowl. (p. 8)

96

It is tragically surreal that seven players from the Superbowl appeared on television to comment on the war while a survey of the sources on the ABC, CBS, and NBC nightly news found that of 878 on-air sources, only one— Bill Monning of Physicians Against Nuclear War—was representative of a national peace organzation (*Fairness and Accuracy in Reporting*, 1991).

TELEVISION REALITY AS THE DISCOURSE OF THE OTHER

> Where we in the West tend to think of our New Testament heritage, where you turn the other cheek and you let bygones be bygones and forgive and forget, the people of the Middle East are the people of the Old Testament, if you will—if the Muslims will let me say that—where there's much more of an eye for an eye and a tooth for a tooth . . . (Edward Peck, former U.S. ambassador to Iraq, cited in "The Media and the Gulf War: Cheerleaders for U.S. Militarism by *Fairness and Accuracy in Reporting*, excerpted from the May 1991 issue in Peace and Freedom, July/August 1991, No. 631.).

Soon after the war ended, our students (from our respective classrooms in Canada and the United States) expressed regret that they could no longer return to their television sets with the same mixture of commitment and enjoyment that many of them reserved only for their favorite soap operas. CNN's staged desire in its coverage of the war had presented them with unamibiguous coordinates to construct *national economies of affect* in the form of binary oppositions (patriot/traitor; good/evil; Christian/Muslim; democracy/dictatorship: liberators/enslaved). Hussein was compared to other dark-skinned leaders such as Idi Amin, Qadafi, and Noriega while the only European who made this rogues gallery was Stalin (Shohat, 1991). As Shohat points out, television anchors in the United States followed George Bush in calling Hussein by his first name—"Sadd'm"—to evoke a series of associations such as Satan, damn, and Sodom. How many television anchors used to refer to George Bush as George? Furthermore, why was Hussein never compared to Hitler when he was armed by the United States or when he used chemical weapons against Iranians and Kurds? Why, for instance, did television archives reveal the brutal consequences of chemical warfare by using images from World War I or from the Iranian war but avoid any images of destruction caused by Agent Orange or napalm during Vietnam strikes (Shohat, 1991: 137)? Shohat further notes that

> The Hussein-Hitler analogy prolonged the historical intertext of Israeli and American imagery linking Arabs to Nazis. This link, both metonymic and metaphoric, had been a staple of didactic Israeli film (*Hill 24 Doesn't Answer, Rebels, Against the Light*) as well as of Hollywood cinema (*Ship of Fools, Exodus, Raiders of the Lost Ark*).

The use of warring oppositions such as "good/evil" and "democracy/dictatorship" to frame associations between Hussein and Hitler served to decontextualize and dehistoricize the events surrounding the war and effectively to "symmetrize" existing relations of power and privilege in the Gulf region. For instance, by establishing chains of equivalences between the war in the Gulf and World War II, the colonial and neocolonial legacy of European nations who "parceled up" the inhabitants of the Ottoman Empire and installed monarchies and regimes loyal to the imperial powers was successfully elided. This made it easier for typical colonial narratives to be constructed such as "the rescue of white or dark women from a dark rapist" under the metaphor "the rape of Kuwait," which followed the "historical oversexualization of Blacks and Indians . . . [which was continued] . . . in the image of Saddam and the Arabs" (Shohat p. 140).

Derian rightly argues that the Gulf War has helped to redefine American identity in the post-Cold War security state by reconstructing patriotism in opposition to the ubiquitous and indomitable radical otherness that marks the global world of difference. The deterritorialization of the state and the disintegration of the bipolar order has left us with a Gulf War syndrome. Within such a syndrome

> the construction and destruction of the enemy other is measured in time, not territory; prosecuted in the field of perception, not politics; authenticated by

technical reproduction, not material referents; and played out in the method and metaphor of gaming, not the history and horror of warring (1994, p. 275).

The colonial narratives played out for American viewers during CNN's production of the Gulf War echo the way in which contemporary forms of media knowledges reproduce national images of citizenship. Such images are modelled on the John-Wayneing of America and captured in the remunerative cliches "Go for it!" (which became the clarion call for the U.S. brand of rugged individualism) and Clint Eastwood's "Go ahead. Make my day!": cliches which adorn the discursive fountainhead of United States bravado culture. These slogans have become cultural aphorisms that reveal a great deal about the structural unconscious of the United States. Both Ronald Reagan and George Bush referred to "Go ahead. Make my day!" while in office. When Clint Eastwood delivered his famous lines in the movie *Sudden Impact* (made during the Reagan presidency) he is daring a Black man to murder a woman so that he (Dirty Harry) can kill him. As Michael Rogin (1990) has pointed out, Dirty Harry is willing to sacrifice women and people of color in the name of his own courage. Reagan had made women and Black people his targets by destroying their welfare-state tax benefits—an act he was defending when he dared his detractors to "Make my day!" Similarly, George Bush made the Black criminal and White rapist of *Sudden Impact* into the figure of Willie Horton, as he attempted for the first time to organize American politics around the ominous image of interracial rape (Rogin, 1990).

98

With the 1992 election campaign in mind, Bush appeared to be using the issue of racial hiring quotas to achieve a similar effect—the fear of darker skinned immigrants taking jobs away from better qualified White people.

The coverage of the Gulf War recalled the warning sounded by the 1975 Trilateral Commission that the electronic media were creating situations of surplus democracy that made the United States more difficult to govern because television was becoming too adversarial and challenging leadership practices and policy initiatives, and delegitimizing established institutions (Kellner 1990: 6–7). In the case of the Gulf War, only 1.5 percent of network sources protested the war, about the same number as the sources who were asked about how the war had affected their travel plans (Naureckas 1991: 5). The Brookings Institute, the most important think tank consulted by the media during the Gulf War, was passed off as a think tank of the left. Representatives from Brookings were called upon to debate those from hard-line conservative think tanks such as the Center for Strategic and International Studies and the American Enterprise Institute. However, the Brookings Institute has been "an institution of the center-right for more than a decade" (Soley 1991: 6). In fact, topping the list of corporate donors to Brookings were media corporations "which drew heavily on Brookings for "liberal" opinions and sound bites" (ibid.).

McLAREN AND HAMMER

It should come as little surprise that views from an authenically progressive think tank such as the Institute for Policy Studies were rarely solicited or cited. In fact, "In seven months of the conflict, IPS was cited 26 times by six major papers (six percent of Brookings's citations); in the first month, not one IPS representative appeared on a nightly newscast" (Soley 1991: 6).

Another example of the repugnantly partisan allegiance of the media to military interests was the conspicuous absence of leftist media analysts and foreign policy experts such as Noam Chomsky. As one of the leading intellectuals in the United States on issues of media analysis and U.S. foreign intervention, Chomsky is too brilliant a rhetorician and too morally honest to be anything but an occasional guest on the US media.

Even our most cherished democracies need to invent "others" upon which to displace the rage of our own failures. Often these "others" were considered at one time to be neighbours or allies. But ultimately these neighbours found each other to be strangers in the midst of their intimacy. As Žižek notes, "The democratic attitude is always based upon a certain fetishistic split: *I know very well* (that the democratic form is just a form spoiled by stains of "pathological" imbalance)" (1991: 168). Even love for the neighboring country necessarily turns into destructive hatred, in accordance with the Lacanian motto *I love you, but there is in you something more than you,* objet petit a, *which is why I mutilate you* (1991: 169).

THE NEW RIGHT AND THE DEFORMATION OF REALITY

And we have now moved what amounts to a medium-size American city completely capable of defending itself all the way over to the Middle East.

>   (President George Bush, statement to the press about the U.S. military
>   deployment in Saudi Arabia, Kennebunkport, Maine, August 22,
>   1990, as cited in O. K. Werckmeister, *Citadel Culture,* p. 187).

An important, if not urgent, reason for students to become media literate has to do with the power of postmodern literacies such as film and television to encode our subjective formations with cultural memory. Since the vector-field of identity has expanded into the electromagnetic spectrum, McKenzie Wark warns that

the encoding of memory in postmodern culture is in the hands of ever more sophisticated cultural technologies. We no longer have roots; we have aerials. George Lukács spoke of a second nature, composed of the products of physical labor, over and against which living labor is formed and struggles. It would seem appropriate now to speak of a third nature, of an environment shot through with the products of intellectual labor, over and against which intellectual labor is formed and struggles. It is this third nature which replicates itself in us, and hence it is no small matter who owns this little piece of America's soul. For we all grew up in America, in a place called Hollywood, a place where movie stars have been replaced in the image-bank by teenage crack-heads and serial killers (1991: 45).

The view that journalism is impartial was so irrefutably belied by the coverage of the Gulf War by all major networks that the term "impartial" takes on an absurd quality rivalled only by the insistence that their complicity with U.S. military censorship was necessary, justified, and even desirable. Competition for readers among the print media fuelled graphic design wars between *Time* and *Newsweek*, which eventually saw pull-out maps of the war zone. These "wars" were not so much designed to inform viewers as to win more subscribers. The extra design costs by the major television networks were also aimed at getting more viewers. In these instances, media war promotion disguised as responsible reporting culminated in such sickening collusions between power politics and the unslakable greed of corporate capitalism as the *Newsweek-Bush* collaboration in which a bylined article by Bush was justified by the hawkish press on the grounds that press conferences and speeches were not sufficent to allow the President to expand his vision of the Gulf crisis. Even *Rolling Stone* cashed in on the war fever by weaving a yellow ribbon through the magazine's logo in the March 21 special college issue. With Dan Rather trying to revive a flagging career by saluting the troops on the air, and many news anchors using the royal "we" when referring to U.S. troops, the world spotlight could be turned on the U.S. as the high-tech weaponry capital of the world and Americans could temporarily forget about the cultural invasion of Sony Walkmans or Japanese car imports (cf. MacArthur 1992). This had a tonic effect on the American people and made it easier to forget that "collateral damage" during air strikes often meant burned and mangled civilians. It encouraged journalists to willfully ignore the fact that the Pentagon is a customer of General Electric (that a successful company paid bribes to Israeli officials to buy its military hardware), which is the parent company of NBC. In fact, so deferent were the media to Schwartzkopf and his minions, that the Fourth Estate readily kissed the patriotic whip which the good General had wielded so tenaciously to menace their journalistic hides, hides already thinned by two decades of accusations that the press were responsible for losing the war in Vietnam.

The New Right has used the media effectively (and affectively) not simply to transform war into a spectacle of national unity based on the Manichean grandeur of good triumphing over evil; nor have they used the media primarily to turn generals into talk show guests through the prodigious use of high tech image consultants (although they have done both very successfully; see Giroux and McLaren, 1989). More impressively, the New Right has been able to seduce Americans through the media to retreat into cultural nostalgia and social amnesia as a way of draining attention away from escalating social problems such as rising incidences of racism in urban settings, growing numbers of

100

homeless, and the devastation of AIDS. Part of this has to do with the media's ability to reduce the historical present to a collage of images, a symbiotic coupling of machine and body, a new cult of the simulacrum. Kellner claims that under the control of multinational capital the media effectively served as ideological mouth pieces for Reagan/Bush disinformation and in so doing helped to forge a conservative ideological hegemony—what Schiller (1989) calls the shadowy but many-tentacled disinformation industry. Kellner writes:

> It is a historical irony that the 1980s marked the defeat of democracy by capitalism in the United States and the triumph of democracy over state communism in the Soviet bloc countries. At present, the "free" television media in the United States are probably no more adversarial and no less propagandistic than Pravda or the television stations in the Eastern European countries, hence the very future of democracy is at stake—and development of a democratic communications system is necessary if democracy is to be realized (1990: 219).

Certainly recent events surrounding the official U.S. media censorship imposed by the military during the Gulf War have largely confirmed Kellner's pronouncement. However, the latest victory of the New Right's media disinformation/propaganda campaign has been through the invention of and concurrent attack upon what has been called the repressive "left mandarin" regime of "political correctness" that is supposedly sweeping North American university campuses. This so-called movement embraces every hate-provoking stereotype of every alleged "radical" imaginable. Educators who work in public schools and universities are currently witnessing a well-orchestrated and singularly scandalous assault on efforts by progressive educators to make race, class, and gender issues central to the curriculum. The new left literacies that have been influenced by continental social theory, feminist theory, and critical social theory in its many forms (postmodernist, post-colonialist and post-structuralist, etc.) are being characterized by New Right critics as a subversion of the political neutrality and ideological disinterestedness that they claim the enterprise of education should be all about.

MEDIA LITERACY AS COUNTER-HEGEMONIC PRACTICE

> Enlightenment, then, is finally bent on leaving nothing extant but its own implicit violence. As it proceeds to blast away each of its own prior pretexts, this explosive rationality comes ever closer, not to "truth"—which category it has long since shattered—but to the open realization of its own coercive animus, purified of all delusions—including, finally, rationality itself. Into the ideological vacuum which it has created so efficiently there rushes its own impulse to destroy and keep destroying.
>
> (Mark Crispin Miller 1988: 315.)

Largely because of the way in which the media function to shape and merchandize orality and to construct forms of citizenship and individual and col-

101

McLAREN AND HAMMER

lective identity, our understanding of the meaning and importance of democracy has become impoverished in proportion to its dissolution and retreat from contemporary social life.

Current forms of collective sociality have been brought under the *nouvelle* aesthetic sign-form of Madonna's hyper bra and Arnold Schwarzenegger's replicant super cut biceps—part of a new politics of voyeurism and exhibitionism that celebrates the culture of commodified flesh over the emancipation of the body politic. We rehearse our lives under these Signs rather than live them; we become curators and custodians of the detritus produced by the radical semiurgy that characterizes our epoch rather than shapers of a new social vision. We have become unwanted visitors in the house of technology.

The fantasies of de Sade have become the urban equivalent of postmodern city life as affluent neighborhoods of the cyber-bourgeoise brush shoulders with the post-holocaust landscape of ravaged inner cities, creating new forms of envy and disgust. In the nihilistic extrapolation of the mass-produced image as the emergent norm of postmodern subjectivity, we witness the eclipse of historical agency and the shrinkage of the democratic imaginary.

A bold indifference to the pain and suffering of its youth has become America's dirty little secret, rotting like a corpse under the floorboards. The stench of this corpse has become so chokingly evident over the past several decades that it is not surprising to see so many of the citizens of the world's richest democracy stricken with despair and disbelief. In affirming the compatibility of individualism, capitalism, and the cultural logic of consumption, America has made its democracy untenable. Yet America desperately needs the idea of democracy to be retained as a necessary, "well founded" illusion. The results have been disastrous. The house of illusions cannot stand. Those destined to suffer the most are our youth.

American youth live in a constant state of emergency. Michael Taussig writes that states of emergency are characterized by "the apparent normality of the abnormal" (1992: 13). Echoing Walter Benjamin, Taussig writes that "in the state of emergency which is not the exception but the rule, every possibility is a fact" (1992: 34).[2] For instance, it is possible to be a healthy, intelligent and creative teenager growing up in the United States and yet have a life expectancy of 18 years. If you happen to be African-American and live in certain neighborhoods of Chicago or Los Angeles the odds could get worse. Similarly, to graduate from a high school in some areas of the nation's capital promises you nothing more than a life of chronic unemployment and misery.

A disquieting silence surrounds the monumentalization of violence in America. As urban youth grope for emotional anchors, we further deplete their already backgroundless lives and meet their often hallowless and empty eyes with a vision of fragmentation and hopelessness. We have solidified for them a reign of impermanence and have begun to heroicize behaviors we, as a nation, once found to be repugnant.

102

McLAREN AND HAMMER

It had crossed our minds that the religious character of the American people was best reflected in its frenzied and often slavish adoration of the internal combustion engine. But nearly a century of addiction to auto-opium has given way to an even more perilous form of veneration. A paranoid reading of an eighteenth-century constitutional provision for a citizen's militia has helped to secure a nearly sacerdotal status for the right to bear arms. The constitutional gangsterism surrounding gun control has helped bring about the naturalization and reification of violence such that, in our society, violence has now acquired the status of a nonevent. What *is* eventful for many of today's youth is surviving throughout the weekend *without* being assaulted, maimed, or murdered. Violence has become one of the few secure ways of stabilizing identity in postmodern culture, one of the few refuges left to escape the even greater horror of living new, radically decentered forms of subjectivity brought on by the reorganization of capitalism and its marriage to the media.

While the cultural state of existence for the middle class in our postmodern culture might be one of competitive consumption, for growing numbers of inner-city youth it is post-traumatic stress disorder. The cold war may be over and, along with it, the nuclear arms race, but the domestic arms race is heightening at an unprecedented rate. The victims of our current urban war can no longer remain hidden behind statistical body counts. We need to remind ourselves that as our nightly newscasts reveal, American youth are real, bleeding, and quivering bodies captured in a contemporary juncture of urban panic, pain, and torment. For anyone who walks the streets at night, it's a reality you *cannot not* know.

The streets of America are currently witnessing a continuous and cumulative massacre of the innocents. While in places like Brasil the authorities murder street children with an unofficial sanction and macabre zeal, in the United States monied interests provoke a similar slaughter through indifference and neglect and a sanctioned social amnesia. Such interests, supported by the moral indignation and self-righteousness of politicians and would-be politicians such as Lynn Martin, Pat Robertson, Pete Wilson, Pat Buchanan, Bill Bennett, Dan Quayle, Phil Gramm, Bob Dole, Lamar Alexander, Dick Cheney, Jack Kemp and others, can attempt to deny the American people universal health coverage while at the same time enhancing their access to guns. Yet none of these moral spokespersons is forced to live in the neighborhoods where drive-by shootings are as inevitable as Roman candles on the 4th of July. Politicians' open affiliation with the Christian Right, the National Rifle Association, and corporate barons signal the resurgence of an authoritarian populism of the likes not seen since the 1950s. Witness the sympathy shown by some Republicans to white separatist, Randy Weaver, and their interest in appeasing the militias who ritualistically denounce the government assault on the Branch Davidians. One examines with consternation and alarm the ef-

103

McLAREN AND HAMMER

forts of many Republicans to gloatingly demonize the White House Administration for supposedly provoking the bombing of the Federal Building in Oklahoma. Ranking officials in charge of Pat Buchanan's populist presidential campaign have been linked to white separatist groups. Politicians are influencing both the way that American identity is being diffused through the capillary powers of the megastate and the manner in which our structures of expectation are being identified by promotional culture.

In recent years it has become increasingly apparent that urban violence is a self-reproducing phenomenon that renders its own disappearance unlikely if not unassailable through its parasitic relationship to the "free" marketplace. Capitalism, in its current, disorganized forms is predicated on winners and losers and haves and have-nots, and on the construction of the citizen as consumer. The notion that capitalism is becoming progressively kinder and gentler is a Hollywood fantasy. Since mono-causal and uni-directional explanations of violence are patently absurd in this age of ungraspable and impalpable hyperreality and pure intensity, we need to understand violence from a number of vantage points as well as understand the relationship among them: the social; the semiotic; the cultural; the political-cultural; and individual perspectives (Sünker 1994).

In a capitalist social order of corporate decision-making in which the quest for empire and markets is rationalized as national "defence," is it so surprising that violence has become the coin of the realm? Youth inhabits a media-generated community of memory which, ironically, is forged out of the empty presence of commodity culture, out of the ruins of our present-day social amnesia, out of the slogans, signs, headlines and sound bites that structure identity around the quest for global market superiority. Youth are building their communities out of figural traces, fading signs and impotent public symbols that reflect and reproduce the dissolution of our shared traditions. The coherence is being drained out of the social worlds of our children. Newscasters, talk radio hosts, spin doctors, and electronic preachers have become counsellors to young people in a desperate search for identity. In a society bereft of decent jobs and hope for a better future, is it surprising that youth who are marginalized by race, class, gender, and sexuality are centralizing themselves through violence?—a violence that has become the new labor power of the excluded, a violence that helps youth to define themselves in a world of radical undecidability and plurality. How can we condemn acts of violence when we celebrate, sexualize, and racialize such acts through the media and when we teach our children to valorize and thrillingly emulate them? The role of the media and its links to global corporate interests are only glancingly recognized by educators and should become the site of a renewed focus of study on the issue of violence.

Urban violence is the savagery of capitalism inscribed at the level of the body; it is a form of agency that exists in the same register as language yet inscribes meaning directly onto the flesh. Acts of violence form the hieroglyphs of inverted, empty hope. They form the runes that diagnose the present and prophesy the future of our spiritual health as a nation. As the forces of the religious right attempt to solidify their hold over the Republican Party and as the pro-gun lobby gloats over its power to hold political sway over Democrats and Republicans alike, we can look forward to the further construction of "moral panics" around issues of family values, the role of religion in schools, and patriotism. We can look forward, as well, to the call for individual protection of person and property becoming the decomposable master marker against which we measure the success of our democracy.

In a society where the monstrosity of daily life is hidden behind the pacifying and fetishistic lure of commodity satisfaction, and where education is treated as simply a subsector of the economy to train students for its economic wars with Southeast Asia and Europe, is it so surprising that a President who suggests that military-style assault weapons be banned in our streets is denounced as a "radical" who is overturning his inaugural oath? The Christian Right refuses to link their personal perspectives to the discourses and social practices that give rise to them. The Right links the breakdown of values to the criminalization of minority youth, and yet at the same time avoids linking crime and violence to the disembedding of the economy, educational tracking, deindustrialization, disinvestment, economic polarization, residential segregation, gentrification, retrograde fiscal responsibility, the privatization of education, and the abandonment of public schools. Conservative discourses attempting to address violence rely on the palpable erasure of the links among violence and capitalist social relations. Are we too afraid of offending big business to make this claim?

While social critics like Marian Wright Edelman[3] do an admirable job of linking violence to disproportionate access to wealth, they typically do not sufficiently address how post-industrial consumer capitalism in the United States is imbricated in and ultimately supports white patriarchal structures of domination which lead both directly and indirectly to urban and domestic violence. We need, in other words, to locate violence within its various socio-historical contexts, within its relational play of forces, economies of mediation, and circuits of capitalist production and consumption (Sünker 1994). As an educated society we need to ask ourselves: What are we educated for? We need to face our complicity in acts of violence because we have ignored their pervasiveness, their constitutive elements, and their far-reaching effects on the lives of a majority of Americans.

In the current historical juncture of democratic decline in the United States, ideals and images have become detached from their anchorage in stable and agreed-upon meaning and associations and are now beginning to assume a reality of their own. The self-referential world of the media is one that splinters, obliterates, peripheralizes, partitions, and segments social space, time,

McLAREN AND HAMMER

knowledge, and subjectivity in order to unify, encompass, entrap, totalize, and homogenize them *through the meta-form of entertainment*. What needs to be addressed is the way in which capitalism is able to secure this cultural and ideological totalization and homogenization through its ability to insinuate itself into social practices and private perceptions through various forms of media knowledges. Questions that need to be asked include: How are the subjectivities and identities of individuals and the production of media knowledges within popular culture mutually articulated? To what extent does the hyperreal correspond to practices of self and social constitution in contemporary society? Do we remain sunk in the depressing hyperbole of the hyperreal (Poster 1990: 66), encysted in the monologic self-referentiality of the mode of information? Or do we establish a politics of refusal that is able to contest the tropes that govern Western colonialist narratives of supremacy and oppression? What isn't being discussed is the pressing need within pedagogical sites for creating a media literate citizenry that can disrupt, contest, and transform media apparatuses so that they no longer possess the power to infantilize the population and continue to create passive and paranoid social subjects (McLaren and Hammer, 1991; Hammer and McLaren, 1991).

In its unannounced retreat during the past decade, democracy has managed to recreate power through the spectacularization of its afterimage, that is, through corporatized image management and the creation of national myths of identity, primarily through mass media techniques that give democracy an "after glow" once it has faded from the horizon of concrete possibility. In other words, the mandarins of media have created democracy as a "necessary illusion." Herman and Chomsky note:

> If . . . the powerful are able to fix the premises of discourse, to decide what the general populace is allowed to see, hear, and think about, and to "manage" public opinion by regular propaganda campaigns, the standard view of how the system works is at serious odds with reality (1988, p. xi).

A critical media literacy recognizes that we inhabit a photocentric, aural, and televisual culture in which the proliferation of photographic and electronically produced images and sounds serves as a form of media catechism—perpetual pedagogy—through which individuals ritually encode and evaluate the engagements they make in the various discursive contexts of everyday life (McLaren, 1986; Giroux and McLaren, 1992; Giroux and McLaren, 1991: McLaren, 1988). This form of literacy understands media representations—whether photographs, television, print, film, or other forms—as productive not merely of knowledge, but also of subjectivity. John B. Thompson (1990) has sketched out some elements of the media literacy we have in mind.

Following Thompson, we suggest that a media literacy must elucidate the typical modes of appropriation of mass-mediated products (i.e., the technical media of transmission, the availability of the skills, capacities, and resources required to decode the messages transmitted by particular media and the rules, conventions, and practical exigencies associated with such decoding). In other words, how do particular individuals throughout the course of their everyday existence receive ritualized messages and integrate them on a daily basis (see McLaren, 1985)? Individuals do not soak up messages as passive onlookers or "inert sponges," but rather engage in an ongoing process of interpreting and incorporating such messages. A critical media literacy must therefore be attentive to the social-historical characteristics of contexts of reception and see them as situated practices. Here Thompson refers to the spatial and temporal features of reception (in the case of television, for instance, we would be concerned with who watches, for how long, in what contexts); the relations of power and the distribution of resources among recipients; the social institutions within which individuals appropriate mediated knowledges; as well as the systematic asymmetries and differentials that characterize the contexts of reception.

One important source for developing a perpetual pedagogy justifying the Gulf War—a national curriculum of sorts—was located on the fourth floor of the Time-Life Building in New York City. The curriculum was written in an epic tone, echoing Tom Shales, the *Washington Post* television critic, who described a General Schwarzkopf briefing in Riyadh as "a performance as spellbinding as the toniest of Hamlets." (MacArthur, 1992, p. 108). It was in this building that Roger Rosenblatt's special column in *Life*, "Letter to a Child in Baghdad," was conceived: a column that John MacArthur has dubbed "the outstanding example of big-media rationalizations for the slaughter of innocent civilians" (1992: 104).

In the manner of an overly earnest pedagogue, seeking philosophical candor, Rosenblatt writes:

> I must tell you right off, so that we do not misunderstand each other, that I believe this war was brought on by the leader of your country. *By him and only him.* He is a taker; he takes what he wants. And he kills what impedes him . . . Look at the antiquities of your country, the statues and reliefs, and see how many celebrate men killing men. (italics original, cited in John MacArthur 1992: 103–4)

ABC's anchorman, Peter Jennings, also tried to assume the role of the pedagogical agent in his special, "War in the Gulf—Answering Children's Questions" in which Jennings used a literal "walk on" map of the Middle East (which failed to demarcate Israel's occupied territories) that was the size of two tennis courts.

Of course, what Rosenblatt and Jennings managed to achieve as national educators was to reproduce the worst dimension of bad teaching: the failure to provide sufficient context to enable students (viewers) to reflectively en-

107

gage the competing discourses about the war that were vying for legitimacy. Missing was any serious discussion of the 1953 coup of Iran's nationalist government that was instigated by the U.S. and Britain. Nothing was mentioned about the arbitrariness of the drawing of the borders of Iraq, Kuwait and Saudi Arabia by the British in 1922. Where was any critical discussion of the CIA involvement in Middle East affairs?

A critical media literacy must also relate the everyday understanding of media messages to social-historical characteristics (i.e., race, class, and gender). It must analyze how mediated messages are discursively elaborated as individuals reject or incorporate them as part of their everyday social practices. And finally, a critical media literacy needs to explore how the appropriation of mediated messages creates virtual communities of recipients that are extended across time and space. Such a media literacy seeks to move beyond Eco's suggestion of creating a "semiological guerrilla movement" based on an anarchistic individualism in which each recipient of mediated messages interprets the transmitted multiplicity of images whichever way he or she chooses (Kearney, 1988). Rather, the critical media literacy that we envision seeks to create communities of resistance, counterpublic spheres, and oppositional pedagogies that can resist dominant forms of meaning by offering new channels of communication, circuits of semiotic production, codifications of experience, and perspectives of reception that unmask the political linkage between images, their means of production and reception, and the social practices they legitimate.

Nick Stevenson (1995) offers lucid advice when he argues that the study of mass communication is important for understanding contemporary society. He advocates three essential intersecting approaches to media literacy: the development of a critical theory of mass communication (i.e., British Marxism, the Frankfurt School) which connects the media with economics and politics; the creation of interpretive approaches to media criticism which examines audience research and reinforces the pedagogical imperative of the self-reflexive subject who is able to interrogate hegemonic knowledges and practices; and the study of the media of communication which examines media cultures as social practices which are both autonomous from and interwoven into other social and cultural practices and have a "structuring impact" on such practices.

However, the credibility of our critical pedagogy of media literacy is handicapped by a formidable paradox: Within certain academic and pedagogical circles, the very recognition of media as powerful hegemonic apparatuses impairs the validity of doing media studies in that those who critique television and other media apparatuses are often seen as complicitous with those very structures of domination that they seek to contest. In addition to constructing a model of media power that speaks to the legitimacy of engaging in a cultural studies approach, a critical media literacy needs to address sufficiently the *specificity and partial autonomy of media discourses,* that is, a model that "would analyze how the media produce identities, role models, and ideals; how they create new forms of discourse and experience; how they define situations, set agendas, and filter out oppositional ideas; and how they set limits and boundaries beyond which political discourse is not allowed" (Kellner 1990: 18).

Of serious concern in our own work is how e1ectronic prophets who manufacture personalities and manage personal images have been able to turn wimp presidents into wrathful avengers and an often frustrated and self-hating citizenry into phallomilitary warrior citizens who are conditioned to redirect a media-instilled hatred of "Sad'am" and various dark-skinned others against a familiar enemy within its own ranks: the poor, the homeless, peop1e of color, those who comprise the detritus of capitalism and white man's democracy, those who are already oppressed by race, gender, caste, and circumstance. After all, what is the mission of postmodern media if not the attempt to "Americanize the un-American" through particular forms of cultural assertion linked to capital and patterns of consumption but also on a grander scale to interlocking international networks of finance and surveillance?

Needed is a counterhegemonic media literacy in which subjectivities may be lived and analyzed outside the dominant regime of official print culture— a culture that is informed by a technophobic retreat from emerging techno-aesthetic cultures of photography, film, and electronically mediated messages. Different media knowledges manage to reveal in different ways what is at stake in naming ourselves as gendered, sexual, and desiring body/subjects. Not only would a critical media literacy warn us of the dangers in constructing social practices that enforce misogynous, homophobic, and patriarchal acts of naming, it would also construct the grounds for a transformative and emancipatory politics of difference (McLaren, 1995). Much of this work necessarily involves not only understanding the disabling and emancipatory potential of the media knowledges that are available to us, but also the importance of struggling to overturn current arrangements of extra-communicational forms of power and the social relations that undergird—and in some instances help to overdetermine—the production of such knowledges. In this regard, a critical pedagogy of media literacy seeks to produce partial, contingent, but necessary historical truths that will provide some of the necessary conditions for the emancipation of the many public spheres that make up our social and institutional life, truths which—unlike those created and sponsored by the media—recognize their social constructedness and historicity and the institutional and social arrangements that they help to legitimate.

In his book *Common Culture* (1990), Paul Willis argues that we live in an era in which high culture or official culture has lost its dominance. Official culture—the best efforts of Allan Bloom and E. D. Hirsch, Jr., notwithstanding—cannot hope to colonize, dominate, or contain the everyday and mundane aspects of life. Formal aesthetics have been replaced by a grounded aesthetics. The main seeds of cultural development are to be found in the commercial provision of cultural commodities. According to Willis, one way to work for the dialectical development of cultural knowledge is by giving everyday culture "back to its owners" and letting them develop it. "Let them control the conditions, production, and consumption of their own symbolic resources" (p. 129). This, however, is no easy task, and there are no guarantees, especially given that symbolic resources "are lodged in their own historical patterns of power and logics of production." But if the grounded aesthetics of everyday cultural life for youth are concretely embedded in the sensuous human activities of meaning-making, there are implications for a critical approach to media literacy. Media literacy must help students "to increase the range, complexity, elegance, self-consciousness and purposefulness of this involvement"—in symbolic work (pp. 130–131). It must provide them with the symbolic resources for creative self and social formation in order that they can more critically re-enter the broader plains of common culture.

Symbolic work within informal culture is unlike the symbolic work of school in fundamental ways.

> Where everyday symbolic work differs from what is normally thought of as "education" is that it "culturally produces"—from its own chosen cultural resources. Psychologically, at least, the informal symbolic workers of common cultures feel they really "own" and can therefore manipulate their resources as materials and tools—unlike the books at school which are "owned" by the teachers. (p. 136)

For these reasons, creative symbolic work within informal culture offers important possibilities for "oppositional, independent or alternative symbolizations of the self." Moreover, human beings must not be regarded merely as human capital or labor power, but as "creative *citizens*, full of their own sensuous symbolic capacities and activities and taking a hand in the construction of their own identities." The pursuit of emancipation and equality, therefore, requires more than being made equal as workers. It calls for all to be fully developed as *cultural producers*. (p. 150)

We feel strongly that citizens should have control over their symbolic economies as cultural producers. Of course, what kind of symbolic economy will be produced is another matter. One of us (McLaren), living in West Hollywood, notes the current offerings on public access television: one show that aired recently involved a female host in her twenties interviewing a feather-clad man in his forties about his life. For an hour the man casually discussed killing people, dissecting their bodies, and placing bodies in oil drums and welding them shut, as "good learning experiences." The host smiled throughout, and concluded by asking her guest to share his tattoos and body piercings with her viewers. During another show, a female host in a garter belt and Gstring provided advice about sex to (mostly male) viewers who called during the show. Two men in their twenties host another popular show, which features interviews with female porn stars who defy the censors by baring their breasts to the camera and mock humping the hosts.

McLaren has appeared as a guest on two trash TV syndicated shows—Jerry Springer and Dennis Praeger. The Springer show dealt with the topic of school censorship, while Praeger's discussed issues of multiculturalism (it also failed to air because, as one person working on the show put it, McLaren sounded too academic. McLaren's attempts at offering some meta-commentary about the show as part of the show itself were quickly dismissed by the hosts). As Charles R. Acland points out, these syndicated shows remind viewers "of the order that is outside and supposedly disappearing" (1994: 99). He notes, further:

> In the final analysis, they are always about "big, important issues," though their individual topics may seem inconsequential. This is because in the talk show, the aberrant is laced with the seeds of social disturbance and the paranoia of the shaken order (1994: 98).

These shows operate on the "display value of the confession," which is, we argue, among the most passionate forms of television ritual because it often deals with "the pathologization of the nuclear family" (ibid: 113). The normal American family is a family of dark, hidden secrets. We have all engaged in acts we would prefer remained private. We have all been remiss in raising our families. We all have secrets. Youth are always, therefore, crises about to happen in a climate endlessly under moral assault. As Foucault has observed, the confession is the site of the self as it is formed by disciplinary power of the state (c.f., ibid). Trash television, as the new postmodern "theater of public confession," now has the power to incriminate the entire public as it reflects a perverse and already widespread normalcy. We all become, like Hugh Grant, just a sound bite away from public exposure. This form of public confession normalizes our private pathologies. Americans can comfort themselves with: At least we don't shell innocent victims in Sarajevo, or release poison gas on Kurds (conveniently forgetting, if it was ever acknowledged, that US agencies have directly funded the killing and maiming of tens of thousands of innocent Nicaraguans and Guatemalans—among many others—and napalm was used freely in Vietnam). Our national salvation is bound up with punishing the "real" offenders, the dark-skinned infidels—the Iraqis, the Serbs. We have the precision weaponry, like cruise missiles, to make sure innocent people don't get hit. The national conscience can be purged and purified by transferring its own self-hate onto others, and then annihilating them.

Critical media literacy is essential, in several ways, in understanding this situation. We need to be sufficiently media literate to deny the injunctions by

111

McLAREN AND HAMMER

which identities are constructed through official media culture—in whatever form it appears. This presupposes that we create what Judith Butler calls "alternative domains of cultural intelligibility . . . new possibilities . . . that contest the rigid codes of hierarchical binarisms" (Willis 1990: 145). Within such hybrid pedagogical spaces educators and cultural workers can give greater attention to the everyday artefacts of popular culture and forms of knowledge that avoid the elitist tyranny of the center. Critical media literacy enables us to rearticulate the role of the social agent so that she or he can make affective alliances with forms of agency that provide new grounds of popular authority, grounds from which to give voice to narratives of human freedom.

Critical media literacy helps us identify and answer the question: How do essentially arbitrarily organized cultural codes, products of historical struggle among not only regimes of signs but also regimes of material production, come to represent the "real," the "natural," and the "necessary?" A critical literacy reveals that signs do not correspond to an already determined metaphysical real, nor are they transhistorically indeterminable or undecidable. Rather, their meaning-making possibilities and their meaningfulness are legitimized through the specificity of discursive and material struggles, and the political linkages between them. A critical perspective of the media also enables teachers and students to understand the dangers in considering literacy to be a private or individual competency—or set of competencies—rather than a complex circulation of economic, political, and ideological practices that inform daily life; that invite or solicit students to acquiesce in their social and gendered positions within a highly stratified society and accept the agenthood assigned to them along the axes of race/class/gender.

To this extent critical media literacy becomes the interpretation of the social present for the purpose of transforming the cultural life of particular groups, for questioning tacit assumptions and unarticulated presuppositions of our current cultural and social formations and the subjectivities and capacities for agenthood that they foster. Critical media literacy is directed at understanding the ongoing social struggles over the signs of culture and the definition of social reality—what is considered legitimate and preferred meaning at any given historical moment.

Perhaps it has never been more urgent for students to begin to understand how the process of representation and identification works. Precisely because they have the power to constitute our subjective identifications in particular ways, media literacies possess the power to influence political life. To become media literate in a world of postmodern literacies means that students must become historians and archaeologists of representation who realize that the shared systems of ideological representations we carry with us as agents of history become our history.

What is needed so desperately at this present historical conjuncture is a pedagogy that is not simply a condition of the heart, but which is also an exercise of historical will. Such a will itself needs to be tempered by forms of critical social theory and informed by a praxis of hope underwritten by a struggle for new forms of democratic possibility.

NOTES

1. This is a revised and expanded version of an article that appeared in *Polygraph* 5, 1993, pp. 46–66; also published in *Journal of Urban and Cultural Studies* 2, 2, 1992, pp. 41–77, and in *Journal of Curriculum Theorizing* 10, 2, 1992, pp. 29–68. The original version appears as Rhonda Hammer and Peter McLaren, "Le Paradoxe de L'Image: Connnaissance Mediatique et Déclin de la Qualité de la Vie," *Anthropologie et Sociétés* 16, 1, 1992, pp 21–39.

2. See also Paul Virilio, *Speed and Politics.* (New York: Semiotext[e], 1986), 'The State of Emergency', 133–51).

3. Marian Wright Edelman (1994), Cease Fire! Stopping the Gun War against Children in the United States. *Religious Education* 89, 4, pp. 461–481.

REFERENCES

Acland, Charles, R. (1994). *Youth, Murder, Spectacle: The Cultural Politics of Youth in Crisis.* Boulder and Oxford: Westview Press.

Benjamin, Walter. (1969). The work of art in the age of mechanical reproduction. In his *Illuminations.* Translated by Harry Zohn. (New York: Schocken Books, 1969, p. 242).

Buck-Morss, Susan. (1989). *The Dialectics of Seeing: Walter Benjamin and the Arcades Project.* Cambridge, MA: The MIT Press.

Butler, Judith. (1991). The imperialist subject. *Journal of Urban and Cultural Studies.* vol 2, no. 1, pp. 73–78.

Butler, Judith. (1990). *Gender Trouble.* New York and London: Routledge.

Cohn, Carole E. (1991). Decoding military doublespeak. *Ms.,* vol. 1, no. 5 (May 28), pp. 88.

Cooke, Miriam. (1991). Phallomilitary spectacles in the DT0. *Journal of Urban and Cultural Studies,* vol. 2, no. 1, pp. 27–40.

Derian, James Der. (1994). Lenin's war, Baudrillard's games. In Gretchen Bender and Timothy Druckrey (eds.) *Culture on the Brink: Ideologies of Technology,* Seattle: Bay Press, pp. 267–76.

Eagleton, T. (1981). *Walter Benjamin: Or towards a revolutionary criticism.* London and New York: Verso.

Ellis, Caroline, Khauun, Saeeda, and Plott, Steve. (1991). Highway to Hell. *New Statesman and Society* (June 21), pp. 21–28.

Ewen, Stuart. (1988). *All Consuming Images,* New York: Basic Books.

Fairness and Accuracy in Reporting, *The Media and the Gulf War: Cheerleaders for U.S. Militarism,* excerpted in *Peace and Freedom,* July/August 1991, no. 631 (np).

Gerbner, George. (1989/90). Media literacy: TV vs. reality. *Adbuster,* vol. 1, no. 2, p. 12.

Gitlin, Todd. (1986). We build excitement, in Todd Gitlin (ed.) *Watching Television.* New York: Pantheon Books, pp. 136–161.

Giroux, Henry. and McLaren, Peter. (1992). Media hegemony—Introduction to *Media*

Knowledge by James Schwock, Mimi White, and Susan Reilly. Albany, New York: State University of New York Press, pp. xv–xxxiv.

Giroux, Henry, and McLaren, Peter. (1991). Leon Golub's radical pessimism: Toward a pedagogy of representation. *Exposure* vol. 28, no. 12, pp. 18–33.

Giroux, Henry, and McLaren, Peter. (1989). Introduction, in their (eds.) *Critical Pedagogy, the State, and Cultural Struggle.* Albany, New York: State University of New York Press.

Grossberg, Larry. (1988). *It's a Sin.* Sydney, Australia: Power Publications.

Hammer, Rhonda and McLaren, Peter. (1991). Rethinking the dialectic. *Educational Theory* 41, 1, pp. 23–46.

Hammer, Rhonda, and McLaren, Peter. (1992). Le paradoxe de l'image: Connaissance mediatique et déclin de la qualité de la vie. *Anthropologie et Sociétés,* special issue, *Pouvoir des Images.*

Hammer, Rhonda and Wilden, Anthony. (1987). Women in Production: The Chorus Line 1932–1980. In Anthony Wilden, *The Rules Are No Game.* London and New York: Routledge and Kegan Paul, pp. 283–300.

Harraway, Donna. (1991). On wimps. *Journal of Urban and Cultural Studies* 2, 1, pp. 41–44.

Herman, Edward S. and Chomsky, Noam. (1988). *Manufacturing Consent.* New York: Pantheon Books.

Jhally, Sut. (1990). *The Codes of Advertising.* London and New York: Routledge.

Kearney, Richard. (1988). *The Wake of Imagination.* Minneapolis: University of Minnesota Press.

Kellner, Douglas. (1990). *Television and the Crisis of Democracy.* Boulder and Oxford: Westview Press.

Kellner, Douglas. (1992). *The Persian Gulf TV War.* Boulder CO: Westview Press.

Larsen, Ernest. (1991). Gulf war TV. *Jump Cut,* no. 36, pp. 3–10.

Lutz, William. (1981). *Doublespeak.* New York: Harper Collins Publishers.

MacArthur. John R. (1992) *Second Front: Censorship and Propaganda in the Gulf War,* New York: Hill and Wang.

McLaren, Peter. (1986). *Schooling as a Ritual Performance.* London and New York: Routledge.

McLaren, Peter. (1988). Critical pedagogy and the politics of literacy. *Harvard Educational Review* 58, 2, pp. 213–234.

McLaren, Peter. (1994). *Schooling as a Ritual Performance* (Second Edition). London and New York: Routledge.

McLaren, Peter. (1994). *Life in Schools.* New York: Longman, Inc.

McLaren, Peter. (1995). *Critical Pedagogy and Predatory Culture.* London and New York: Routledge.

McLaren, Peter and Hammer, Rhonda. (1989). Critical pedagogy and the postmodern challenge: Towards a critical postmodernist pedagogy of liberation. *Educational Foundations* 3, 3, pp. 29–62.

Miller, Mark Crispin. (1988). *Boxed In: The Culture of TV.* Evanston, IL: Northwestern University Press.

Naureckas, Jim. (1991). Gulf War coverage: The worst censorship was at home. *Extra!,* vol. 4, no. 3 (May, 1991), pp. 3–10.

Nelson, Joyce. (1987). *The Perfect Machine: TV in the Nuclear Age.* Toronto: Between the Lines.

Norris, Margot. (1991). Military censorship and the body count in the Persian Gulf War. *Cultural Critique* No.19. pp. 223–245.

Poster, Mark. (1990). *The Mode of Information.* Chicago: The University of Chicago Press.

Poster, Mark. (1991). War in the mode of information. *Cultural Critique* No. 19, pp. 217–222.

Postman, Neil. (1986). *Amusing Ourselves to Death: Public Discourse in the Age of Show Business.* London: Penguin Books.

Rogin, Michael. (1990). Make My Day!: Spectacle as amnesia in imperial politics. *Representations* vol. 29, pp. 99–123.

Said, Edward. (1993). *Culture and Imperialism.* London: Chatto and Windus.

Sanders, Barry. (1994). *A is for Ox: The Collapse of Literacy and the Rise of Violence in an Electronic Age.* New York: Vintage Books.

Schiller, Herbert I. (1989). *Culture, Inc.: The Corporate Takeover of Public Expression.* New York and Oxford: Oxford University Press.

Schulte-Sasse, Jochen and Schulte-Sasse, Linda. (1991). War, otherness, and illusionary identifications with the state. *Cultural Critique* no. 19, pp. 67–95.

Schwoch, James, White, Mimi, and Reilly, Susan. (1992). *Media Knowledge.* Albany, New York: State University of New York Press.

Shohat, Ella. (1991). The Media's War. *Social Text* vol. 9, no. 3, pp. 135–141.

Soley, Laurence. (1991). Brookings: Stand-in for the Left. *Extra!* vol. 4, no. 3 (May 1991), p. 6.

Stevenson, Nick. (1995). *Understanding Media Cultures.* London and Thousand Oaks: SAGE Publications.

Sünker, Heinz. (1994). America as a violent society. Paper delivered at the University of Connecticut at Hartford, 7 April 1994.

Taussig, Michael. (1992). *The Nervous System.* New York: Routledge.

Thompson, John B. (1990). *Ideology and Modern Culture.* Stanford, California: Stanford University Press.

Virilio, Paul. (1986). *Speed and Politics.* New York: Semiotext[e], pp. 133–151.

Wark, McKenzie. (1991). From fordism to sonyism: Perverse readings of the new world order. *New Formations* No. 15, pp. 43–54.

Wark, McKenzie. (1993). Engulfed by the vector. *New Formations* No. 21, pp. 64–79.

Werckmeister, O.K. (1991). *Citadel Culture.* Chicago: University of Chicago Press.

Willis, Paul. (1990). *Common Culture.* Boulder and Oxford: Westview Press.

Wilden, Anthony. (1987). *The Rules Are No Game.* London and New York: Routledge and Kegan Paul.

Žižek, Slavoj. (1991) *Looking Awry: An Introduction to Jacques Lacan through Popular Culture.* Cambridge, MA.: The MIT Press.

LIBERATORY POLITICS AND HIGHER EDUCATION:

A FREIREAN PERSPECTIVE[1]

Peter McLaren

I suggest those who have not read Amilcar Cabral's works on the struggle in Guinea Bissau take up the task of reviewing them. I am much impressed by his works, as well as those of Che Guevara. Furthermore, both shared a mutual respect for the other. It was in Guinea Bissau where the two met for the first time. They kept silence, observing one another. I would call it a revolutionary love with clasped hands (even though Amilcar was short and Guevara was an extraordinary specimen of a man). They both shared a love based on the revolution. And what was most interesting of all, they did many similar things— like being eminent pedagogues, great educators of the revolution.

Paulo Freire in *Paulo Freire on Higher Education* (1994)

chapter 5

It is a shame—since our North American cousins have unspeakable interests in this regard—that we continue to live in Latin America without knowing each other.

Paulo Freire in *Paulo Freire on Higher Education* (1994)

I myself was a university professor for a long time, long before the coup in Brazil. But the professor I have become is not the professor I was. It couldn't be! It would be horrible! Even exile played an important part in my reeducation. It taught me that radicalization is a fundamental course and enabled me to go through different experiences as a university professor in different parts of the world: in Latin America, in the United States, in Canada, in Europe, in Africa, and in Asia.

Paulo Freire in *Paulo Freire on Higher Education* (1994)

I remember in 1968 young people rebelled all around the world without coordinating themselves. Students in Mexico in 1968 were not telephoning young people in Harvard, or Columbia, or Prague, or Brazil. Nevertheless they carried out more or less the same movement. It was impressive. I also remember that communication between world universities was nonexistent, and it was unbelievably easy for dominant classes to repress world wide movements.

Paulo Freire in *Paulo Freire on Higher Education* (1994)

WE ARE living the hallucinatory wakefulness of nightmare reason. It is a time in which U.S. culture and history threaten the autonomy of the human spirit rather than exercise it. Henri Lefebvre (1975) warns that during this present historical conjuncture we are suffering from an alienation from alienation—that is, from a lack of awareness that we exist in a state of alienation.

Educators and cultural workers in the United States living in this twilight of reason are facing a crisis of democracy. The democratic aspiration of U.S. schooling and social, cultural, and institutional practices in general have been carried forth to an unheralded present moment in what retrospectively appears to have been an act of bad faith. The consequences of such an act for future generations are only faintly visible and are bathed in an ethos eerily reminiscent of earlier swindles of hope. The "democratizing" imperatives of private enterprise, wage labor, free trade and other fundamental axes for the new capitalist world system ushered in by the third industrial revolution of computer technology have shrouded individuals in a web of promotional logic patterned by the conquering dynamism of Eurocentrism. Colonization has gone transnational and corporatist (Miyoshi, 1993). As Jacques Attali (1991: 120) warns, "From Santiago to Beijing, from Johannesburg to Moscow, all economic systems will worship at the altar of the market. People will sacrifice for the gods of profit." We live in an age in which desires, formerly tilted inwards, are now constructed on the surface of bodies like pathologically narcissistic tattoos that reflect lost hope and empty dreams—forfeited identifications turned into grotesqueries, unable to escape the circuit of deceit and despair constructed out of capitalist relations and rationalizations and new modes of social regulation that produce not persons nor individuals, but subjects.

Capitalism carries the seeds of its own vulnerability and frailty even though its cunning appears inexhaustible and its mechanisms of production and exchange irreproachable and unchallenged. Its vulnerability is, ironically, the most steadfast and dangerous precondition for its further development. So long as it has bourgeois universal reason and the epistemic privilege of science as its spokesperson and Eurocentrism as its cultural anchor, and whiteness as its foundation of cultural calculability, its very constitution as a discourse of power within an increasingly homogeneous "world culture" needs to be challenged by popular movements of renewal within a polycentric cultural milieu.

Educators in the United States have no special immunity to these conditions but bear a signal responsibility to understand them and, in turn, help their students to do the same. Students are particularly vulnerable in these dangerous times, as they are captured in webs of social and cultural meaning not of their own making, motivated to remember in specific ways, and silently counselled through advertisements, the media, and religious and political "others" to respond to the logic of commodity fetishism as if it were a natural state of affairs. Teachers and students together face New Right constituencies of all types and stripes, in particular, fundamentalist Christians and political interest groups who are exercising an acrimonious appeal to a common culture monolithically unified by a desire for harmony in sameness.

The past decade has witnessed unprecedented levels of struggle over the meaning and deployment of racial "difference," culminating in the Tuesday, November 8th 1994, wide margin of vote (59% to 41% margin overall; 78% Republican, 62% Independent, 36% Democrat) in favor of Proposition 187 in California. The measure is designed to restrict public schooling, welfare, and nonemergency medical services for those persons who are unable to prove their legal immigration or nationality status in the U.S. The measure originated with Orange County political consultant Robert Kiley; his wife, Yorba Linda Mayor Barbara Kiley; and Ron Prince, an accountant who had been unemployed for three years and who recently was forced to file for bankruptcy.

As a blue-eyed Anglophone Canadian from the Great White North, who was issued a green card in 1985, I have little fear of being targeted by the measure, since the campaign ads and rhetoric surrounding the measure were clearly focussed on the southern state border, with Mexico. Marking an historical moment unparalleled in modern Californian history, 8 November 1994 is a day that henceforth shall live in infamy. For this moment signals not only the resurfacing of fascism but also the complete and utter villainization and demonization of the Latino/a immigrant in a manner so ferocious that even the most militant and cynical Raza have been caught unprepared. What is at hand is not simply a further backward step in the sad but steady erosion of ground won by decades of civil rights activism, but rather the triumph of cultural apartheid and the inquisition of the colonial mind. Racial authoritarians have defiantly sloughed off their white cocoons, transformed now into full-blown racist terrorists, whose symbolic projection was captured the morning after the vote in the Governor's cutting of prenatal care to undocumented immigrants, mostly Mexican. A moment of struggle is at hand that has a special political valency and ethical potency. When the law of the land is trotted out as a cover for a form of ethnic cleansing, we need to act. It is plainly time to push western civilization up against the wall and demand that democracy live up to its name.

What is remarkable is that in this dislocated climate of victimization, a spirit has risen up to strike back at the white fangs of gringo justice: we are witnessing a resurgent *indigenismo*, bolstered by the example of the Zapatistas; the new youth *movimiento* that has seen thousands of Raza youth take to the streets in school walk-outs; the discontinuous histories of the powerless have coalesced into a new recognition of the plurality of Chicano/a-ness; new forms of self-creation through an engagement with the social memory of Chicano/a struggle have occurred; and the political mobilization and system-

119

McLAREN

atic cultural activism of Latino/as, often in concert with other groups, has continued. And professors in places like California State L.A., and U.C.L.A. have committed themselves to positions of civil disobedience, and to offering to start up sanctuary schools, should the measure finally be implemented. It is obvious that Proposition 187 is another blow to the very meaning of public education, another assault on the public sphere as a place for the practice of equality for all individuals, even the strangers in our midst, regardless of their legal status.

For educators and cultural workers this current historical moment refracts through a series of unstable standpoints which represent a broad canvas from which to frame our struggle for liberation; it is a bold summons to re-examine our commitment to the forging of history, rather than just its representation, translation, or interpretation. As nihilism and despair begin to impose their own inevitability we need to construct a counter-memory, a counter-discourse, a counter-praxis of liberation. It is a time that calls us to examine how we, as cultural workers, have been invented by Western culture within the process of colonization and the formation of Eurocentrism. To examine how we, as citizens committed to public education and the rights of children, can allow ourselves to be positioned as INS agents in universities and schools.

The call for the educator and cultural worker to act is not a call for a new Chicano/a centrism or subaltern collectivity centering around the return to Atzlan—a treasurehouse of Chicano/a authenticity waiting to be unlocked—for any centrism, be it Afrocentrism, Eurocentrism, phallocentrism, or androcentrism, obeys an epistemology hospitable to myths of originary unity, an unsullied historical time, and an eternally stable racial self around which a redemptive narrative of heroic struggle pivots; such centrisms are themselves infected by and complicitous with Western codes, assumptions, and conventions. Rather, it is a call not merely to challenge our strategies of representation but to dismantle the ineffable structures of terror that pervade both the politics of the public and the popular, that are inextricably bound up with global economic developments, and that form the structural unconscious of the United States.[2] I am talking here about discourses of power and privilege and social practices that have epistemically mutated into a new and terrifying form of xenophobic nationalism in which the white male Euro-American becomes the universal subject of history.

Such a dilemma points to a necessary displacement of the US as the center of analysis and the development of a more inclusive, global perspective. It suggests, too, that as critical educators for social justice, we must no longer advance our view of what it means to be American on the graveyards of other people's cultures; nor can we view ourselves as disinterested chroniclers, as detached entertainers, as agents who operate in a realm outside the messy web of ethics and politics.

We practice our craft within expressive culture, but such a culture needs to

McLAREN

be located within a systemic entity known as global capitalism. As such, we never leave its circuits of subordination, of commodification, of simulacra. Educators, especially, need to politicize their readers against the violent thrall of capital, to menace their social apathy and haunt their "comfort zones" like a surly stranger. The educator as social agent needs to challenge the white media's attempts to commodify black rage, Latino militancy, and Asian resistance, and to resist its attempt to hellify their world as it continues to establish an equivalence between youth of color and full-throated deviancy. In a society in which prison has become the most realistic educational alternative for African Americans and Latinos, the educator as activist cannot stand on the sidelines and hide in the false binarism of objectivity/subjectivity. Rather, the educator must assume a standpoint from which, as Paulo Freire asserts, to read both the word and the world.

Without much of an economic base to work from in our inner cities, we are faced with strategies and tactics of diversion from conservatives who try to focus the blame for social problems on the breakdown of family values. Interestingly and perhaps terrifyingly, a July *Los Angeles Times* poll of 1,500 people nationwide suggests that the political influence of culturally divisive groups associated with the Democrats (feminists and gay activists, for instance) cause more concern to voters than the religious right. In fact, more people see the breakdown of moral values as the root of social strife in the US than they do economic constraints. Within such a right-leaning climate, it is not surprising that some conservative school districts in Los Angeles are denying hungry students breakfast programs because such programs are viewed as "anti family." In other words, starving is good for young students' characters. A Los Angeles program to help black inner-city youths through organized golf attempts to counter the behavior of youth who sport the bad, black LA Raiders fashion with the cultural capital of a good white sport.[3] Whiteness has located itself in those discourses of the public and the popular in such a way (whiteness is everywhere and nowhere) that our definition of the normal and the commonsensical has been colonized. If we do nothing to contest the Republican initiative that will place the children of those on social assistance in orphanages, how will we be able to resist when the initiative calls for forced sterilization? Or internment camps for illegal Latino/as? We need to remember that few spoke out when Jewish students were forced out of German universities or when Jewish faculty were expelled.

In such circumstances, we as educators need to move beyond a notion of multiculturalism as liberal pluralism because pluralism always has an ideological center of gravity which rarely gets defined for what it is: liberal pluralism as the politics of white supremacist patriarchal capitalism. This is the same pluralistic society whose system of capitalism is paying its workers in underdeveloped countries salaries which amount to little more than slave wages. Not to mention its own sweatshops in New York and elsewhere. It is the same

121

McLAREN

system that calls for the privatization and corporatization of education and signals the end of public education as we know it. It is hard to develop the form of class consciousness necessary for contesting current conditions because, as Brosio has noted, after Jameson, the current postmodernist culture, "characterized by disconnected and decontextualized images," and its "celebration of randomness, heterogeneity, and claims of unprecedented complexity," does little more than to "reinforce the difficulty in understanding the, as yet unrepresentable, capitalist totality" (1993: 480). This situation enables Newt Gingrich to call on the ghosts of Father Flanagan and Whitey Marsh to provide us with the moral fortitude to struggle on in the name of truth and justice, and Mortimer B. Zuckerman, Editor-in-Chief of *U.S. News and World Report*, 12 December 1994, to proclaim that US immigration policy discriminates against Europeans and that the "standard of living in a California jail is higher than that in many Latin American villages" (p. 123).

The forms of ethical address which have been constructed by the sentinels of our dominant political, cultural, and educational systems—even under cover of abstract endorsements of diversity—are bent on draining the lifeblood out of difference by installing an invisible ideological grid through which appeals to normalcy, decency, and citizenship may be filtered and differences extorted into reconciliation. They are effectively limiting the range of meanings which are being stockpiled in the name of democracy. E. D. Hirsch wants to reduce culture to a paraphrasable core of necessary ideas; the English Only movement desires to ontologically and epistemologically fix the relationship between citizenship and language so that "real Americans" won't be bothered anymore by the babel of foreign tongues; educational reformers under the sway of marketplace logic are implored to get youth off the streets and into the declining job markets where they can then be conscripted into the corporate wars with Germany and Japan.

Insinuated into grand narratives of progress, these contestable sets of assumptions and social practices effectively reproduce the systems of intelligibility that further the interests of the privileged and powerful.

Against the backdrop of the global underclass, the growing influence of neoconservatism and neoliberalism in political life in general and education in particular, and the struggle for democracy, exists the work of Paulo Freire, one of the great revolutionaries of our generation. Freire's name encrypts the contested encounter among capitalism, schooling, and democracy, and his work is traversed by a call to rethink the concepts of education and liberation. The meaning of Freire's work among those who seek liberty and democracy perhaps can be partially captured by the words that Theodor Adorno used to describe Walter Benjamin: "Anyone who was drawn to him was bound to feel like the child who catches a glimpse of the lighted Christmas tree through a crack in the closed door" (Adorno 1967, p. 230).

It is important to make clear that Freire's work cannot be articulated out-

McLAREN

side the diverse and conflicting registers of indigenist cultural, intellectual, and ideological production in the Third World. The "Third World" is a term used most advisedly here after Benita Parry and Frantz Fanon to mean a "self-chosen phrase to designate a force independent of both capitalism and actual-ly existing socialism, while remaining committed to socialist goals" (Parry, 1993: 130). As such, it offers a starting point for a critique of imperialism and "retains its radical edge for interrogating the Western chronicle."

Of course, one of the powerful implications surrounding the distinction between First and Third Worlds involves the politics of underdevelopment. Andrew Ross (1989) describes the classic model of underdevelopment as one that benefits the small, indigenous elites of Western developed nations. For-eign markets such as those in Latin America provide a consumption outlet for the developed nations of the First World so that they are able to absorb the ef-fects of a crisis of overproduction in the core economy. According to Ross, the peripheral economy (Latin America) underproduces for its domestic pop-ulation. He reports that "The economic surplus which results from peripher-al consumption of core products is appropriated either by core companies or by the domestic elites; it is not invested in the domestic economy of the pe-ripheral nation" (1989: 129). Of course, what happens as a result is that the domestic economies of Latin America fail to possess the productive capacity to satisfy the most basic needs of most of the population. This is because "the only active sector is the one that produces commodities either for the indige-nous elite or exotic staples for the core metropolitan market" (Ross 1989: 129). The contact between Latin America and foreign capital certainly does encourage peripheral economies to develop, but such development—if you can call it that—is almost always uneven and consequently such contact forces the peripheral economy to undevelop its own domestic spheres.

When there is economic dependency, cultural dependency often follows in its wake. However, the capitalist culture industry is not simply superstructural but constitutive in that the masses—in both First and Third Worlds—do not simply consume culture passively as mindless dupes. There is often resistance at the level of symbolic meaning that prevents the culture industry from serv-ing simply as a vehicle of repressive homogenization of meaning (Martin-Barbero, 1992; McLaren, 1995). According to Ross (1989), the elites of the peripheral nations are the first to acquire access to Westernized popular cul-ture, but because of the limited access of the indigenous population to the media, the media generally serve to encourage affluent groups to adopt the consumer values of the most developed countries. The elites basically serve in a supervisory capacity when it comes to the cultural consumption of the in-digenous peasantry. However, the continuing ties of the peasantry to their own ethnic cultures does help them become less dependent on Western in-formation. Foreign mass-produced culture is often interpreted and resisted at the level of popular culture, and we must remember that cultural values of the

First World can also be affected by contact with the cultures of less developed countries. And, further, not everything about contact with Western culture is to be shunned, although the emergence of a new, transnational class appears to have all the ideological trappings of the older, Western bourgeoisie. For instance, my own contact with Brazilian feminists has revealed to me that oppositional feminist critique in the U.S. can be successfully appropriated by Brazilian women in their struggle against the structures of patriarchal oppression, structures which can permit men to kill their wives if they suspect them of infidelity on the grounds that their "male honor" has been violated.

The image of Freire that is evoked against this recurring narrative of the decline and deceit of Western democracy and the cultural hegemony of developed nations is a distant voice in a crowd, a disturbing interloper among the privileged and powerful—one who bravely announces that the emperor has no clothes. Ethically and politically Freire remains haunted by the ghosts of history's victims and possessed by the spirits that populate the broken dreams of utopian thinkers and millenarian dreamers—a man whose capacities for nurturing affinities between disparate social, cultural and political groups and for forging a trajectory towards moral, social and political liberation challenge the disasters that currently befall this world.

Freire's internationally celebrated praxis began in the late 1940s and continued unabated until 1964, when he was arrested in Brazil as a result of a literacy program he designed and implemented in 1962. He was imprisoned by the military government for seventy days, and exiled for his work in the national literacy campaign, of which he had served as director. Freire's sixteen years of exile were tumultuous and productive times: a five-year stay in Chile as a UNESCO consultant with the Chilean Agrarian Reform Corporation, specifically the Reform Training and Research Institute; an appointment in 1969 to Harvard University's Center for Studies in Development and Social Change; a move to Geneva, Switzerland in 1970 as consultant to the Office of Education of the World Council of Churches, where he developed literacy programs for Tanzania and Guinea-Bissau that focused on the re-Africanization of their countries; the development of literacy programs in some postrevolutionary former Portuguese colonies such as Angola and Mozambique; assisting the governments of Peru, Nicaragua, and Grenada with their literacy campaigns; the establishment of the Institute of Cultural Action in Geneva in 1971; a brief return to Chile after Salvador Allende was assassinated in 1973, provoking General Pinochet to declare Freire a subversive; and his eventual return to Brazil in 1980 to teach at the Pontificia Universidade Católica de São Paulo, the Universidade de São Paulo, and the Universidade de Campinas. These events were accompanied by numerous works, most notably, *Pedagogy of the Oppressed, Cultural Action for Freedom,* and *Pedagogy in Process: Letters to Guinea-Bissau.* Little did Freire realize that on November 15, 1988, the Partido dos Trabalhadores (Workers Party or PT) would win the

McLAREN

municipal elections in São Paulo, Brazil and he would be appointed Secretary of Education of the city of São Paulo by Mayor Luiza Erundina de Sousa.

Relentlessly destabilizing as *sui generis* and autochthonous mercenary pedagogy—i.e., spontaneous pedagogy wantonly designed to stimulate the curiosity of students, yet imposed in such a bourgeois manner so as to "save" those who live in situations of domestication only when they are reinitiated into the conditions of their own oppression—Freire's praxis of solidarity, that is, his critical pedagogy, speaks to a new way of being and becoming human. This "way of being and becoming" constitutes a quest for the historical self-realization of the oppressed by the oppressed themselves through the formation of collective agents of insurgency. Against the treason of modern reason, Freire aligns the role of the educator with that of the organic intellectual. It should come as no surprise, then, that against perspectives generated in the metropolitan epicenters of education designed to serve and protect the status quo, Freire's work has, even today, been selected for a special disapprobation by the lettered bourgeoisie and epigones of apolitical pedagogy as a literature to be roundly condemned, travestied, traduced, and relegated to the margins of the education debate. That Freire's work has been placed under prohibition, having been judged to be politically inflammatory and subversive and an inadmissible feature of academic criticism, is understandable given the current historical conjuncture. But it is not inevitable.

It is not the purpose of this essay to address the often egregious misrepresentations of Freire's work by mainstream educators, nor to simply situate Freire unproblematically within the context of First World efforts to ground liberation struggles in pedagogical practices. This chapter seeks merely to elaborate on one of the central themes of Freire's work, the role of the educator as an active agent of social change.

CRITICAL PEDAGOGY VS. THE ACADEMY

While their political strategies vary considerably, critical educators of varying stripes (many of whom have been directly influenced by Freire's work) generally hold certain presuppositions in common which can be summarized as follows: pedagogies constitute a form of social and cultural criticism; all knowledge is fundamentally mediated by linguistic relations that inescapably are socially and historically constituted; individuals are synecdochically related to the wider society through traditions of mediation (family, friends, religion, formal schooling, popular culture, etc.); social facts can never be isolated from the domain of values or removed from forms of ideological production as inscription; the relationship between concept and object and signifier and signified is neither inherently stable nor transcendentally fixed and is often mediated by circuits of capitalist production, consumption, and social relations; language is central to the formation of subjectivity (conscious and unconscious awareness); certain groups in any society are unnecessarily and often

125

McLAREN

unjustly privileged over others and while the reason for this privileging may vary widely, the oppression which characterizes contemporary societies is most forcefully secured when subordinates accept their social status as natural, necessary, inevitable or bequeathed to them as an exercise of historical chance; oppression has many faces and focusing on only one at the expense of others (e.g., class oppression vs. racism) often elides or occults the interconnection among them; power and oppression cannot be understood simply in terms of an irrefutable calculus of meaning linked to cause and effect conditions, and this means that an unforeseen world of social relations awaits us; domination and oppression are implicated in the radical contingency of social development and our responses to it; and mainstream research practices are generally and unwittingly implicated in the reproduction of systems of class, race, and gender oppression (Kincheloe and McLaren, 1994; McLaren 1992).

Freire's work certainly reflects this list of assumptions to different degrees and while his corpus of writing does not easily fall under the rubric of poststructuralism, his emphasis on the relationship among language, experience, power and identity certainly give weight to certain poststructuralist assumptions. For instance, Freire's work stresses that language practices among individuals and groups do more than reflect reality, they effectively organize our social universe and reinforce what is considered to be the limits of the possible while constructing at the same time the faultlines of the practical. To a large extent, the sign systems and semiotic codes that we use are always already populated by prior interpretations since they have been necessarily conditioned by the material, historical, and social formations that help to give rise to them. They endorse and enforce particular social arrangements since they are situated in historically conditioned social practices in which the desires and motivations of certain groups have been culturally and ideologically inscribed, not to mention overdetermined. All sign systems are fundamentally arbitrary but certain systems have been accorded a privileged distinction over others, in ways that bear the imprint of race, class and gender struggles (Gee, 1993). Sign systems not only are culture-bound and conventional but also are distributed socially, historically and geopolitically (Berlin, 1993). For U.S. educators, this implicates our language use in Euro-American social practices that have been forged in the crucible of patriarchy and white supremacy (Giroux, 1993).

Knowledge does not, according to the view sketched above, possess any inherent meaningfulness in and of itself but depends on the context in which such knowledge is produced and the purpose to which such knowledge is put. If there is no pre-ontological basis for meaning that is extralinguistically verifiable, no philosophical calculus that can assist us in making choices— then we can come to see language as a form of power that apprentices us to particular ways of seeing and engaging the self and others and this, in turn, has particular social consequences and political effects (McLaren and

Leonard, 1993). Few educators have helped us to judge the political effects of language practices as much as Paulo Freire. And few educators have been as misused and misunderstood. Clearly, Freire does not see individuals and groups to be agentless beings invariably trapped in and immobilized by language effects. Rather, human beings are politically accountable for their language practices and as such, agency is considered immanent (McLaren and Lankshear, 1994; McLaren and Giroux, 1994). Freire's position reflects Gramsci's notion that the structural intentionality of human beings needs to be critically interrogated through a form of conscientization or conscientização (this Portuguese word is defined by Freire as a deep or critical reading of commonsense reality).

THE EDUCATIONAL INSTITUTION AS (A) MORAL AGENT

When the surgical pick of Egas Moniz was poised to perform the first medical lobotomy (a procedure that, it may be recalled, won him the Nobel Prize and which led reactionary advocates to consider lobotomies for individuals subversive of good citizenship practices) it was inconceivable to think that such an act of cerebral terrorism could be achieved at a cultural level more effectively and much less painfully through the powerful articulations of new and ever more insidious forms of capitalist hegemony. The emancipatory role of university and public intellectuals has been greatly diminished by this process, as well as the function of the organic intellectual. In fact, emancipatory praxis has been largely orphaned in our institutions of education as educators are either unable or refuse to name the political location of their own pedagogical praxis. Part of the problem is that postmodern traditions of mediation have become simulacra whose ideological dimensions cannot easily be identified with or organically linked to the most oppressive effects of capitalist social relations and material practices. The redoubled seduction of new information technologies not only rearticulates a submission to multinational financial strategies, but creates possibilities for a resignification of, resistance to, and popular participation in, the politics of everyday life. The fact that relationships between the specific and the general have become blurred by these new electronic forces of mediation has not only increased a reorganization and liberation of difference but has also posed a danger of further cultural fragmentation and dissolution limiting the struggle for strategic convergences among sites of intellectual production, the formation of new moral economies, and the expansion of new social movements. This disaggregation of public spheres and the massification of mestizae identities makes it difficult to establish the solidarities necessary for developing liberating idioms of social transformation (Martin-Barbero, 1992; McLaren, 1995). Rey Chow poses an urgent question to U.S. intellectuals: How do intellectuals struggle against a hegemony "which already includes them and which can no longer be divid-

127

McLAREN

ed into the state and civil society in Gramsci's terms, nor be clearly demarcated into national and transnational spaces?" (1993: 16). Chow remarks that most oppositional university intellectual work derives from strategies which deal (after de Certeau's conceptualization of urban spatial practices) with those who wish to solidify a place or barricade a field of interest. What we need instead of strategies, argues Chow, are tactics to deal with calculated actions outside of specific sites. Strategic solidarities only repeat "what they seek to overthrow" (p. 17). In discussing de Certeau's distinction between strategies and tactics, Michael Shapiro notes that strategies belong to those who have legitimate positions within the social order and consequently are part of "a centralized surveillance network for controlling the population" (1992: 103). Tactics, on the other hand, "belong to those who do not occupy a legitimate space and depend instead on time, on whatever opportunities present themselves" (1992: 103). Tactics are associated with the performative repertoire—i.e., "the slipperiness of the sophistic stance"—of displaced, disenfranchized, and dominated people (Conquergood, 1992: 83). Tactics, in other words, are the "techniques of the sophist" in which the ethos of the formal meaning of sophistry is replaced by a resistant praxis of the contingent, the available, the possible (Conquergood, 1992: 82). In a world of scarce options, tactics can serve to camouflage resistance as a form of what Conquergood calls "improvizational savvy" (1992: 82). There are the actions of the class clown, the student who "goofs off," the teacher who seizes the space of a classroom lesson to engage in a dialogue with students about issues not on the formal curriculum. de Certeau describes tactical operations and maneuvers as follows:

128

> [A] tactic is a calculated action determined by the absence of a proper locus. . . The space of a tactic is the space of the other. Thus it must play on and with a terrain imposed on it and organized by the law of a foreign power. It does not have the means to keep to itself, at a distance, in a position of withdrawal, foresight, and self-collection: it is a maneuver "within the enemy's field of vision," . . . and within enemy territory. It does not, therefore, have the option of planning, general strategy. . . It operates in isolated actions, blow by blow. It takes advantage of opportunities and depends on them, being without any base where it could stockpile its winnings, build up its own position, and plan raids. . . . This nowhere gives a tactic mobility, to be sure, but a mobility that must accept the chance offerings of the moment, and seize on the wing the possibilities that offer themselves at any given moment. It must vigilantly make use of the cracks that particular conjunctions open in the surveillance of proprietary powers. It poaches in them. It creates surprises in them. . . . It is a guileful ruse. (cited in Conquergood, 1992: 82).

According to Conquergood, rationality itself is linked to the domain of strategy in that it derives its legitimacy (after de Certeau) in an established locus or place. Against the strategic imperatives of formal rationality founded on established rights and property, Conquergood posits what he calls "sophistic tactics" that "resist systematizing and totalizing discourses because they are dispersed and nomadic; they are difficult to administer because they cannot be pinned down." He further adds: "Artful dodgers and tacticians of resistance are branded disreputable by proprietary powers because they are always on the move and refuse to settle down" (1992: 83). It should be emphasized that the realm of resistance that can be tactical is not only classroom behaviors deemed counter-hegemonic but also the practice of theory, as Giroux has pointed out (1983; 1992).

Chow elaborates on the distinction between strategies and tactics as it relates to the politics of insurgent university educators:

> We need to remember as intellectuals that the battles we fight are battles of words. Those who argue the oppositional standpoint are not *doing* anything different from their enemies and are most certainly not directly changing the downtrodden lives of those who seek their survival in metropolitan and nonmetropolitan spaces alike. What academic intellectuals must confront is thus *not* their "victimization" by society at large (or their victimization-in-solidarity-with-the-oppressed), but the power, wealth, and privilege that ironically accumulate from their "oppositional" viewpoint, and the widening gap between the professed contents of their works and the upward mobility they gain from such words. (When Foucault said intellectuals need to struggle against becoming the object and instrument of power, he spoke precisely to this kind of situation.) The predicament we face in the West, where intellectual freedom shares a history with economic enterprise, is that "if a professor wishes to denounce aspects of big business . . . he will be wise to locate in a school whose trustees are big businessmen." Why should we believe in those who continue to speak a language of alterity-as-lack while their salaries and honoraria keep rising? How do we resist the turning-into-propriety of oppositional discourses, when the intention of such discourse has been that of displacing and disowning the proper? How do we prevent what begin as tactics—that which is "without any base where it could stockpile its winnings" (de Certeau: 37)—from turning into a solidly fenced off field, in the military no less than in the academic sense? (1993: 17).

Chow reminds us that oppositional tactics within the university—often undertaken as the practice of Freirean "critical pedagogy"—can become dangerously domesticated precisely because they can be conscripted by leftist educators into the service of career advancements. Even employed with best of intentions, Freirean pedagogy can unwittingly locate itself as a voguish set of systematized strategies that carries with it the imprimatur of leftist high theory. Its adoption can be used for accruing academic property rights by those who wish to keep resistance a form of ludic play, a form of mimesis as distinct from praxis. To enact resistance as a tactical performative undertaking, a subversive maneuver designed to rupture and displace the unitary cohesiveness of the acad-

129

McLAREN

emy's master discourses and develop a pedagogy that operates outside of mainstream pedagogy's founding binarisms, would be considered too risky for educators who wish to enjoy the appearance of being radical without facing the hard decisions that could risk one's job security or possibilities for tenure. It is to a deeper understanding of the strategic and tactical relationships between the role of hegemony in the formation of public intellectuals and the function of the university itself in the context of wider social and political formations that Freire's work needs to be engaged. Freire's work also needs engagement with oppositional discourses dealing with higher education and the role of the intellectual that appropriate postmodernist criticisms.

What can be loosely described as postmodern social theory has been influential in, among other things, offering criticisms of material and economic causality and the Cartesian notion of subjectivity by placing an emphasis on reading social reality as a text, on language as a model of representation that helps "construct" social reality, on power as both a condition and effect of discourse, on world-construction as an interplay of signifying relations and on unmasking Enlightenment conceptions of truth as the aesthetic effectiveness of the rhetoric of reading and writing practices. Freire's work has not addressed in any extended commentary current political debates surrounding the pedagogy and politics of postmodernism (McLaren and Leonard, 1993), but recent remarks situate these debates as ongoing "discoveries" that center around two possibilities: the denial of history and human agency or the recognition of history as a necessary human experience, one that is historically constituted (Freire, 1993a; 1993b). Freire writes:

> I would like to actively follow the discussions about whether the issue of postmodernity is an historical province in itself, a kind of *sui generis* meant in History as the starting point of a new History, almost without continuity with what went before or what is to come; without ideologies, utopias, dreams, social classes or struggles. It would be a "round time," "filled out," "smooth," without "edges," in which mean and women would eventually discover that its main feature is neutrality. Without social classes, struggles or dreams to fight for, without the need for choice or, therefore, for changes, without the game of conflicting ideologies, it would be an empire of neutrality. It would be a denial of history itself.
>
> I would like to discover whether, on the contrary, postmodernity, like modernity, and traditionalism, on which presses a substantial number of connotations, implies a necessary continuity which characterizes History itself as a human experience whose form of being can filter from one moment in time to another. In this sense, each moment in time is characterized by the predominance and not by the exclusivity of its connotations.
>
> For me, postmodernity today, like modernity yesterday, by conditioning men and women caught up in it, does not destroy nor did it destroy what we call their nature, which not being a priori of History, has been socially constructed exclusively through it. (1993a: 2).

McLAREN

Freire describes pedagogical practice within postmodernity as "one that humbly learns from differences and rejects arrogance" (p. 3). It is a practice that does not forcefully reject prior historical struggles, but rejects the arrogance and certainty that often accompanied them.

Writing from a postmodernist perspective, Sande Cohen (1993) has recently offered a forceful challenge to the timid and frequently duplicitous role which university intellectuals have assumed in relation to the sociality of capital and the "catastrophe of socialized expectations." Cohen's analysis has much to offer Freirean educators who wish to enter into conversation with postmodern social theory and who also wish to situate the challenge of critical pedagogy within university settings.

Following the persistent contentions of Baudrillard, Nietzsche, and others, Cohen maintains that objectivity can no longer hide or deny its subjectively-based interests—a situation that has serious implications for the role of the intellectual in contemporary North American society. He writes:

> For intellectuals it is suggested that our texts and objects now fail to connect with everything *but our own simulacra, image, power, formation of exchange.* In doubting and negating everything, in affirming and consecrating everything, intellectuals remain prisoners of the futile role of the subject-in-consciousness and enforce the pretense that our efforts translate and represent for the truth of others, the reality of the world. (Italics original, 1993: 154).

For Cohen, as for Freire, the dilemma of the intellectual lies in the failure to forcefully challenge the perils of capitalism. In response to this dilemma, Cohen mounts an articulate and vigorous attack on the U.S. professoriate. University discourse and practices are condemned as mobilizing the academicization and domestication of meaning through a modernist process of historicization—a process which, in effect, amounts to creating various self-serving theologies of the social that enable professors to speculate on the future in order to justify their social function as intellectuals. Resulting from this process are acute forms of antiskepticism leading in many instances to a debilitating cynicism. According to Cohen, universities and their academic gentry operate as a discursive assemblage directed at creating a regime of truth, a process that fails to undertake the important task of "inventing systems independent of the system of capital" (p. 3). In this instance, academic criticism is crippled by its inability to break from conventional categories such as "resemblance." Critical languages forged in the theoretical ovens of the academy simply and regrettably pursue their own hegemony through the production of pretense and the desire for power. Further, in face of the cultural logic of late capitalism, "the category of the intellectual is disengaged from any possible antimodernist argument" (p. 68). This situation recenters "high status" knowledge within the liberal tradition of therapeutic discourse. According to Cohen, "Universities cannot speak to their own participation

131

McLAREN

in the destruction of events without undoing their "need" and control structures" (p. 114).

Even Habermas' now popular appeal for a rational means of resolving differences and restoring democratic social life in the ideal speech situation is
described by Cohen as "psychologically based moral economy" (p. 67) in
which "intellectuals are empowered so long as they stay in the precut grooves
of providing resocialization with concepts, theory, sophistication, the seduc-
tions, one might say, of bureaucratic integration" (p. 70). With this dilemma in
mind, Cohen asserts:

> Why isn't capitalism—which makes mincemeat of real argumentation by its ho-
> mogenization of signifiers, accomplished, for example, by the media's ordinary
> excessive displacement of analysis or the marginalization of unfamiliar cultural
> and social voices—rendered more critically? . . . Why is the economic mode so
> accepted in the first place as an unalterable form of social relation? Why is criti-
> cism so often an opposition that acts under the identity of a "loyal opposition?"
> (p. 70).

In order to escape the inevitability under capitalism of a modernist histori-
cist recoding of knowledge, Cohen astutely adopts Lyotard's notion of "dispossession." Dispossession is recruited in this context in terms of "the dispossession of historicizing, narrating, reducing, demanding" (p. 72). More specifically, it refers to a form of "uncontrolled presentation (which is not reducible
to presence)" (p. 73). It also points to the suspension of identification—including negative identification. Cohen also conscripts into the service of a
critique of capitalism Hannah Arendt's concept of "active critique" of ends
and goals "that never identif[ies] with time valuations which are, unavoidably,
always already atrophied" (p. 113). We are advised here to "strangify"—a term
he employs in tandem with an unyielding commitment to resubjectifica-
tion—to making subjectivity different outside the acts of negation and opposition through the creation of insubordinate signifiers which loosen and
"neutralize . . . the Platonic control on the power to select" (p. 118). To
strangify is to engage in a non reduction of meaning that terrorizes all forms
of equational logic, positive and negative (p. 119).

Cohen's project of strangification—a type of postmodern extension of
Freire's term of conscientization—is directed at destabilizing and decentering
the monumentalization of the already known and the militarization of existing sign systems established by the academic gentry and mandarins of high
status knowledge whose participation is aimed at the legitimization of their
own power. Along with smashing through the Western arcs of destiny—those
supposedly unassailable narratives of individual freedom arching towards Dis-
neyland, Aztecland, Inca Blinka, San Banadov, or Gangsterland—strangification unsettles foundational myths which anchor meaning in a sedentary web
of contradictory appearances and pre-code the world in such a way that en-

132

McLAREN

trance to the world of "success" depends on the imprimatur of one's cultural capital and the potential for earning power.

A number of questions are raised by Cohen's analysis for those who are developing Freirean based pedagogical work. These questions include, among others:

> What importance do "postmodern theory" and "resistance postmodernism" have for the Brazilian sociopolitical context?
>
> The recent thesis on "the death of the subject" advanced by many poststructuralists (the individual is constituted by discourse or is simply a position in language, systems of signification, chains of signs) has called into question the feasibility of historical agency of political praxis. How can we think of agency outside of a transhistorical and prediscursive "I" and yet not fall into the cynical trap that suggests that individuals are simply the pawns of the interpretive communities in which they find themselves? If the subject has been aestheticized and reduced to simply a "desiring machine," how are we to address the concepts of morality and ethics and multidimensional forms of agency?
>
> How are we to react to those who proclaim the "death of History" thesis which decries the meta-narratives of the Enlightenment as misguided beliefs in the power of rational reflection? If we are to reject "grand theories" that essentialize others and speak for their needs from a perspective that refuses to critically interrogate its own ideological constitutiveness, then are we simply left with a micropolitics of local struggles? In other words, is it possible to build global alliances in the postmodern era that do not produce the same forms of technocratic capitalism that are part of the problem?
>
> If master narratives are colonizing practices that repress differences and the recognition of multiple identities, and if it is virtually impossible to represent the real outside the constraints of regimes of representation, how should we begin to rethink and practice liberation?
>
> While postmodern theorists have developed new understandings of desire as a means of criticizing the disabling effects of instrumental reason, how can we address pragmatically the project of human freedom?

Postmodern critiques of educational institutions such as those advanced by Cohen can be helpful to Freirean educators in placing social and educational critique within a wider contemporary problematic.

THE NOCTURNAL ACADEMY AND THE POLITICS OF DIFFERENCE

Western intellectuals need to further understand that while affirming the experiences of subaltern groups is exceedingly important within a praxis of liberation, it is a highly questionable practice to render the "other" as transparent

McLAREN

by inviting the other to speak for herself. Freire and other critics make this point very clear (Freire and Macedo, 1987; Freire, 1971; 1985). As Gaurav Desai (following Gayatri Spivak, Lata Mani, and Partha Chattergee) notes, the position of permitting the other to speak for herself is uncomfortably "complicitious with a Western epistemological tradition that takes the conditions of the possibility of subaltern counterinvention for granted without engaging in a critique of the effects of global capitalism on such counterinvention" (1993:137). Since the oppressed speak for themselves within a particular sign structure, the language of critique adopted by the insurgent intellectual needs to be able to analyze the embeddedness of such a sign system in the larger episteme of colonialism and white supremacist, capitalist patriarchy. Insurgent intellectuals must apply the same critique to their own assumptions about the other as they do to the other's self-understanding. In fact, critical educators need to counterinvent a discourse that transcends existing epistemes (Desai, 1993). "We can," Linda Alcoff argues, "engage in a 'speaking to' the other that does not essentialize the oppressed and nonideologically constructed subjects." Summarizing Spivak, Alcoff points out that Western intellectuals must allow "for the possibility that the oppressed will produce a 'counter-sentence' that can then suggest a new historical narrative" (1991–92: 23). We need to question how events "position" Western intellectuals as authoritative and empowered speakers in ways that reinscribe the oppressed in discourses of colonization, patriarchy, racism, and conquest (Alcoff, 1991–92).

Jim Merod (1987) poses the challenge of the intellectual as follows:

134

> The critic's task is not only to question truth in its present guises. It is to find ways of putting fragments of knowledge, partial views, and separate disciplines in contact with questions about the use of expert labor so that the world we live in can be seen for what it is (1987: 188).

The problem, as Merod sees it, is that there exists within the North American academy no political base for alliances among radical social theorists and the oppressed. He writes:

> The belief among liberal humanists that they have no "liberation strategy" to direct their steps is a vivid reminder of the humanities' class origin. Yet intellectuals always have something to fight for more important than their own professional position. North American intellectuals need to move beyond theory, tactics, and great dignified moral sentiments to support, in the most concrete ways possible, people harmed or endangered by the guiltless counter-revolutionary violence of state power. . . The major intellectual task today is to build a political community where ideas can be argued and sent into the world of news and information as a force with a collective voice, a voice that names cultural distortions and the unused possibilities of human intelligence (1987: 191).

One important task of the critical educator is to translate cultural difference. This is certainly the challenge for Freirean educators. The act of transla-

McLAREN

tion is, in Bhabha's (1990) terms, "a borderline moment" (p. 314). As Walter Benjamin pointed out, all cultural languages are to a certain extent foreign to themselves and from the perspective of otherness it is possible to interrogate the contextual specificity of cultural systems (Bhabha, 1990). It is in this sense, then, that "it becomes possible to inscribe the specific locality of cultural systems—their incommensurable differences—and through that apprehension of difference, to perform the act of cultural translation" (ibid.: 314).

All forms of cultural meaning are open to translation because all cultural meanings resist totalization and complete closure. In other words, cultural meanings are hybrid and cannot be contained within any discourse of authenticity or race, class, gender, essences. Bhabha describes the subject of cultural difference as follows:

> the subject of cultural difference is neither pluralistic nor relativistic. The frontiers of cultural differences are always belated or secondary in the sense that their hybridity is never simply a question of the admixture of pregiven identities or essences. Hybridity is the perplexity of the living as it interrupts the representation of the fullness of life; it is an instance of iteration, in the minority discourse, of the time of the arbitrary sign—"the minus in the origin"—through which all forms of cultural meaning are open to translation because their enunciation resists totalization (ibid).

The subaltern voices of minority cultures constitute "those people who speak the encrypted discourse of the melancholic and the migrant" (ibid.: 315). The transfer of their meaning can never be total. The "desolate silences of the wandering people" (ibid.: 316) illustrate the incommensurability of translation which confronts the discourse of white supremacist and capitalist patriarchy with its own alterity.

As translators, critical educators must assume a transformative role by "dialogizing the other" rather than trying to "represent the other" (Hitchcock, 1993). The site of translation is always an arena of struggle. The translation of other cultures must resist the authoritative representation of the other through a decentering process that challenges dialogues which have become institutionalized through the semantic authority of state power. Neither the practice of signification nor translation occurs in an ideological void, and for this reason educators need to interrogate the sign systems that are used to produce readings of experience. As Joan Scott notes, "experience is a subject's history. Language is the site of history's enactment" (1992: 34). It is Freire's particular strength that he has developed a critical vernacular which can help to translate both the other's experience and his own experience of the other in such a way that ideological representations may be challenged. The challenge here is to rethink authoritative representations of the other in a critical language that does not simply reauthorize the imperatives of "First World" translation practices. To do otherwise would open translation to a form of cultural imperialism. Experiences never speak for themselves, and certainly not those of the oppressed. Freire is careful to make sure his language of translation provides the oppressed with tools to analyze their own experiences while at the same time recognizing that the translation process itself is never immune from inscription in ideological relations of power and privilege (Freire and Gadotti, 1995).

While Freire's dialogue does not centrally address the politics of race, his message can none the less be elaborated through an engagement with the work of Black insurgent intellectuals. Cornel West blames what he perceives as a decline in Black literate intellectual activity on the "relatively greater Black integration into postindustrial capitalist America with its bureaucratized, elite universities, dull middlebrow colleges, and decaying high schools, which have little concern for and confidence in Black students as potential intellectuals" (hooks and West 1991: 137). He is highly critical of "aspects of the exclusionary and repressive effect of White academic institutions and humanistic scholarship" (p. 137) and, in particular, "the rampant xenophobia of bourgeois humanism predominant in the whole academy" (p. 142).

West sketches out four models for Black intellectual activity as a means of enabling critical forms of Black literate activity in the United States. The bourgeois humanist model is premised on Black intellectuals possessing sufficient legitimacy and placement within the "hierarchical ranking and the deep-seated racism shot through bourgeois humanistic scholarship" (p. 138). Such legitimation and placement must, however, "result in Black control over a portion of, or significant participation within, the larger White infrastructures for intellectual activity" (p. 140).

The Marxist revolutionary model, according to West, is "the least xenophobic White intellectual subculture available to Black intellectuals" (p. 140). However, West is also highly critical of the constraints Marxist discourse places on the creative life of Black intellectuals in terms of constructing a project of possibility and hope, including an analytical apparatus to engage short-term public policies. According to West,

> The Marxist model yields Black intellectual self-satisfaction which often inhibits growth; it also highlights social structural constraints with little practical direction regarding conjunctural opportunities. This self-satisfaction results in either dogmatic submission to and upward mobility with sectarian party or pre-party formations, or marginal placement in the bourgeois academy equipped with cantankerous Marxist rhetoric and sometimes insightful analysis utterly divorced from the integral dynamics, concrete realities, and progressive possibilities of the Black community. The preoccupation with social structural constraints tends to produce either preposterous chiliastic projections or paralyzing, pessimistic pronouncements (p. 141).

It is important to point out amidst all of this criticism that West does recognize the enabling aspects of the Marxist revolutionary model in its promotion of critical consciousness and its criticisms of dominant research programs within the bourgeois academy.

The Foucaultian postmodern skeptic model invoked by West investigates the relationship among knowledge, power, discourse, politics, cognition and social control. It offers a fundamental rethinking of the role of the intellectual within the contemporary postmodern condition. Foucault's "political economy of truth" is viewed by West as a critique of both bourgeois humanist and Marxist approaches through the role of Foucault's specific intellectual. The specific intellectual, according to West,

> . . . shuns the labels of scientificity, civility, and prophecy, and instead delves into the specificity of the political, economic, and cultural matrices within which regimes of truth are produced, distributed, circulated, and consumed. No longer should intellectuals deceive themselves by believing—as do humanist and Marxist intellectuals—that they are struggling "on behalf" of the truth; rather the problem is the struggle over the very status of truth and the vast institutional mechanism which accounts for this status (p. 142).

West summarizes the Foucaultian model as an encouragement of "an intense and incessant interrogation of power-laden discourses" (p. 143). But the Foucaultian model is not a call to revolution. Rather, it's an invitation to revolt against the repressive effects of contemporary regimes of truth.

Selectively appropriating from these three models, West goes on to propose his own "insurgency model" which posits the Black intellectual as a critical, organic catalyst for social justice. His insurgency model for Black intellectual life recovers the emphasis on human will and heroic effort from the bourgeois model, highlights the emphasis on structural constraints, class formations, and radical democratic values from the Marxist model, and recuperates the worldly skepticism evidenced in the Foucaultian mode's destabilization of regimes of truth. However, unlike the bourgeois model, the insurgency model privileges collective intellectual work and communal resistance and struggle. Contrary to the Marxist model, the insurgency model does not privilege the industrial working class as the chosen agent of history but rather attacks a variety of forms of social hierarchy and subordination, both vertical and horizontal. Further, the insurgency model places much more emphasis on social conflict and struggle than does the Foucaultian model. While Freire's critique of domesticating forms of pedagogy gives a specifically Latin American context for the development of the insurgent intellectual, West's own typology extends some central Freirean themes in order to deepen its engagement with issues of race.

bell hooks describes an intellectual as "somebody who trades in ideas by transgressing discursive frontiers . . . who trades in ideas in their vital bearing on a wider political culture" (hooks and West 1991: 152). However, hooks argues that White supremacist capitalist patriarchy has denied Black women, es-

137

McLAREN

pecially, "the opportunity to pursue a life of the mind." This is a problem that is also firmly entrenched in the racist White university system that involves "persecution by professors, peers, and professional colleagues" (p. 157). hooks rightly notes that "any discussion of intellectual work that does not underscore the conditions that make such work possible misrepresents the concrete circumstances that allow for intellectual production" (p. 158). She further elaborates:

> Within a White supremacist capitalist, patriarchal social context like this culture, no Black woman can become an intellectual without decolonizing her mind. Individual Black women may become successful academics without undergoing this process and, indeed, maintaining a colonized mind may enable them to excel in the academy but it does not enhance the intellectual process. The insurgency model that Cornel West advocates, appropriately identifies both the process Black females must engage to become intellectuals and the critical standpoints we must assume to sustain and nurture that choice (p. 160).

I have employed criticisms of the academy by West, hooks, and Cohen because concerns dealing with postmodern social conditions and theory and those of race and gender help to widen Freire's criticisms by situating his insights more fully within the context and concerns of North American liberation struggles, specifically as they address struggles of the poor, of women, and people of color (McLaren and Leonard, 1993; Freire, 1993a). Of course, there is room to broaden the context even further in relation to the struggles of indigenous peoples, of gays and lesbians, and other cultural workers within and outside of university settings. Freirean-based educators need to raise more questions related to race and gender so that these issues are given a more central focus in the struggle for social transformation. These include:

> In what ways have pedagogical practices been colonized by racialized discourses?
>
> What is the relationship between racial differentiation and subordination and dominant discourses about race and ethnicity? How are these relationships reproduced by white supremacist discursive regimes and communicative practices?
>
> While the struggle for racial and gender equality is deemed worthwhile, those who struggle on behalf of this worthy goal are often deemed deviant when they step outside of the legitimating norms of what is considered to be the "common culture." How are race and gender inequality reproduced within liberal humanist discourses?
>
> If there is no necessary racial teleology within the educational practices of most U.S. schools, how does the reproduction of racist discourses occur in most school sites?
>
> How does the hypervisibility of white cultures actually hide their obviousness in relations of domination and oppression?

138

How does race constitute a boundary constraint on what is considered normal and appropriate behavior?

In what ways are the conditions within the dominant culture for being treated justly and humanely predicated on utilitarian forms of rationality and the values inscribed and legitimated by bourgeois, working-class and elite forms of white culture? How do these forms of rationality work within the episteme of a larger discourse of colonialism?

Despite these absent discourses, Freire's work remains vitally important in the current debates over the role of universities, public schools and educational sites of all kinds throughout North America (Freire, 1985). Freire warns educators that the activity of reading the word in relation to the social world has been regrettably pragmatic rather than principled (Freire and Macedo, 1987). In other words, schooling (in relation to both universities and public schools) revolves around the necessity of differentially reproducing a citizenry distinguished by class, race, and gender injustices. The challenges of educators in both First and Third World contexts is to transform these reproductive processes. This idea needs to be nuanced.

Freirean pedagogy is set firmly against what Kristin Ross calls "the integral 'pedagogicizing' of society", by which she refers to the "general infantilization" of individuals or groups through the discourses and social practices of "the nineteenth-century European myth of progress" (1993: 669).

Ross conceives of critical pedagogy through what she refers to as the "antidisciplinary practice" of cultural studies. Drawing upon revisionist theories of allegory of Walter Benjamin, Paul de Man, and others, Ross moves away from the essentialist conceptions of cultural identity informed by a symbolic (mimetic and synechdochical) model of experience and representation in which one part timelessly and ahistorically reflects the whole. According to this model, the plight of, say, white women in New York reflects the plight of Black women in the southern U.S. Rather than viewing this relationship as an unmediated one in which the plight of black women constitutes an authentic reflection of the plight of white women, Ross prefers to see this and similar relationships as allegorical rather than mimetic.

According to Ross:

Allegory preserves the differences of each historically situated and embedded experience, all the while drawing a relationship between those experiences. In other words, one experience is read in terms of another but not necessarily in terms of establishing identity, not obliterating the qualities particular to each. (1993: 672).

E. San Juan, Jr. maintains that allegory as a formal device has specific advantages for shattering illusion:

McLAREN

> What happens in allegory is this: instead of inducing an easy reconciliation of antimonies, an existential leap into faith where all class antagonisms vanish and rebellious desire is pacified, allegory heightens the tension between signifier and signified, between object and subject, thereby foiling empathy and establishing the temporary distance required for generating critical judgment and, ultimately, cathartic action (San Juan, Jr., 1988: 46.).

Further, San Juan notes that allegory constitutes "a process of misaligning opposites." As such, it:

> . . . focuses on the crux of the contradictions and discharges a call, a polemical challenge. It images the transitional movement of difference from passive contemplation to active involvement, converting objects into process: the process of social production rupturing social relations (San Juan, Jr., 1988: 46).

Allegory, according to Terry Eagleton, is a "figurative mode which relates through difference, preserving the relative autonomy of a set of signifying units while suggesting an affinity with some other range of signifiers" (1990, p. 356). This challenges the Lukácsian idea of expressive totality and brings to mind Adorno's idea of constellation. For Adorno, the contradictory accomplice of the bourgeois Enlightenment—dominative reason—is challenged by totality. To engage totality from the perspective of a negative dialectics is to view totality allegorically, and in doing so defending totality against totalitarianism because the materialism of the aesthetic is never abandoned and, therefore, totality is never reduced to totalizing idealism. I stand with Eagleton when he notes that "those who indiscriminately demonize such concepts as unity, identity, consensus, regulation have forgotten that there are, after all, different modalities of these things, which are not equivalently repressive" (1990, p. 355).

Laura E. Donaldson remarks on the importance of allegorical vision in a feminist approach to the issues of homogeneity and universality. She does this by articulating allegory as a form of metanarrative that can negotiate "the contradiction between a radical politics of identity and a postmodern skepticism, an unqualified opposition and purely affirmative action, which threatens feminism from within" (1994: 20).

According to Donaldson, "Allegory not only exposes the ideological underpinnings of discourse, but also problematizes a symbolic metaphysics of presence, or in the case of a feminist stand point, a radical politics of identity" (1994: 21). Whereas symbol is anti-paradoxical, excluding the logic of its two opposing units, allegory "implies a much more discontinuous relation between signifier and signified, since an extraneous principle rather than some natural identification determines how and when the connection becomes articulated."

Donaldson's characterization of allegory in relation to feminism proves instructive:

Allegory creates meaning metonymically by temporally displacing reference from one sign to the next; in other words, it's always mobile. Construction of meaning resists a representational truth or the attempt to find an invariant signified for the narrative which can then be placed before the reader for acceptance or rejection. Likewise, an allegorical feminism resists not only a representational view of women's truth but also the unified Cartesian subject which such a view presupposes. Allegory highlights the irrevocably relational nature of feminist identity and the negations upon which the assumption of a singular, fixed, and essential self is based (1994: 22).

Citing James Clifford, Donaldson goes as far as asserting that all meaningful levels of a text, including theories and interpretation, are allegorical or are composed of multiple allegorical registers or "voices" (p. 22). No one register necessarily privileges the rest. Donaldson's comments echo Walter Benjamin's attack on the German Romantic theory of the symbol with its emphasis on the totalizing mystical instant in which the signifier fuses with the signified:

> There is a great difference between a poet's seeking the particular from the general and his seeing the general in the particular. The former gives rise to allegory, where the particular serves only as an instance or example of the general; the latter, however, is the true nature of poetry; the expression of the particular without any thought of, or reference to, the general. Whoever grasps the particular in all its vitality also grasps the general, without being aware of it, or only becoming aware of it at a later stage (Cited in Taussig, 1992, p. 152).

141

Benjamin's concept of allegory (seeing the general in the particular) does not permit the redemption of nature through transcendence since in allegory the signifier is held apart from its signified by "a jagged line of demarcation" which is both history and death (Taussig, 1992: 153). Ross conscripts similar insights about allegory into the service of a critical teaching about cultural identity. Since it is impossible to represent every cultural group in the curriculum, the task of critical pedagogy, in Ross' terms, is to construct cultural identity allegorically—for each group to see his or her cultural narrative in a broader and comparative relation to others and within a larger narrative of social transformation.

For students to recognize the historical and cultural specificity of their own lived experiences allegorically—i.e., in allegorical relations to other narratives—is especially urgent, especially, as Ross puts it,

> at a time of growing global homogenization [in which] the non-West is conceived in two, equally reductive ways: one whereby differences are reified and one whereby differences are lost. In the first, the non-West is assigned the role for the repository for some more genuine or organic lived experience; minority cultures and nonwestern cultures in the West are increasingly made to provide something like an authenticity rush for blase or jaded Westerners, and this is too

McLAREN

heavy a burden for anyone to bear. In the second, nonwestern experiences are recorded and judged according to how closely they converge on the same: a single public culture or global average, that is, how far each has progressed toward a putative goal of modernization (1993: 673).

An emancipatory curriculum cannot present First and Third World cultures in the context of binary oppositions as relations of domination and resistance, since this move usually permits the First World perspective to prevail as the privileged point of normative civilizations (Ross, 1993). While Freire's work calls attention to the danger of a reductive dichotomization of First and Third World cultures, his interpreters often attempt simply to transplant Freire's perspective into First World contexts as a fortuitous equivalence or natural counterpart to subaltern resistance without recoding Freire's arguments sufficiently in terms of First World contexts (Giroux, 1992). This leads to an unwitting embrace of pedagogy as a Western "civilizing" practice.

As a teacher, Freire has provided the pedagogical conditions necessary to better understand how Enlightenment humanism and its specifically Eurocentric (and EuroAmerican) "voice of reason" has not always been insightful or even reasonable in exercising its transcontinental thinking in the service of truth and justice (Giroux, 1992). Freire's work helps us to further confront this issue as well as many others of concern to educators and cultural workers.

The perspectives of Freire can help deepen the debate over the role of the university in contemporary North American culture and, by extension, can also help to situate the struggle of Latin American educators within the concerns of postmodern and insurgent criticisms of the academy as exemplified by the perspectives of West, hooks, and Cohen.

In a world of global capitalism we need global alliances through cultural and political contact in the form of critical dialogue. Samir Amin (1989) notes that we collectively face a problem that "resides in the objective necessity for a reform of the world system; failing this, the only way out is through the worst barbarity, the genocide of entire peoples or a worldwide conflagration" (p. 114).

In attempting to develop a project premised on the construction of an emancipatory cultural imaginary that is directed at transforming the conditions that create the victims of capitalist expansion, educators need to go beyond simply severing their arterial connections to the forces of production and consumption that defraud them through the massification of their subjectivities. They need to create new alliances through a politics of difference. Otherwise, they face the prospect of becoming extensions of multinational corporations within the larger apparatus of capitalist expansion in the service of unequal accumulation and further underdevelopment in the peripheral and semi-peripheral countries of Latin America. In short, what is needed is a politics of radical hope. Hope needs to be conjugated with some aspect of the

142

McLAREN

carnal, tangible world of historical and material relations in order to be made a referent point for a critically transformative praxis.

We are reminded by Freire and his colleagues not to engage in controversies about difference, but rather to be encouraged to dialogue about difference. It is in this sense that the university is invited to become truly plural and dialogical, a place where students are not only required to read texts but to understand contexts. A place where educators are required to learn to talk about student experiences and then form this talk into a philosophy of learning and a praxis of transformation.

I have recently witnessed in Brazil an experiment using Freire's work in conjunction with contributions by critical educators in Europe and the United States at Escola 1.° e 2.° Graus José César de Mesquita (a public school and high school consisting of 1,000 students who live in an industrial zone in Porto Alegre). The project is currently supported by the Sindicato des Trabalhadores nas Indústrias Metalúrgicas, Mecânicas e Material Elétrico de Porto Alegre and directed by Nize Maria Campos Pellanda. Here, the curriculum has been forged out of dialogues among teachers, researchers, and scholars from many different countries in both First and Third Worlds. Both elementary and high school students are encouraged to make active alliances with social movements and link their classroom pedagogies directly to social issues facing the larger community. While there exists a great deal of political opposition to this school for workers from both reactionary and neoliberal educators, administrators, and politicians, the experiment itself is a testament to the Freirean vision of transcultural alliances and geo-political realignment.

Freirean pedagogy argues that pedagogical sites, whether they are universities, public schools, museums, art galleries, or other spaces, must have a vision that is not content with adapting individuals to a world of oppressive social relations but is dedicated to transforming the very conditions that promote such conditions. This means more than simply reconfiguring or collectively refashioning subjectivities outside of the compulsive ethics and consumerist ethos of flexible specialization or the homogenizing calculus of capitalist expansion. It means creating new forms of sociality, new idioms of transgression, and new instances of popular mobilization that can connect the institutional memory of the academy to the tendential forces of historical struggle and the dreams of liberation that one day might be possible to guide them. This is a mission that is not simply Freirean, but eminently human.

Rather than ground his pedagogy in a doctrinal absolutism, Freire's attention is always fixed on both the specific and generalized other. Categories of identity, when confronted by Freire's practice of conscientization, are vacated of their pretended access to certainty and truth (Giroux, 1993). What has endeared Freire to several generations of critical educators, both in terms of a respect for his political vision and for the way he conducts his own life, is the

143

McLAREN

manner in which he has situated his work within an ethics of compassion, love, and solidarity.

To disentangle hope from the vagaries of everyday life, to disconnect human capacity from the structures of domination and then to reconnect them to a project where power works as a form of affirmation and a practice of freedom is, these days, to invite more cynical critics to view Freire's work as a nostalgic interlude in a world whose modernist dream of revolutionary alterity has been superseded by the massifying logic of capitalist accumulation and alienation. Yet Freire's work cannot be so easily dismissed as an anachronistic project that has failed to notice history's wake-up call from recent postmodernist critiques. Many, but not all, of these critiques have relegated human agency to the dustbin of history, along with modernist projects of emancipation including those, like Freire's, that continue to be informed by socialist and humanistic ideals. To argue in this climate of the simulacrum, as does Freire, that freedom can be both true and real is to instantly arouse skepticism and in some quarters, to provoke derision.

As educators who take Freire's message to heart, we need not only to create oppositional Chicano, white, African-American, and Asian ethnicities but, indeed, to reinvent the very notion of ethnicity. This is because current approaches to pluralism in the schools often masquerade as democratic education. Further, we need to address not only the discursive constructions of race but also economic exploitation and the manner in which such forms of ethnicity are structurally imbricated and intertwined. In this way, educators can participate in analyzing our cultural and social present and decolonizing the Euro-American mind, and, moreover, in organizing affectively our responses to and encounters with the world. We need to remember that the forms of pleasure we produce and the economies of affective investment we create as educators and cultural workers will have political consequences by which history will remember us. Are we going to invest in society's weakest and most vulnerable members? Are we prepared to take on the responsibility of making history?

The answer to this question may well depend on the extent to which we see the possible historical present described by Subcomandante Marcos as pertinent not merely to Mexico, but to the entire world:

Para construir un mundo feliz: Cuando la angustia llegue a su pecho, siga las siguientes instrucciones para cambiar al mundo. Primero, construyase un cielo más concavo, píntese de verde o café, colores terrestres y hermosos; salpíquese de nubes a discreción, cuelguese con cuidado una luna llena de occidente, digamos a tres cuartos partes sobre el horizonte respectivo donde oriente inicia lentamente, el ascenso de un sol brillante y poderoso, traiga a hombres y mujeres, abrales el paso con cariño y ellos empezaran a andar por si sólos. Contemple con amor el mar. De estancia en el séptimo día.

Segunda parte: Reuna los silencios necesarios, forjelos de sol, mar y lluvia y polvo y noche; con paciencia vayase dando uno de sus extremos; elija un traje marrón y un pañuelo rojo, espere al amanecer y con la lluvia por irse marche a la gran ciudad. Al verlo, los tiranos huiran atrerrorizados, atropellandose unos a otros, pero no se detenga. La lucha apenas inicia[4]

> Subcomandante Marcos.
> Aguascalientes de la Selva Lacandona
> Chiapas, Mexico

To construct a happier world: When anguish reaches your heart, follow these directions for changing the world. First, create a more concave sky; paint it with beautiful earthy colors, green or brown; splatter it with clouds accordingly; carefully hang a moon full of the West, say about three quarters over the respective horizon from which the East slowly begins the rising of a brilliant and powerful sun; bring men and women, open the path to them with affection and they will begin to walk on their own, contemplate the ocean with love. Be at rest on the seventh day.

Secondly, unite the necessary silences, forge them with the sun, ocean, and rain and dust and the night; with patience begin extending one of your extremities, choose a dark suit and a red hankerchief, wait for the dawn and with the parting rain march toward the great city. Upon seeing you, the tyrants will flee, terrorized and running over each other. But don't stop. The fight has just begun. (Translation Carlos Tejeda and Claudia E. Ramírez)

> Subcomandante Marcos
> Aguascalientes de la Selva Lacandona
> Chiapas, Mexico.

145

For both the oppressed and nonoppressed alike, Freire's life and work have served as a life-affirming bridge from private despair to collective hopefulness to self and social transformation. Just as United States foreign policy towards Latin America over the last two decades has been directed at defeating Guevarist-inspired struggle on behalf of the suffering poor, United States educational policy has consisted essentially of defeating the threat of Freirean-inspired pedagogical vision within its own borders. Freire's army of educators, far larger than Che's Bolivian *foco* of fifty guerrillas, is facing a late capitalist crisis of struggle. Captured in a tiny schoolhouse in La Higuera and executed, Che's political spirit is still alive even as his image continues to be mass-marketed and exploited by the forces of capital. The spirit of Freire's pedagogy, while still cultivated from schoolhouses like those of La Higuera, to university seminar rooms and electronic journals on the internet, has yet to inspire a revitalization of public schooling, as the mass appeal of public education has been dwindling under capital's seductive sign of privatization. Undaunted, Freire continues to provide a language of demystification and reenchantment in our flightpath of self-making, one that has no endpoint but nevertheless has a critical direction.

McLAREN

The political optic that guides Freire's work is fashioned not so much from dialectics (with its emphasis on collectivity and scientific objectivity vs. false consciousness), as it is from dialogue (with its emphasis on reciprocal engagement, subjectivity, and performance/community), and in this light he is closer to Levinas, Buber, and Bakhtin than he is to Marx. In so far as he addresses individuals as more than the capricious outcomes of historical accident, or exceeding the abstract boundaries of metaphysical design, Freire's work presupposes a subject of history and a culture of redemption.

At a time in U.S. culture in which history has been effectively expelled from the formation of meaning and hope has been quarantined in the frenetic expansion of capital into regions of public and private life hitherto unimaginable and unthinkable, Freire's pedagogy of liberation is one we dismiss at our peril.

NOTES

1. This essay is forthcoming in *Cultural Critique.*

2. For an analysis of this process in the context of schooling, see Peter McLaren (1995), *Critical Pedagogy and Predatory Culture: Oppositional Politics in a Postmodern Age*, London and New York, Routledge; Peter McLaren (1994), *Schooling as a Ritual Performance*, London and New York, Routledge; Peter McLaren (1994), *Life in Schools*, White Plains, NY, Longman Inc; Henry Giroux and Peter McLaren eds. (1994), *Between Borders*, London and New York, Routledge; Henry Giroux and Peter McLaren eds. (1989), *Critical Pedagogy, the State, and Cultural Struggle*, Albany, NY, State University of New York Press; and Peter McLaren and Colin Lankshear eds. (1994), *Politics of Liberation*, London and New York: Routledge.

3. See Charles Acland (1994), *Youth, Murder, Spectacle: The Cultural Politics of "Youth in Crisis".* Boulder, CO: Westview Press, p. 136.

4. *La Jornada*, 21 September 1994, p. 14.

REFERENCES

Acland, Charles.(1994). I. *Youth, Murder, Spectacle: The Cultural Politics of "Youth in Crisis".* Boulder, CO: Westview Press.

Adorno, Theodor. (1967). *Prisms.* Cambridge, MA: The MIT Press.

Alcoff, Linda. (1991–92). The problem of speaking for others. *Cultural Critique,* no. 20, 5–32.

Amin, Samir. (1989). *Eurocentrism.* New York: Monthly Review Press.

Attali, Jacques. (1991). *Millennium.* New York: Random House, Inc.

Berlin, Jim. (1993). Literacy, pedagogy, and English studies: Postmodern connections. In Colin Lankshear and Peter McLaren (Eds.), *Critical Literacy: Politics. Praxis. and the Postmodern* (pp. 247–270). Albany, NY: Suny Press.

Bhabha, Homi K. (1990). *Nation and Narration.* London and New York: Routledge.

Chow, Rey. (1993). *Writing Diaspora: Tactics of Intervention in Contemporary Cultural Studies.* Bloomington and Indianapolis: Indiana University Press.

Cohen, Sande. (1993). *Academia and the Luster of Capital.* Minneapolis, MN: University of Minnesota Press.

Conquergood, Dwight. (1992). Ethnography, rhetoric, and performance. *Quarterly Journal of Speech* 78, 80–123.

de Certeau, Michel. (1984). *The Practice of Everyday Life.* Trans. Steven Rendall. Berkeley: University of California Press.

Desai, Gaurau. (1993). The invention of invention. *Cultural Critique.* 24, 119–142.

Donaldson, Laura E. (1988–89). (Ex)changing (wo)man: Towards a materialist feminist semiotics. *Cultural Critique.* 11 5–23.

Eagleton, Terry. (1990). *The Ideology of the Aesthetic.* London: Basil Blackwell.

Freire, Paulo and Macedo, Donaldo. (1987). *Literacy: Reading the Word and the World.* South Hadley, MA: Bergin and Garvey.

Freire, Paulo, and Gadotti, Moacir. (1995). We can re-invent the world. In Peter McLaren and Giarelli, Jim (Eds.), *Critical Theory and Educational Research.* Albany, NY: State University of New York Press, pp. 257–270.

Freire, Paulo. (1971). *Pedagogy of the Oppressed.* New York: Seabury Press.

Freire, Paulo. (1985). *The Politics of Liberation: Culture. Power. and Liberation.* South Hadley, MA: Bergin and Garvey.

Freire, Paulo. (1993a). *A Note From Paulo Freire.* Communication and Development in a Postmodern Era: Re-Evaluating the Freirean Legacy. International Conference Programme. University Sains Malaysia, December 6–9, Penang, Malaysia.

Freire, Paulo. (1993b). Forward. In *Paulo Freire: A Critical Encounter,* Peter McLaren and Peter Leonard (Eds.). London and New York: Routledge, pp. ix–xii.

Freire, Paulo. (1994). *Paulo Freire and Higher Education.* Miguel Escobar, Alfredo Fernández and Gilberto Guevara-Niebla (Eds.) with Paulo Freire. Albany, NY: State University of New York Press.

Gee, Jim. (1993). Postmodernism and literacies. In Colin Lankshear and Peter McLaren (Eds.), *Critical Literacy: Politics. Praxis and the Postmodern* (pp. 271–296). Albany, NY: Suny Press.

Giroux, Henry. (1992). Paulo Freire and politics of postcolonialism. *Journal of Advanced Composition.* 12(1), 15–26.

Giroux, Henry. (1993). *Border Crossings.* New York: Routledge.

Hitchcock, Peter. (1993). *Dialogics of the Oppressed.* Minneapolis: University of Minnesota Press.

hooks, bell, and West, Cornel. (1991). *Breaking Bread: Insurgent Black Intellectual Life.* Boston, MA: South End Press.

Kincheloe, Joe and McLaren, Peter. (1994). Rethinking critical theory and qualitative research. In Norm K. Denzin and Yvonna S. Lincoln (Eds.), *Handbook of Qualitative Research.* Newbury Park, CA: Sage Publications, pp. 138–157.

Lefebvre, H. (1975). *Metaphilosophie.* Frankfort: Suhrkamp.

Martin-Barbero, Jesus. (1992). *Communication. Culture. and Hegemony: From Media to Mediation.* London: Sage Publications.

McLaren, Peter (1995). *Critical Pedagogy and Predatory Culture: Oppositional Politics in a Postmodern Era.* London and New York: Routledge.

McLaren, Peter and Giroux, Henry. (1994). Forward. In Moacir Gadotti (Ed.), *Reading Paulo Freire: His Life and Work.* Albany, NY: State University of New York Press, pp. iii–xvii.

McLaren, Peter and Lankshear, Colin. (Eds.). (1994). *Politics of Liberation: Paths from Freire.* London and New York: Routledge.

147

McLAREN

McLaren, Peter and Leonard, Peter. (Eds.). (1993). *Paulo Freire: A Critical Encounter.* London and New York: Routledge.

McLaren, Peter. (1992). Collisions with otherness: Multiculturalism, the politics of difference, and the enthographer as nomad. *The American Journal of Semiotics.* 2(2–3), 121–148.

Merod, Jim. (1987). *The Political Responsibility of the Critic.* Ithaca and London: Cornell University Press.

Miyoshi, Masao. (1993). A borderless world? From Colonialism to Transnationalism and the decline of the nation-state. *Critical Inquiry* 19, 726–751.

Parry, Benita. (1993). A critique mishandled. *Social Text* 35, 121–133.

Ross, Andrew. (1989). *No Respect: Intellectuals and Popular Culture.* New York and London: Routledge.

Ross, Kristin. (1993). The world literature and cultural studies program. *Critical Inquiry* 19, 666–676.

San Juan, Jr., E. (1988). *Ruptures. Schisms Interventions: Cultural Revolution in the Third World.* Manila, Phillipines: De La Salle University Press.

Scott, Joan W. (1992). Experience. In Judith Butler and Joan W. Scott (Eds.), *Feminists Theorize the Political* (pp. 22–40). New York and London: Routledge.

Shapiro, Michael J. (1992). *Reading the Postmodern Polity: Political Theory as Textual Practice.* Minneapolis: University of Minnesota Press.

Taussig, Michael. (1992). *The Nervous System.* New York: Routledge.

Torres, Carlos Alberto. (1993). *Democratic Socialism, Social Movements and Educational Policy in Brazil: The Work of Paulo Freire as Secretary of Education in the Municipality of São Paulo.* Manuscript in progress.

CRITICAL PEDAGOGY AND CYBERSPACE

Colin Lankshear, Michael Peters, and Michele Knobel

"We are living through a movement from an organic, industrial to a polymorphous, information system—from all work to all play, a deadly game"

(Donna Haraway, 1990)

chapter 6

INTRODUCTION

THIS CHAPTER will project practices of critical pedagogy into cyberspace, and consider the viability of critical pedagogy within an environment where a range of new technologies and practices have converged to produce the "communications revolution" (Hinkson 1991).

In line with our commitment to an educational project of critical pedagogy, we offer here a portrayal and a speculative analysis which are basically sympathetic. We will argue that critical pedagogy is most definitely a viable educational enterprise within cyberspace. Indeed, many of its foundational concepts and principles are made more explicit and more relevant within educational expanses of cyberspace. Critical pedagogy does not, however, enjoy an easy transition from the space of conventional printed texts to that of the digitally coded ether. On the contrary, it undergoes something of a sea change: elements need to be rethought and reworked.

Our argument develops in four sections. The first addresses briefly some characteristic features of critical pedagogy within (what we call) "modernist spaces of enclosure." The second backgrounds distinctively postmodern spaces emerging with discourses of postindustrialism, the information society, and cyberspace. In the third section we address four themes (from a potentially much larger pool) which provide fruitful bases for generating new possibilities for critical pedagogy in cyberspace. Finally, ideas from these three sections are used to indicate a range of theoretical and practical extensions of critical pedagogy into cyberspace.

CRITICAL PEDAGOGY IN MODERNIST SPACES

"Critical pedagogy" names a generic concept for a family-related set of critical practices in and around education originating, most visibly, with Paulo Freire's work in the 1960s (Freire 1970, 1973). Freire's work was taken up and developed from the late 1970s as a distinct(ive) educational project, especially in North American settings. In this generic sense, "critical pedagogy" subsumes the various practices which fall under its younger sibling, "critical literacy" (Peters and Lankshear 1994). Critical pedagogy, then, includes more than a critical study of the text or text relations alone, extending the scope of critical study to take in the wider educational structures and relations within the overall set of socio-cultural practices that constitute the life of social groups and entire societies.

In part, critical pedagogy is grounded in a view of schooling as a form of *cultural politics.* That is, schooling "always represents an introduction to, preparation for, and legitimation of particular forms of social life" (McLaren 1989: 160). Furthermore, schooling always involves power relations, social practices, and privileged forms of knowledge "that support a specific vision of past, present and future", and "rationalize the knowledge industry" in ways that "reproduce inequality, racism and sexism [and] fragment democratic social relations" by emphasizing "competitiveness and cultural ethnocentrism" (ibid: 161).

In response to the cultural politics of schooling, critical pedagogy engages students and teachers collaboratively in making explicit the socially constructed character of knowledge, and asking in whose interests particular "knowledges" are thus constructed. This automatically introduces concepts and issues of social class, of cultures—dominant and subordinate—and of gender. The twin concepts of hegemony and ideology operate together within modernist constructions. The task of critical pedagogy, in this regard, is to unmask hegemonies and critique ideologies with the political and ethical intent of helping to empower students and, more generally, the social groups to which they belong: by fostering awareness of conditions that limit possibilities for human becoming and legitimate the unequal distribution of social goods (Gee 1991); and by unveiling the origins and the historical contingency of these ideologies/hegemonies and the social relations and practices they simultaneously beget and sustain. This task was, of course, writ large in Freire's founding work within peasant communities in Brazil (see Freire 1970, 1973).

At the same time, critical pedagogy has the larger—and necessarily related—task of engaging students and teachers in transformative social practices: practices which, by their very nature, challenge unequal and antidemocratic structures and processes, and seek to establish more egalitarian and "humanizing" alternatives in their place. This transformative ethos is grounded in an epistemology which defines knowledge as a praxis of reflection and action (c.f., Freire 1970). From this perspective, we can only know the world—whether the social-cultural world or the natural world—by acting on it in ways that would change it, and observing the consequences of our action. Thus, only by challenging "limit situations" of inequality or oppression can we *know* the world in its hierarchical or oppressive aspects, and bring that knowledge to understanding. By taking up active roles as knowing *agents*—or acting knowers—and *changing* the world, learners can affirm their empowerment by creating material conditions in which they can share in the production and distribution of power and other social goods on (more) equal terms with others.

As intimated, the theme of empowerment is central to late modernist conceptions of critical pedagogy (c.f., LeCompte and deMarrais 1992). Ira Shor, for example, frames critical pedagogy for empowerment in terms of an education for self and social change, since "the self and society create each other" in a recursive, dialectical manner. Accordingly, critical pedagogy must relate personal growth to public life, and do so by developing "strong skills, academic knowledge, habits of inquiry, and critical curiosity about society, power, inequality, and change" (Shor 1992: 15).

Throughout the 1980s numerous accounts of theory and practice of critical pedagogy in school and tertiary classroom settings were advanced (see, for example, Shor 1980; Bee 1984, 1989; Elsasser and Irvine 1985; Giroux and McLaren eds. 1989; Shor and Freire 1987; among others). Many followed Freire's lead explicitly and insisted that critical pedagogy adopt a "problem posing" approach. In general, they advocated approaching all subject matter "as historical products to be questioned rather than as universal wisdom to be accepted" (Shor 1992: 32). Hence knowledge, society, and human beings themselves are to be viewed as "unfinished products in history, where various forces are still contending" to determine what will constitute standard knowledge and the shape of society and its inherent relationships and distributions (p. 35). Ideally, by approaching the world, and knowledge of the world, as inherently problematic, students and teachers together could "reinvent . . . their relationship to learning and authority" (p. 35). This entails framing aspects of everyday reality and what passes for knowledge as problems to be addressed and resolved, not as immutable "givens." In this way participants can consider the world, and knowledge of the world, as being "up for grabs." They can inquire about the consequences of different "makings/namings" and representations of reality as opposed to others, and pursue alternative namings and representations that accord more fully with democratic and emancipatory ends.

This "problem posing" approach to critical pedagogy focuses on drawing from students' experiences and concerns to generate themes and derive issues that reveal inequalities, oppressions, and injustices woven into the very fabric of the politics of education and everyday life. These "generative" themes, and the issues constructed out of them, are to provide bases for a praxis of reflection-analysis and action, wherein teacher and students become actively involved in addressing and transforming oppressive relations and practices within in the educational process of *coming to know* the world. Until recently, most accounts of critical pedagogy identified generative themes and issues as clustering around the "Big 3" organizing categories of the 1980s critical tradition: race, gender and class.

The pedagogical strength of generative themes and the issues they provoke is that they emerge directly from student cultures and conversations and reflect "unresolved social problems" in classrooms and communities. Hence, they can stimulate and focus investigation around the relationship between personal life and larger issues, and provide genuinely "student-centred foundations for problem-posing" (Shor 1992: 47, 55; also Freire 1970; Shor and Freire 1987).

Ideally, generative themes and issues would comprise the primary subject matter of critical teaching and learning. While this is the ideal in theory, some pressing impediments are imposed in practice by exigencies of the classroom setting, curriculum and syllabus demands, the organization of learning around conventional text forms modelled, paradigmatically, on the book, and by the historically evolved role and identity of the teacher. Not surprisingly, proponents of critical pedagogy have had to deal with a series of difficulties and challenges associated with the almost inescapable demands on (critical) teachers to mediate both official curriculum and text/literacy/content requirements, and the standards and criteria for (genuinely) *critical* inquiry, analysis, and understanding.

Those working within and otherwise sympathetic to the broad paradigm of critical pedagogy identified and wrestled with a range of issues and concerns emerging from the theories and practices of critical pedagogy that evolved during the 1980s. Those most relevant to our immediate purposes are as follows.

(i) While the emphasis on building critical inquiry as far as possible around generative themes considerably reduces teacher-*centredness*, 1980s critical pedagogy nonetheless often remained strongly teacher-*controlled* or orchestrated. Teachers continued to assume responsibility for conceptualizing issues to be discussed, for distilling key themes incipient in students' generative experiences, and, very often, for locating and assembling the resources (typically printed texts of one type or another) in accordance with her or his perceptions of what will be useful and appropriate for critical exploration of themes. Even allowing for considerable variation from case to case, the residual picture is very much one of teachers orchestrating proceedings on the basis of their own critical awareness.

How far this was a function of what Elizabeth Ellsworth identifies as rationalist assumptions underlying the goals of critical pedagogy (1989: 303–304) is open to question. What is beyond question is the fact that critical pedagogy is inescapably vulnerable to compromises inherent in the "essentially paternalistic project of education itself." There is the constant risk that "strategies such as student empowerment and dialogue" may "give the illusion of equality," but, in effect, leave "the authoritarian nature of the teacher/student relationship intact" (ibid: 306).

ii) Practices of critical pedagogy within formal settings remain bounded by curriculum and syllabus demands. Themes framed as links between students' prior learnings and the demands of an (official) ongoing curriculum, but which still enable a critical social focus to enter in, are inevitably circumscribed by the norm of a coherent, sequenced official program of study. This also holds generally wherever critical pedagogy has to negotiate sanctioned scholastic, professional, and technical bodies of knowledge (i.e., subject content).

Curriculum predicated on recourse to the book as the central medium and mediator of knowledge and knowledge production imposes an additional form of constraint on critical pedagogy. The book/text (and the curricular knowledge embodied in the book) stands between the learner and the world, with several limiting consequences. Learners' experiences of much of "the world to be known" is in danger of remaining "bookish": the World is reduced to Words, and remains "known" at the level of words. In addition, learners' own lived and material experiences have to be related to and filtered through books in order to have educational legitimacy and currency. Books and other curricular texts must necessarily become major, if not sole, objects of critique, thereby deflecting critical transformative energy and action away from its "true object": the world itself, or at least the word-world relation as *lived*.

(iii) Critical pedagogies as described in practice were often restricted by the inevitably limited and partial scope of *local* and *immediately available* concerns, experiences, expertise, subjectivities, and identities. Most obviously, student interests and their translation into generative and topical themes, and their treatment, were restricted to the range of possibilities available within the community of experiences and being that comprises the class.

(iv) The social identities assumed to provide the necessary empowering

153

base for moral deliberation and social action were often unduly simplified to the extent that critical pedagogy seeks to make available empowering social identities by affirming student's race, class, and gender positions. Commentators subsequently argued that these identities were too "centered" and reductionist: individuals were increasingly seen as inhabiting "intersections of multiple, contradictory, overlapping social positions not reducible either to race, or class, or gender, and so on" (Ellsworth 1989: 302. See also Aronowitz and Giroux 1988; Giroux 1988; McLaren 1986, 1988). Centered and reductionist social identities screened out many important issues and masked the contradictory and overlapping nature of social positions and identities: leaving students with a limited perceptual and experiential base from which to frame and enact moral and political challenges. This created the added risk that students would effectively be left to operate with teachers' framings of social identities and moral-political perspectives (LeCompte and deMarrais 1992).

(v) The social, moral and political ideals intended to provide direction for critical pedagogy as a whole, and to inform critical judgments of specific issues and viewpoints, often remained abstract and decontextualized: e.g., emancipation, liberation, social justice, radical democracy.

(vi) Reports of critical pedagogy in practice often expressed the difficulties experienced in effecting transformative action and in changing in significant ways the social relations of authority and knowledge production within formal settings. In many cases the pedagogy in practice hived ideology critique off from material practices of change. Students would be introduced to new perspectives on beliefs and belief systems, and could often articulate changes in their own ideological repertoires. This, however, very often marked the extent of the change (LeCompte and deMarrais 1992).

We suggest that these problems largely originate in "spaces of enclosure" that characterize the modernist institution of school education. The book, the classroom and the curriculum can be viewed as intermeshed fixed enclosures which operate in concert to separate educational engagement from wider spheres of social practice: substituting reliance on texts for an integrated experience of word in relation to world, and in the process conferring heavy responsibility on the teacher to organize curricular activities and materials, and interpret meaning and experience.

The status of the book as the text paradigm of modernity underwrites the social construction of school as a quintessential modernist institutional space of enclosure. The book has typically been seen to enclose meaning and experience and, thereby, to promise the possibility of bringing the world into the classroom. It is precisely this that underpins the project of educating learners for life in the world by means of an "age-specific, teacher related process" which requires "full-time attendance at an obligatory curriculum" (Illich 1971: 32). The demands of the obligatory curriculum require that critical teachers "accommodate" generative themes to curricular "needs," and force the teacher's controlling hand in distilling and managing the themes around which critical pedagogy is organized. Likewise, the assumption that books and other texts enclose meaning, and that the task of readers is to extract this meaning, legitimates the role of teacher as the presumed authority on matters of interpretation and accuracy: the teacher "standing in" for the author and for the (experiential) world. Together with students, teachers who are involved in critical pedagogy can (and do) name these constraints. But these same teachers are almost inescapably caught in performative contradictions by the very acts of naming them within prevailing educational settings.

In a more complex way, perhaps, the characteristics of the book might be seen to be reflected in the reductionist and overly centered (conceptions of) social identities critiqued by numerous proponents of critical pedagogy (e.g., Brady and Hernández 1993; Giroux 1988, 1991; McLaren 1988; McLaren and Hammer 1989). The "totalized and totalizing" categories of class, gender, race and the like, correspond to the "freeze-framed" and inescapably simplified ways in which issues and themes tend to be managed in print. In order to establish coherence on the model of linear arguments, authors of print texts are almost inevitably obliged to forego much of the fluidity, dynamism and complexity of their subject matter: e.g., by employing static and generic categories, and ellipses, as framing mechanisms and as means for carrying detail. The abstraction noted with regard to the ideals and principles of critical deliberation and action is a further symptom of this condition.

Finally, the tendency for critical pedagogy to be strongly circumscribed by the local and immediate is an almost unavoidable consequence of learning being confined to classrooms and their close environs, mediated by conventional text forms. While books and other texts can potentially expand the range of information, meaning, and conveyed experience considerably beyond what is materially available in the classroom, the world is nonetheless removed from immediate access—being carried textually—and the use that can be made of such texts is constrained by the knowledges, subjectivities, and life experiences of those immediately connected to the classroom.

Theorists committed to the broad project of critical pedagogy and informed by insights from postmodern and poststructuralist theories have increasingly attempted, in recent years, to address shortcomings identified here. Brady and Hernández (1993), Giroux (1993), Grossberg (1994; Grossberg and Nelson 1988), McLaren (1986, 1993), McLaren and Lankshear (1993), Rockhill (1993), Shor (1992), and Weiler (1992), among many others, have sought in particular to decenter student and teacher identities and to enlarge the range of student voices and printed texts to be given play in critical pedagogy classrooms. By such means they hope to broaden the range of potential issues and themes addressed critically, and the moral, social and political perspectives from which they are addressed.

Outcomes here include richer and more realistic accounts and theoretical

155

LANKSHEAR, PETERS, AND KNOBEL

models of human subjectivity and identity, which increase the likelihood of students identifying issues and arguing for moral positions on the basis of their own multiplicity and contradictoriness. This, in turn, reduces students' dependence upon and vulnerability to teachers' moral perspectives and positions. Moreover, the increased emphasis given to narratives and texts deriving from students' diverse cultural and moral traditions increases the role of generative themes within the subject matter of critical pedagogy—by expanding the generative "base" with which to integrate and relate the more formal demands of the official curriculum.

Even so, the most highly developed accounts of critical pedagogy in modernist spaces have remained hobbled in important ways. Ellsworth, for example, decentered student and teacher subjectivities as an antidote to the silencing of diversity she detected in earlier accounts of critical pedagogy. She and her class searched for commonalities across differences which could provide a basis for challenging racism and other oppressive formations on campus without, however, compromising the distinctive realities and effects of personal experiences of differences. She reports, however, that many of her students did not encounter the classroom as a safe space in which to "speak out or talk back about their experiences of oppression" inside and outside the classroom (1989: 315). The pedagogy employed generated such diverse social positionings that students variously felt afraid of being misunderstood, and/or inhibited by memories of negative prior experiences of speaking out, and/or resentment that some oppressions were marginalized by the explicit emphasis on addressing racism. Interestingly, certain student groupings who experienced silencing and marginality *within* the classroom established "informal and overlapping affinity groups" *outside* the class setting. In their own spaces they were able to realize many of the objectives intended for the pedagogy but which could not be achieved inside the classroom. Ellsworth concluded that "power relations between raced, classed and gendered students and teachers are unjust," and distort communication in ways that simply "cannot be overcome in a classroom" (p. 316).

In an important further development, Giroux mounts a concerted attack on the "canon" of cultural literacy and advocates a pedagogy of difference that offers students opportunities to cross borders. In this way students are presented with critical resources "for rethinking how the relations between dominant and subordinate groups are organized . . . and how such relations might be transformed in order to promote a democratic and just society" (1993: 375). Giroux's argument provides clear signposts toward a pedagogy in which multiple voices and narratives are given space for expression, informed moral appraisal, and legitimate development.

Yet, the enclosures of the curriculum-centred, book-based classroom make it difficult for teachers to escape strong orchestrating roles. The challenge of developing revitalized and better-informed practices of critical pedagogy in classrooms calls for "organizing curricula in ways that enable students to make judgments" about the historical and social construction of society, the operation and effects of existing power relations, and the possibilities that might exist outside of these relations in a different kind of society (see Giroux 1993: 374). The challenge identified by Giroux is, precisely, how curriculum *organization* can be undertaken in ways that meet the democratic principles of critical pedagogy, and that build in emancipatory ways on difference and diversity. This means looking beyond modernist spaces of enclosure: being open to developing emergent postmodern spaces in ways that employ and enhance their distinctive potential for critical practices of learning and educating.

POSTMODERN SPACES: POSTINDUSTRIALISM, THE INFORMATION SOCIETY AND CYBERSPACE

During the past decade numerous scholars have sought to name the space of transition between "modernity" and "postmodernity," between "modernist" and "postmodernist" culture (see Chapter 1 above). David Harvey (1989), for instance, talks of the transition in terms of the latest round "of time-space compression" of late capitalism. Fredric Jameson (1984) theorizes the signs of change in terms of postmodern developments instantiating the cultural logic of late capitalism. In a third variation on this broad theme, Manuel Castells (1989) hypothesizes a change within capitalism from a traditionally modern goods-and-services producing economy to an increasingly sophisticated and developed mode of information, against which the global restructuring processes of the late 1980s can be understood.

157

It is interesting that notions and theories of "postindustrial society" and the "information society," first realized and developed in the 1960s and 1970s, are resurfacing in current theoretical debates which will have considerable impact on the future development of education and on advanced industrial economies more generally. The notion of "the information society" and its preceding paradigm, "the postindustrial society," were promulgated in the early 1960s by theorists like Alain Touraine and Daniel Bell, and may in fact date as far back as 1917 (see Rose 1991). In recent history, however, the concepts and theories of postindustrial and/or information society belong to the era of optimism that was the 1960s: when it seemed there were no limits to growth, or to the increasing affluence of the "long boom."

We can distinguish three "generations" of thought since the 1960s concerning the emergence of what is variously referred to as the "information," "postindustrial," or "knowledge" society.

The first generation was impressed by the progressively increasing significance throughout the twentieth century of "knowledge producing occupations" within modern economies, and issues associated with this. People like Machlup (1962) advocated policies which emphasized pursuit of productivity gains through investment in research and development and programs of educational reform designed to raise the general level of accomplishment.

In the second "generation," theorists building on the influential works of Daniel Bell (1973) and Alain Touraine (1974) developed accounts of "the postindustrial society" which identified theoretical knowledge as the axis around which new technology, economic growth, and social stratification would be organized. In many ways, Bell and Touraine emerged as "prototype" theorists for their generation: Bell representing a sub-tradition in which postindustrialism is portrayed in celebratory terms; Touraine representing a sub-tradition characterized by a spirit of critique and the hope that society as presently constituted would evolve into more emancipatory and sustainable forms.

The former group, which includes people like Peter Drucker and Alvin Toffler, and entire organisations like the OECD, announced approvingly the arrival of a new kind of society marked by shifts from a manufacturing toward a service economy and blue-collar toward white-collar work; from the dominance of business corporations to the prominence of the university; from an ideology of growth to one which emphasized quality of life; and so on. The latter group, encompassing people like Illich, Rozak, Schumacher and Dickson, saw these shifts as outgrowths of industrial society rather than as hallmarks of a new *kind* of society: a postindustrial society. Such a society would—following Touraine—be associated with increasing decentralization and popular participation, and the "demythologizing" of science: ideals and qualities not yet extant, and which we are urged to mobilize around by, for instance, Illich's (1971) call to "convivial production," and Schumacher's plea for appropriate technologies (Schumacher 1975).

This divergence—across spectrums between celebration and critique; optimism and "darker views"—remains a feature of the "third generation" of thought about information and postindustrialism which has come in the wake of Jean-François Lyotard's influential book, *The Postmodern Condition: A Report on Knowledge* (1984). Lyotard addresses the changing status of science and technology in the most highly developed societies, focusing particularly on the *control* of knowledge and information. His philosophical perspective, influenced strongly by French poststructuralism, problematizes anew the legitimation of science. The strategic value and significance of his analysis is that it allows us to see the effects of the transformation of knowledge on public power and civil institutions in ways which challenge dominant conceptions.

By the mid-1970s the optimism of the two previous decades and the idea of continuous economic growth on which it depended, seemed both misplaced and naive. The oil shocks of the mid-1970s, the bite of world-wide economic recession and the process of de-industrialization, charted a shift in discourse from optimism to preoccupation with economic crisis. During this period also, ecological arguments began to find their mark. Within the discourse of economic decline, visions of a postindustrial society appeared to many who dwelled on such matters more distant and, even, ethically irresponsible. Even so, during that same period new forms of postindustrial theory were being developed around the introduction and apparent effects of new information and communications technologies.

These theories have come to fruition in the 1990s, dominating contemporary social, cultural and economic debates. Today's debates may be more cautious than those of the 1960s, but they are no less optimistic. Certainly, they continue to cling tenaciously to the idea that advanced industrial societies are witnessing a set of interrelated changes at least as significant as those accompanying the shift from agrarian to industrial societies (c.f., Wark 1993; Ross 1991; Stone 1993; Davis 1993; Rheingold 1994).

The debates, however, are complex: schizophrenic, even. The notion of the "information"—or "communication"—society has recaptured the air and quality of social and utopian promise it originally conveyed. Indeed, many communication theorists seem to radiate the same "hype" that pervades the jargon used as descriptors of the information society: hypertext, hypermedia, hyperculture.

At the same time, contemporary social analysis has its darker, pessimistic, foreboding side. This points to increasing economic rationalization (e.g., see Pusey 1991) which is said to have submerged the traditional concerns of the social democratic state under the economic imperative to compete in the global market. Within processes of capitalist restructuring and economic rationalization, formal models are seen to have prevailed over issues of practical substance and the economic system has assumed a reified independent, objective, and autonomous status: so much so, that civic society is now seen as a resisting, idealized opponent of "the economy." Pusey (1991: 21) remarks here as follows:

> Culture and identity dissolve into arbitrary individual choices, and, moreover, institutional arbitrariness is no longer a sign of failure but is instead put forward with deadly seriousness as a necessary condition, at the steering level, for the smooth and rational operation of a self-referential system.

Returning to the more optimistic side of the theoretical and analytical divide, an eclectic coterie of (largely American) theorists are exploring and promoting the democratic potential of the new communications revolution. These theorists argue that the new communications technologies redefine our notions of textuality and our textual practice, and proceed to theorize how these redefined notions and practices are part of a wider reconfiguration of subjectivity, and cultural forms. Mark Poster (1990), for instance, follows a poststructuralist line of argument and echoes—in a deliberate play—Marx's metaphor of the mode of production in talking of the "mode of information." According to Poster, the mode of information reconfigures communication as symbolic exchange and, thereby, also reconfigures subjectivity and entire networks of social relations.

Many left literary and humanist scholars now talk confidently of a remarkable convergence between poststructuralism, the new communications technologies, and democracy. George Landow (1992: 2) speaks of the paradigm shift taking place in the writings of Jacques Derrida and Theodore Nelson, or Roland Barthes and Andries van Dam, arguing that "we must abandon conceptual systems founded upon ideas of center, margin, hierarchy, and linearity, and replace them with ones of multi-linearity, nodes, links and networks." Paul Delaney and George Landow (1993) use poststructuralist theory to explain some of the fundamental features of text-based computing which are shaping the emergent world of digitized and networked information. In like vein, Richard Lanham suggests that "poststructuralism and the common digital code seem part of the same event" (1993: xi). He observes an historical convergence among democracy, technology, theory and the university curriculum. The word, the image, and the sound have been reduced to a common digital denominator which seemingly provides a new synthetic unity for the liberal arts curriculum. This generative common code permits experimentation with new forms of textuality and greater flexibility which, together, undermine models of consciousness based upon the finiteness and fixity of the book.

If we take Landow's characterization seriously—and we think there are good grounds for doing so—it follows that practicing critical pedagogy in cyberspace must build upon sophisticated notions of multiplicity. Critical educators must recognize that there are multiple paths for reading and writing, and possibilities for multiple and nonlinear forms of learning and teaching interactions. Correspondingly, they must also reconfigure teaching and learning in terms of the concepts of "links" and "networks" which have the power to redefine the roles of teachers, administrators and learners. Here, the notion of virtual communities holds interesting possibilities for greater democratization of education. It clearly enables not only greater access to on-line information which is continuously available, but also participation in a range of information activities and learning experiences.

We see these developments falling under the imaginary category of "cyberspace," a term first employed in the science fiction of William Gibson's *Neuromancer* (1984). It is a space which names a new social and technological imaginary, both utopian and dystopian, and brings together the speculative writings of science *fiction* with science *fact*, in the form of developments in media studies and computer science. Rheingold (1994: 5) defines cyberspace as "the name . . . for the conceptual space where words, human relationships, data, wealth, and power are manifested by people using CMC [computer-mediated communications] technology." As an educational project, critical pedagogy needs some reshaping in this new context of transformation. We begin here to theorize this reshaping under a set of four "contemporary" themes.

FOUR CONTEMPORARY THEMES

1. The "Decoupling" of Body and Subject

Critical pedagogy in its archetypal modernist formulations was largely theorized around models of consciousness based on the book as the text paradigm. Subjects tended to be conceived as stable, fixed, continuous identities in a manner roughly analogous to that by which the book—as a physical object—incorporated a set of authorial intentions within the axes of top-down, left-right, beginning-end orientations. Just as the book was seen to be the stage for a kind of authorial agency, so models of consciousness based upon the book as text paradigm viewed the subject as the author of its own political intentions. This is a little unkind to variants of critical pedagogy which attempted to theorize beyond the subject in terms of a set of relations such as the student to the teacher, and other students, and the citizen to the State. Nonetheless, the central concern of critical pedagogy with the empowerment of groups and individuals does seem to predicate a core of essence which, metaphorically speaking, corresponds to conceptions of words and meanings as fixed and stable.

Cyberspace calls into question the stability and coherence of the book and forms of narration enacted upon it. Equally, it calls precisely these same features into question in relation to the subject. New forms of textuality and intertextuality—hypertext and multimedia—indicate promising directions for reconstruing consciousness and, hence, the subject. In the new reader-controlled environment the limits, scale, size, and topography of the text unit are manipulated by the reader within wide parameters circumscribed by software programs. Indeed, the distinction between the reader and the writer disappears as the reader can add, delete, edit, and modify the text in so many ways as to make her or him the manifest creator of meaning. Almost infinite possibilities exist for multiple subjectivities and multiple forms of authority, with important implications for practices of critical pedagogy.

Of course, many poststructuralist writers—notably feminists, and media and culture theorists—have re-examined the question of the subject directly in terms of decentering and multi-vocality. The social spaces of cyberspace enable subjects to re-examine, play and experiment with, and ultimately transform their *own* multiplicity. Mark Taylor and Esa Saarinen (1994: Shifting Subjects 1) celebrate the fluidity of identity in cyberspace:

> In cyberspace I can change my self as easily as I change clothes. Identity becomes infinitely plastic in a play of images that knows no end. Consistency is no longer a virtue but becomes a vice; integration is limitation. With everything always shifting, every one is no one.

161

LANKSHEAR, PETERS, AND KNOBEL

Fundamental to this theorization of multiple and shifting subjectivities is what—following Allucquere Stone (1991: 99ff)—we call "decoupling the body and the subject." Drawing on Francis Barker's *The Tremulous Private Body* (1984), Stone suggests that with the impact of the Restoration, the human body ceased to be perceived as public spectacle and became privatized and self-constituted in such (types of) texts as the diary, the lady's journal, and the confessional genre more broadly. In the same way, says Stone, Barker's work resonates with Donna Haraway's (1985, 1990) accounts of the collapse of subject categories and of boundaries of the body, through the interventions of twentieth-century technologies. (NB: We prefer to talk about new formations and the proliferation of the subject rather than its collapse, which implies an imploding and disabling metaphor.) As both Baudrillard and Haraway suggest, "the boundaries between technology and nature are themselves in the midst of a deep restructuring" (Stone 1991: 101). In Stone's words (ibid)

> This means that many of the usual analytical categories have become unreliable for making the useful distinctions between the biological and the technological, the natural and artificial, the human and mechanical, to which we have become accustomed.

The result is seamless and ceaseless osmotic flows between the social and the natural, and between biology and technology, that constitute new forms of consensual social spaces. In a useful metaphor, Mackenzie Wark (1993) spells out a conception of "third nature" which resonates with Stone's principal thesis. For Wark, "second nature" is epitomized in the modern period by the infrastructure of railways and newspapers, which integrated space (read "nature') economically, politically and culturally. "Third nature," by extension, is invoked in the move from the telegraph to telecommunications, producing a new and "fluid" geography superimposed on both nature and second nature. So,

> [W]hen information can move faster and more freely than people or things, its relation to those other movements and to space itself changes. No longer a space of places we move to a space of flows . . . (Wark 1993: 120).

For Wark, this "third nature" is *cyberspace*. The postmodern aesthetic simply maps the symptoms of third nature, and "cyberspace" provides a literary description of its subjective effects. Wark (1993: 120–1) continues:

> One can imagine a delirious future: beyond cyberspace. Not the future of Marx's communism: from each according to their abilities to each according to their needs. Rather the future of the rhizome [Deleuze & Guattari 1983] made concrete: where every trajectory is potentially connected to every other trajectory, and where all other trajectories are equal and equally rootless. Where, truly, we

no longer have roots; we have aerials. Where we no longer have origins; we have terminals.

Of course we do not need recourse to Wark's science fiction scenario to acknowledge that we are already in a world of information flows, relays and feedback cycles, and that these have begun to reshape our subjectivities in ways that are fundamentally important to understanding critical pedagogy in cyberspace. Just as the deep restructuring of the boundaries are taking place between technology and nature, so too the boundaries between the formal/informal, teacher/student, classroom/home, and print/electronic text are in the throes of change. These changes impact upon education directly, yet can preserve the project of critical pedagogy by making explicit and concrete the ways in which models of consciousness and agency can no longer be theorized in terms of the ideology of individualism and the omniscience of the book—for the couplets individual/community and citizen/state undergo profound transformations in cyberspace.

2. Democratization and the Virtual Community

Ever since John Dewey (1916) proposed that education was the means to reinvent and instantiate democracy for each generation—to relive it, so to speak, and in reliving it to revitalize its practices—theorists of critical education have made the practices of democracy central to education. They have commented on education in terms of democratic process and content, and have talked repeatedly of democratizing authority by means of shared decision-making, peer group discussion, self-evaluation, and by actively redistributing speaking chances in classrooms along lines which recognize the dimensions of class, race, and gender. In all of this, the ideal of democracy has been afflicted with interpersonal perceptions of the "Other," and banking conceptions of education predicated on the teacher-student hierarchy.

In cyberspace, we might say, democracy is realized implicitly and as an underlying principle. Marshall McLuhan (1968; McLuhan and Powers 1992) was among the first to broadcast this theme in terms of the concept of a "global village." His speculative concept is now instantiated in the information network and the virtual communities which comprise it. This conception is currently overblown and dramatized. At the level of traditional political economy it ignores questions of ownership, information barriers, and the growing gap between "information-poor" and "information-rich" schools, societies, and economies. Even so, if we look at the rapid expansion and ownership of personal computers since their first development in the early 1970s, we might hypothesize a rapidly expanding pattern of ownership which makes the personal computer, or access to a terminal, as common and as indispensable as the telephone and television.

For those of us fortunate enough to have access to an on-line terminal and can log onto the Internet via the World Wide Web—and the number who can do so is growing at an exponential rate—the world has become a virtual community. While this is to date predominantly a Western phenomenon, it is nonetheless true that very many people now have access to on-line library catalogues and specialist user and discussion groups. Increasingly the "great books" are available in electronic form, and a diverse range of hundreds of electronic journals and newsletters exists. These facilities and webs—along with electronic shopping, community information bulletin boards, civic information guides and directories, email address lists, and the like—name the different spaces of the Internet: the Network of networks. Cyberspace is constituted by a logic which is both participatory in nature and interactive in terms of format. We confidently predict the rise of collaborative, multi-authored publications which, in new hybrid discourses, erase the distinction between informal communication on the one hand, and traditional forms of scholarly publication on the other (Odlyzko 1994; Okerson 1994). By such means the democratic impulse formulated by Dewey, and its participatory and collaborative logic outlined by theorists of critical pedagogy, can be preserved and enhanced—albeit transposed—in the mode of information.

Furthermore, the "decoupling of body and subject" abstracts variables of gender, race and class, thereby preserving anonymity at will and democratizing discussion and interaction. For example, assuming access to a modem, and the wish to do so (!), it is not at all difficult to envisage a peasant-born woman of color from a remote village conversing on equal terms with a white male professor located in one of the world's most prestigious universities. Similarly, individuals with various forms of "disability" which can and do disadvantage them in conventional forms of interaction, often experience more equitable processes and relations of interchange through mediated decoupling of body and subject (c.f., Stone 1991 for examples).

3. The Word-World Relation in Cyberspace

The notion of a Word-World relation captures the insight that textual practices and the making, transmitting, giving and receiving of meanings in and through *language* (word) are contiguous with and co-constitutive of the "larger" embodied and enacted meanings that constitute social-cultural practice(s) *per se*. Our daily practices of encoding and decoding meanings from literal texts (i.e., language and literacy practices) are part and parcel of the myriad webs of social practice that comprise our social-cultural reality ("World"): the world of biological humans "made" and "remade" discursively as social and cultural beings. There can no more be language outside of social practice than there can be social practice without language (Wittgenstein 1953). Language, indeed, is [a] social practice; although it is by no means *all* of social practice (c.f., Kress 1985, 1988).

By invoking and elaborating the notion of a Word-World relation, critical theorists like Freire draw attention to the relationship between "reading the word" and "reading the world" as, precisely, dialectical "moments" or constitutive elements of socio-cultural practice.

> Reading is not exhausted merely by decoding the written word or written language, but rather anticipated by and extending into knowledge of the world. Reading the world precedes reading the word, and the subsequent reading of the word cannot dispense with continually reading the world. Language and reality are dynamically intertwined. The understanding attained by critical reading of a text implies perceiving the relationship between text and context (Freire 1991: 139).

Accordingly, critical pedagogy has always emphasized activities and processes concerned with clarifying this relationship and making it explicit, in the face of the tendency of mainstream educational practices to mystify it.

The very spaces of modernist institutional enclosure militate against an easy recognition of the Word-World relation. The institution of school, with its constitutive "sub-institutions" of book, textbook, classroom, and curriculum—all instances of modernist spaces of enclosure—separate out and constitute a set of bounded social practices as *educational*, and differentiate them from other sets of similarly bounded social practices: such as those based on the institutions of the family, the workplace, the corporation, the law, the church, and the various political institutions of the public sphere. This mystifies and masks the Word-World relation in at least four ways.

(i) As literacy, Word is taught in school predominantly as a disembodied, decontextualized—and, therefore, neutral—tool, skill (or set of skills), or technology: whole language approaches notwithstanding. Learners come to see literacy as discrete from the practices in which it is employed: as being *brought to* these practices rather than being an *inherent aspect* of them. Thus conceived, literacy teaching drives a wedge between word and world, hiving literacy teaching off from the world of social practices in which literacy practices are organically embedded. Hence, it is often assumed that learners will become better writers by reading more, rather than by greater engagement in social practices that comprise the proper contexts of this or that form of writing!

(ii) In a related confusion, meaning itself is widely misconstrued. In part, meanings tend to be seen as belonging to the realm of Word/"book" alone, rather than as being produced and communicated in social practices that unite word and world. Furthermore, meanings are construed as being enclosed within texts and to be accessed and validated by recourse to some kind of authority: e.g., an etymological source or a person presumed to have authoritative entry to authorial intent, etc.

(iii) Understood as neutral skills or technologies, language and literacy are presumed to be properties of *individuals*. That is, the ways individuals use lan-

LANKSHEAR, PETERS, AND KNOBEL

guage are seen as matters of individual choice and control. Effective and ineffective language use are construed as matters essentially of *personal* efficacy or deficiency rather than as a function of differential language socialization practices and experiences. Studies of language and literacy practices undertaken from a critical perspective reveal the extent to which these alleged personal language attributes are in fact functions of people's discursive histories, which vary markedly across the many indices of difference.

(iv) The text-dominated school curriculum encourages partial and distorted understandings of the relations and practices that constitute the World. Students are subjected to idealized and interest-serving representations of reality. The World tends to be portrayed as a setting of linear processes and hierarchical social relations and groupings. "Reality" is represented as fixed (or static), transcendent and "given," immutable and "natural," rather than as contingent, historical, constantly in the process of being made and remade and, as such, capable of being remade in quite different forms from those which currently prevail. Furthermore, official curriculum texts purvey dominant versions of everyday Discourses (Gee 1990), which are at odds with the discursive histories and experiences of students from nondominant social groups. This process effectively denies these students equitable access to academic success, while denying the reality and validity of their own Discourses, cultural meanings, language practices, and experiences.

In cyberspace, however, electronically mediated communication tends to break down such spaces of institutional enclosure and subvert their mystification of the Word–World relation. Working with digital texts in networked and (other) interactive media settings makes very explicit the interpenetration of reading and writing within those larger webs of social practice that *are* the World.

The social construction of the interactive reader engaged in the act of meaning making with texts becomes concretely manifest in the textual interchanges of cyberspace. The shift from book to screen breaks down the distinction between reader and writer, and implicitly questions all forms of authorial control. On-line networking is an embodied *visceral* experience of the practice of meaning-making as active engagement: the practice can literally be traced as reader-writers modify digital texts available in the ether, and as scholarly peers construct collaborative texts.

We are suggesting that the presumptions and deep presuppositions which come with the book as the paradigm form of *the text* underwrite all modernist educational spaces of enclosure. These, however, are forced into the open and called critically into question in cyberspace—in ways that historically have become inhibited in bookspace. They include the fixity and stability of the word, its left-right/top-down/beginning-end axes of enclosure, the text as an author-controlled environment, the teacher as authoritative bearer of textual meaning (author surrogate), and so on. In the present conjuncture the very bases of modernist institutionalized spaces of enclosure are open—and are *explicitly* open—to critique. The radical interactiveness and convertibility of digital text undermines at the level of lived textual practice the very notion of a static, immutable, transcendent reality pictured by the book.

With the burgeoning of cyberspace, reader-writers of digital texts increasingly experience themselves as living through a profound cultural transformation: recognizing that cyberspace is a socio-cultural and political construction, and that they are actively involved in constructing and reconstructing the social relationships and the purposes and operating principles of the networks, webs, and communities of cyberspace (Rheingold 1994). The very conception of cyberspace as a virtual *community* denies possibilities of individuals operating in isolation. The model of consciousness based on the book as text paradigm—implying the unity, stability, and coherence of the subject—is, to that extent, undermined: or, at least, seriously challenged and readily problematized. Alternative models based on different text forms (including intertextuality, multi-textuality, hybrids of all kinds) can now be entertained, along with new notions of collective and interactive agency and new political possibilities (Smith 1994).

Cyberspace comprises an open, far-flung, fluid, dynamic, networked, and radically connected space which comprises a burgeoning web of "worlds" within its overarching World. Pioneers of the Internet and its constitutive networks—a mass of user groups, bulletin boards, information services, etc.—speak almost as one the language of interconnectedness, creative formative engagement, system building, and the iteration of actions and effects. The fractal—with all its connotations—has emerged as a central motif. "Cyberians" talk of putting in place processes and actions that will "iterate everywhere" (Rushkoff 1994).

Cyberspace scholars and theorists in the cast of Taylor and Saarinen (1994) and Howard Rheingold (1993, 1994), for example, proclaim that we have the historical option *now* of determining future relations, principles, and principles of communication and socio-cultural construction; and that we can build a future that differs from the modernist enclos(ur)ed past in very much the ways advocated by the theorists and practitioners of critical pedagogy. Regular users of bulletin boards, on-line discussion groups, and the like express enthusiasm for the possibilities of operating inside rules and relations that are more egalitarian, purpose-driven, and self-imposed and self-monitored than those which have come to characterize dominant educational practices. They esteem the fact that the ends and purposes of communicative engagement are essentially established and monitored by the *user communities themselves*. In cyberspace we encounter endless groups of individuals creating and maintaining, as a matter of course rather than as exceptions to the rule, the very kinds of affinity groups Ellsworth sought through critical pedagogy; but which she

167

believed could only be established *outside* the inhibiting social relations and processes of teacher and curriculum-driven classrooms.

Growing accounts depict communities of collaborating users creating rules and principles as they go along, building from the ground up a connected environment that literally spans the world of continents and societies (Rushkoff 1994; Rheingold 1994; Taylor and Saarinen 1994). In these communicative exchanges participants are engaged in reading and writing their world as they read and write their texts. Indeed, they are actively developing new words to express, scaffold, and "institute" the new practices and relations ("worlds") they are constructing. Interesting "ecological" features emerge here. Participants convey a strong sense of location and purpose in relation to other locations and purposes. So, for example, when activity inside a user group merges into purposes that fall outside the "jurisdiction" of that particular site (e.g., a conference space), the users will agree to move their conversation to a more appropriate cyber space (such as email, chat mode, or bulletin boards), whilst retaining an overall perspective of their temporal locations within the larger space that is cyberspace.

Such descriptions resonate strongly with Illich's vision of education being remade via learning webs and networks developed within an ethos of conviviality and interrelatedness, rather than reflecting an ethos of manipulation-compulsion, consumerist individualism, and learned passivity he saw as definitive of "schooling" (Illich 1971).

In addition, communicative interactions in cyberspace permit a radical transcendence of "the local," and the relative anonymity available to participants creates opportunities to explore a diverse range of fluid and experimental roles and identities. Such access to diverse worlds makes readily available the kind of scope and scale that can inform inquiry and critique with enlarged generative experiences and themes, and to discover commonalities across difference. These possibilities are of the essence of critical pedagogy.

4. *Knowledge, Information and Understanding: Problems of Regulation and Legitimation*

The traditionally prevalent analysis of knowledge within Anglo-American epistemology and pedagogy has been the "justified true belief" account, which dates back to the Greeks. This view has dominated within modernist enclosures developed around the book, classroom, and larger curriculum structures. According to this analysis, for someone (A) to know something (P)—where P is a proposition—A must believe that P (the "belief" condition); P must be true (the "truth" condition); and A must be justified in believing that P (the "justification" condition) (c.f., for example, Scheffler 1965).

This remains central to the analytic creed. It is an individualist account, based on a disembodied and abstract subject and involving Truth as a consequence of moves made by knowers within closely circumscribed discipline-based approaches to knowledge typically given to positivist formulations. Within formal educational philosophy and theory the notion of "forms of knowledge" has been grafted on to this account (Hirst 1974). These forms of knowledge are subject/discipline-centered, rather than person (or even interest)-centered. Each has its own specific set of criteria for establishing truth and its own authorized/authoritative canon of literature—the stock of true propositions as hitherto established. According to this educational epistemology, and the pedagogy based upon it, individuals become capable of distinguishing knowledge from error, truth from falsehood, by being apprenticed to forms (and their derivative "fields") of knowledge at the hands of teachers, who are presumed to have "mastered" the forms related to their curriculum subject specialisms (e.g., Olson 1977).

The innovation from critical pedagogy was initially to invoke a marxist account of scientific truth grounded in a species of materialism and a realism. This was thought to provide a basis for distinguishing *ideology* from *knowledge*. For many, knowledge became "marxism" as *science*. In contradistinction to the more strictly analytic dogma, this stressed the situatedness and embodiedness of the knower, together with the importance of reflexivity. Some accounts, notably those derived from Freire, stress knowledge as praxis. "The true word" (Truth) was seen to comprise a dialectical unity of reflection and action, continually made and remade.

In both the "justified true belief" formulation and the original formulation within critical pedagogy, formal criteria, standards, and procedures for distinguishing clearly between knowledge and information—as well as "truth" and "falsehood," "ideology" and "science", "critical consciousness" and "false" or "naive consciousness"—were established and implemented. These provided at the same time norms for regulating and legitimating knowledge as against mere pretensions to knowledge: including information.

When we recast these conceptions in cyberspace, however, the typical easy distinction between knowledge and information seems to disappear. Indeed, the emphasis on and faith invested in *information* often make earlier concerns with knowledge appear anachronistic. It is almost as if "now we have information, who cares about knowledge?" Certainly, none of the conditions referred to in the justified true belief account seem to have necessary application to information. For something to count as information it is not necessary for it to be believed, for it to be true, or even for a believer to have justification for any belief of it over and above the fact that it has become an item in the information bank. Rather, what we have is simply the engineering distinction between "information," on the one hand, and "noise" on the other (c.f., for example, Poster 1990: 14. See also Jameson 1984, on the multiplication of messages). In addition, there is some concern to distinguish information from "mis-information" and "dis-information." "Mis-information" is information that doesn't accord with the "facts," and "dis-information" denotes the act of issuing mis-information with the conscious purpose of misleading (think "CIA"). The latter is intentional; the former not necessarily.

In the computing and systems literatures, "information" is conceived as what results from data processing (its assembly, analysis). For instance, Paul Beynon-Davies (1993: 1–2) defines information in the following terms.

> Data is facts. A datum, a unit of data, is one or more symbols that are used to represent something.
> Information is interpreted data. Information is data within a meaningful context.
> Knowledge is derived from information by integrating information with existing knowledge [coherence theory of truth?]
> Information is necessarily subjective. Information must always be set in the context of its recipient. The same data may be interpreted differently by different people on the basis of their existing knowledge.

Benyon-Davies also talks of information systems in terms of semiotics, where the sign is considered as a convention linking the signifier (symbol) to the signified (what it is representing).

This, however, is highly problematic for anyone who retains serious concerns for ethical, cultural, political, and general "quality of life" matters that call for more than a (literally) mechanical distinction between information and "noise." In an important critique of limitations in the "engineering" approach, Umberto Eco (1989: 67–8) argues that

> information theory provides us with only one scheme of possible relations (order-disorder, information-signification, binary-disjunction, and so on) that can be inserted into the larger context. . . . [the scheme] is valid, in its specific ambit, only as the quantitative measurement of the number of signals that can be clearly transmitted along one channel. Once the signals are received by a human being, information theory has nothing else to add and gives way either to semiology or semantics since the question henceforth becomes one of signification.

The engineering definition of "information" reduces it to bits and bytes, but does not provide us with a theory of signification or a theory of knowledge—both of which we need, and particularly so from the standpoint of commitment to critical inquiry. Taylor and Saarinen warn that it is important not to confuse information and meaning.

> Though not necessarily opposites, they are inversely proportional: as information increases, meaning decreases. One of the distinctive features of the information age is the proliferation of data whose meaning becomes obscure. The more we accumulate the less we have (1994: Net Effect 4).

Meaning, by definition, is the medium and outcome of social practice. Without a theory of signification we literally cannot make sense of our lives. Information yields data, but without sense that data is useless.

Equally, we need a theory of knowledge, otherwise all meaning-mediated information becomes of a piece, and the notion of an examined life is rendered unintelligible. Critique becomes impossible. In cyberspace, however, practices of knowledge/knowing and their inherent social relations and norms of regulation and legitimation must differ greatly from those that characterize modernist spaces of enclosure. Here again, the urgency and the broad contours of the situation are best communicated by Taylor and Saarinen.

> One of the most significant mistakes of modernists was to believe in the autonomy of culture . . . Without the autonomy of culture, negative dialectics seemed impossible.
>
> . . . Postmodernity discloses the illusion of cultural autonomy. Culture is inextricably bound to and by the psycho-social conditions of its creation. But the denial of cultural autonomy does not necessarily imply the impossibility of critique. In the absence of any Archimedean point from which to view and criticize society, it is necessary to develop strategies of criticism that deploy available modes of production and reproduction.
>
> . . . If the global classroom simply replicates the structures of power that have made it possible and provides no critique of contemporary socio-political configurations, it is a failure (1994: Pedagogies 6).

In cyberspace, meaning-making and communication practices admit a distinction between (realms of) information and knowledge which undercuts the sorts of norms and procedures of regulation and legitimation that have prevailed within enclosures of bookspace. While much more work needs to be done than can be done here, we would suggest that the "logics" and purposes of user groups, news groups, on-line discussion groups, and conferences, etc., and other virtual communities provide the basis for a "first cut" at a qualitative distinction.

Within virtual communities of cyberspace, membership is voluntary and convivial—in Illich's sense of "conviviality" (1971). Members log onto facilities and interact for as long (or as briefly) as participation meets their purposes. There is no compulsion to "attend" or to remain a member of a user group. No one can force the acceptance of texts or messages (although destructive and otherwise aversive "presences" do occur and can be upsetting. See Rushkoff 1994; Dibbell 1993). Participants are free to remain anonymous, and most never meet face to face. They produce, co-produce, and reproduce considerable information, including mis- and dis-information. Information will become integrated into their daily practices to the extent that it meets users' purposes. In the process, purposes and values may—and likely will—evolve and change. Communities of "practitioners" emerge, and maintain themselves so long as purposes and interests are met and remain fulfilling. Examples of communities of practitioners include the Electronic Frontiers Foundation, the Whole Earth 'Lectronic Link (WELL), and a diverse array of

171

MOOs (multi object-oriented spaces) and MUDs (multi user dimensional spaces).

In this way, some information abides. It gets taken up, used, and lives and identities are constructed around it—freely: without coercion or subjection to externally imposed authority. Much information, of course, remains unused. It falls between cracks, is erased, or becomes modified into useful, usable forms. If we think of this abiding, useful, "employed" information as knowledge we have a basis for reconfiguring knowledge. Knowledge becomes legitimated in the self-directing, self-monitoring practices of virtual communities and sub-communities of collaborators in communicative practice. (It should be noted that not all cyber-spaces are thus convivial. See Rheingold, 1994 Chapter 10, for examples that caution against romantic uncritical, uninformed carte blanche acceptance.) The social relations of knowledge production, the constitution of particular items as knowledge, and the taking up of knowledge under convivial conditions are entirely different from those which dominate within modernist enclosures of the text.

As such, knowledge is born and reborn as *praxis*, meeting Taylor and Saarinen's demand that "in the praxis-dominated world of ultra-tech the politics of critique must take a new form." Cyber citizens become what they call media philosophers, attempting "to move beyond existing institutions to imagine *and refashion* possibilities that **might be**" (1994: Media Philosophy 17, 20; our italics, bold in original).

This calls for *understanding*, in addition to information and knowledge. Taylor and Saarinen ask how we might create understanding in a world that desperately needs it, but where information and knowledge are out of control. Whereas understanding "presupposes information and knowledge," they "less and less lead to understanding." Extending critical pedagogy into cyberspace can assist here by helping to transform "institutional technologies dedicated to the production of information that is not knowledge to the production of knowledge that advances understanding" (Taylor and Saarinen 1994: Communicative Practices 12–13).

Within the characteristically self-directed, purpose and interest-driven communications of cyberspace, cyber citizens enjoy uncoerced opportunities to make *explicit* their individual and collective purposes and means to achieving them. Collaborative partners—who they are, what they are, and what makes them partners to practice—also become explicit in the process of building such virtual communities of practice. Explicitness provides here the key to *understanding*. Understanding is grasping what you are wanting to do (achieve, etc.); why you want to do it; how you are doing it (or what you have to do to do it); what the impediments to success are and where they originate; etc. Communicative practices of this type presuppose openness, self-monitoring, and constant reflexivity on the part of participants.

Engaging differences, locating similarities, and discovering commonalities across difference enhance the explicitness of values, beliefs, and purposes operating in particular communicative practices, and their variance from alternative practices. With this comes the quintessence of understanding as a basis for critique and transformative action: namely, a meta-level awareness of Discourse or social practice *per se*, of particular Discourses, and of the sheer variety, range, and historical contingency of actual and possible Discourses (Gee 1990, 1991, 1993. See below). This meta level understanding is enhanced and affirmed in the very *acts* of engagement built upon it. This is the heart of moving from what is to envisaging what might be, and to creating what might be within practices of communicative collaboration that are critical and transforming.

POSSIBILITIES FOR CRITICAL PEDAGOGY IN CYBERSPACE

In Chapter 2 above, Henry Giroux argues that we need to expand the definition of pedagogy so as "to move beyond a limited emphasis on the mastery of techniques and methodologies" and "enable students to understand pedagogy as a configuration of textual, verbal and visual practices that seek to engage the processes through which people understand themselves and the possible ways in which they engage others and their environment." From Giroux's perspective, pedagogy represents "a form of cultural production implicated in and critically attentive to how power and meaning are employed in the construction and organization of knowledge, desires, values and identities" (supra: 52). Giroux also stresses the importance of educators operating as border intellectuals who can travel "within and across communities of difference working in collaboration with diverse groups" (supra: 54), and argues that educational projects grounded in cultural studies perspectives need to interrogate the production and operation of new information systems (p. 55).

Our perspective in this chapter indicates that these concerns are tightly interwoven, and that cyberspace offers fruitful terrain on which to revitalize, expand, and reconceive theories and practices of critical pedagogy. By way of concluding, we will draw on ideas presented in earlier sections to advance a range of possible developments for the theory and practice of critical pedagogy.

1. *Some Theoretical Developments*

(i) Cyberspace has enormous potential for rendering the Word–World relation clear and explicit in quite unique ways. It also has important potential for enabling students to grasp the historical and contingent nature of Discourse(s) and discourse(s). In this context, James Gee's account of D/discourse is helpful. Gee defines Discourses as

ways of thinking-believing-acting-interacting-speaking-listening-valuing (sometimes, too, reading and writing) at appropriate times and places with appropriate objects so as to signal membership in (to be "in synch with") a particular social group. There are many different Discourses, ranging from (certain sorts of) African-Americans, boardroom executives, feminists, Soviets, doctors, street gang members, physicists, and so forth (Gee and Lankshear 1995: 12).

Discourses, then, are social practices involving sets of values and viewpoints, beliefs and purposes, rules and languages. One must speak, act, believe, etc. in accordance with those belonging to a Discourse in order to count as being in that (particular) Discourse—and thus to take up the roles, subjectivities, and identity partially constituted by participation in that Discourse. (NB. Gee employs "discourse", with a small "d", to refer specifically to the language components of Discourses: stretches of language that make sense within their associated Discourses—like essays, conversations, speeches, minutes of meetings, etc. C.f., Gee 1993: 14. This, incidentally, provides a further interesting angle on the Word-World relation.)

Bearing Gee's comments in mind, two points stand out with regard to the clarity and explicitness of the Word-World relation in cyberspace.

(a) The status of language and literacy as social practices—as *cultural* through and through—becomes readily apparent. This works against technicist misperceptions of language as a tool, technology, or some other unitary essence which is put to manifold uses at the individual user's discretion. This is partly a consequence of Net users experiencing themselves as creators, refiners, and sustainers of *social practices* within the very acts of encoding and decoding symbols and images.

174

To function as a user involves acknowledging explicitly the norms and etiquette of appropriate use, as an individual member of a self-monitoring and self-regulating community. As noted above, it is common, for example, to find segments of "conversation" among participants in cyberspace activities suggesting that it is time to move to a new "venue," because the conversation is moving into purposes or activities that fall outside the bounds of the current "space." Failure to do so risks censure, of varying degrees of severity. At the other extreme, users quickly learn recognized "counter" forms of involvement, like "flaming" and "ranting" (c.f., Dery 1994: 4), which have their own names and are explicitly known and understood as distinctive practices and genres. In such ways, members of virtual communities are involved in forms of social interaction in which "words" are always manifestly components of purpose-related and value-laden social practices associated with roles, identities, and forms of production (i.e., aspects of "world'). Idiosyncratic vocabularies of cyberspace are integral to this general phenomenon. Users have to master specialized vocabularies that go along with doing and being in certain ways. This involves explicit knowledge which helps, in turn, to make explicit the relationship between language, forms of engagement in social practices, and the taking up of particular types or elements of identity.

Participating in structured practices within cyberspace also has the capacity to clarify in important ways the nature of meaning. This involves understanding meaning as comprising much more than linguistic or textual meaning alone but, rather, as *embodied*, and as constructed, transmitted, negotiated, and embedded within social practices. Moreover, the possibilities of digital text explode the notion that meaning is encased within texts and consists in objective authorial intent. Digital text positively invites participants to transcend the false dichotomy of author-writer-transmitter vs reader-receiver. Instead, digital text is experienced overtly as *being available* for rewriting, reconfiguring and, in general, as a resource for *making* meaning. Such an orientation is intrinsic to any viable conception of critical social practice.

(b) The historical and contingent nature of all discursive practice is readily apparent within cyber spaces. To experience oneself as engaged with others in constructing, refining, and monitoring social practices which comprise amalgamations of reading-writing-imaging, values, purposes, theories, roles, identities, etc., is necessarily to envisage one's activity as simply so many representations of what social practice(s) *might* be; and to be aware of alternative possibilities within and outside cyberspace. It is to realize there is nothing *necessary* about inhabiting any particular discursive space or spaces: all such spaces are contingent and historical. This insight is central to meta-level awareness of discursive practice, and possibilities for transformative praxis predicated upon it.

The same insight is enabled by the immediacy available in icon-assisted windows-type applications, and CD-ROM, hypertext, hypercard stacks, and morphing facilities, which can convey the vast sweep and transitoriness of Discourses and entire discursive formations at the click of a mouse. The electronic processes that make almost endless human variety accessible in visual and textual forms instantaneously, carries in an overt way the "message" that social practices come and go: they emerge and evolve in particular contexts, under given conditions, for certain purposes and in association with specific values, beliefs and theories; they give way to other practices under different constellations of purposes, beliefs, values and conditions. While this awareness is in principle available in similar ways via engagement with more conventional text forms, it is nonetheless much more *readily* apparent and, indeed, is practically *unavoidable*, where electronic hardware and relevant software are employed.

(ii) Experiences, interactions, and information available within cyberspace environments tend to "objectify" the complexity, diversity, and sheer multiplicity of human subjectivities, together with the highly fluid nature of identity and the extensive possibilities for constructing personal identity. Cyber networks abound with "spaces" in which people communicate freely—typically from the safety of anonymity or pseudonymity—about aspects of subjectivity and identity, and their associated implications, consequences and challenges. Even allowing for the likelihood of considerable mis-information and dis-information here, the access provided within electronically mediated environments to difference, experimentation with identity, experiences of contradictory subjectivities, and so on, generate rich possibilities for insights and transformative practices that are important from a critical pedagogy perspective.

Four brief comments must suffice here. First, insights into the complexities of human subjectivity and identity can heighten awareness of risks involved whenever we invoke broad social constructs and categories, assign populations unproblematically to these categories, and use this as a basis for explaining social causes and effects and for advancing social and political agendas. General constructs like class, race, and gender are important and useful—if not necessary—for social analysis and for helping developing agendas for social struggle and change. At the same time, they have their limits. Informed social action requires paying due attention to matters of similarity/commonality and difference alike. Speaking for and mobilizing on behalf of entire groups involves historical risks, even if it is quite often practically effective in the political short run (c.f., former Balkan states and Soviet republics in our own time).

Second, cyberspace environments can offer rich possibilities in "safe places" for learners to discover and develop commonalities across difference, and to "speak out" and "talk back" about experiences of oppression or marginality (Ellsworth 1989). The sorts of difficulties experienced by Ellsworth's students, might be ameliorated by conducting interactions and inquiries within cyberspace. At the same time, virtual communities offer extensive possibilities for forming affinity groups within which experiences can be analyzed and shared, responses framed, and activity mobilized.

Third, the contingency of human identity and the ever present possibilities for actively taking up and constructing new identities, become readily apparent from interactions in virtual communities. At one level this militates against myths and "easy explanations" of social phenomena and outcomes—such as in conservative appeals to the causal power of human nature. At another level, learners can be freed to approach their identities and lives as being subject in interesting ways to their "own authorship": within the bounds of these identity-constitutive social practices/Discourses they choose to engage. This is linked to a fourth point, that the relationship between identities and discursive practices can be uncovered and made explicit relatively easily in cyberspace. Exploring subjectivity and experimenting with possibilities for identity are always in part a matter of relating the personal to the discursive.

In these ways cyberspace can be seen to offer enhanced access to important forms of meta-level understandings of social practices in relation to subjectivity, identity, and agency (or agenthood). Engendering such understandings is absolutely fundamental to theories and practices of critical pedagogy.

(iii) The principle of commitment to transformative action is affirmed through active participation in virtual communities of cyberspace, and the possibilities this offers for organic extensions of activity to "real world" spheres of everyday life and citizenship.

From early formulations of critical pedagogy to the most recent accounts, it has consistently been recognized that misperceptions of "reality" as fixed and immutable present major obstacles to individuals and groups framing and enacting transformative change. Insights into the historical and contingent nature of social practices and their inherent structures, processes and relationships, illuminate the possibility of intervening in daily routines to bring about change. Moreover, processes of informed change are demystified by experiences of collaborative activity, and the historical role of acting as a change agent becomes clearer and is experienced as being manageable. The activities of "children" as young as 10 years of age instigating bulletin boards and collaborating in their ongoing development indicates the potential of extending critical pedagogy into cyberspace for "apprenticing" learners to the role of creating new social and cultural practices and procedures.

Furthermore, new electronic technologies allow users to access a vast pool of diverse agendas, practices, and data pertaining to concerns and responses. Users can contact people all over the globe who have encountered shared or similar issues and experiences, and who have framed and addressed these in various ways. The information and accounts of experience available provide ideas for action as well as the experience of support and solidarity that can be vital in mobilizing and sustaining social, cultural, and political-civic action. Virtual communities can also provide the assurance of ongoing support for a critical praxis of reflecting further on the outcomes of action, and acting further on the basis of this reflection. This is not to forget—and we should always remember—that cyberspace also provides a forum for groups who represent antidemocratic and otherwise ethically obnoxious values and predilections. We are not turning romantic or utopian blind eyes to the darker possibilities and realities of cyberspace. Rather, we choose to "surf" on the side of optimism and to theorize pedagogical options available to educators who are broadly in agreement with our purposes here.

(iv) The present conjuncture is propitious for shifting the weight within conceptualizations of pedagogy from teaching toward learning. There is, of course, a burgeoning rhetoric which advocates learning-focused pedagogies which are increasingly purpose-driven and self-directed. The fact that many classroom learners are more informed about and competent within cyberspace environments than their teachers creates interesting possibilities for "rebirthing" the educator-educatee/educatee-educator relationship (Freire 1970, 1973). Student learners can access themes, issues, and information that extend far beyond the enclosed capacities of individual teachers, textbooks, and curriculum details. At the same time, teachers are positioned in such a way that the notion of their genuinely learning in collaboration with students

177

and pursuing knowledge into areas beyond their expertise, becomes positively *factored into* pedagogy. This frees teachers up to operate in more "generic" ways within classroom-based critical inquiry. They will not so much organize curricula, distil issues and themes from students' generative experience and official demands, and act as authorities on matters of knowledge and "critical consciousness." Rather, they will assume responsibility for maintaining an ethos of interrogation; as well as for assisting students to *conceptualize/*frame up their questions and ideas; for ensuring that learning becomes as *explicit* as possible.

Extending critical pedagogy into cyberspace offers valuable opportunities for students and teachers to reveal the narrowness, partiality, and the "sampling" character of formal and official learning resources associated with school curricula in general. Even the most liberal lists of references and topics can readily be seen as extremely limited in their thematic, interpretive, and informational and experiential range. This permits the enclosed forms of knowledge, information, and understanding that coalesce around modernist pedagogical spaces to be problematized and interrogated with relative ease and maximum insight. Moreover, cyberspace brings the world into classrooms in close and very direct approximations to its richness, complexity and "seamlessness." With this capacity available, students and teachers can make explicit the extent to which education/learning has been compartmentalized, and knowledge itself fragmented. This is largely a function of the fluidity and "hypertextuality" of information within cyberspace. Critical skills also enjoy enlarged prospects for development, in virtue of the fact that many of the "sources" of the information and theory being employed in critical pedagogy within cyberspace are available on-line. Perspectives, claims, and interpretations can be questioned and reframed in networked dialogue: screen to screen.

(v) Finally, we can frame a broad agenda for critical pedagogy within three "realms" of cyberspace: namely, realms of information, knowledge, and understanding. These realms are, of course, inter-related.

Within the realm of information, critical pedagogy is concerned with investigating the nature and role of information within electronic media. In part this involves problematizing information in relation to meaning, and considering how and why particular elements of information available in cyberspace become integrated into social ways of being and acting. Beyond this, critical pedagogy should: (i) tackle the question of how (or whether) information might be distinguished from mis-information and dis-information; (ii) investigate how information is controlled and regulated within electronically-mediated environments; and (iii) explore cases where regulation and control of information result in people being served up mis-information or dis-information by electronic media in cyberspace.

Comparisons might also be undertaken between the nature, regulation, and control of information within more traditional text types and "spaces," and cyberspace respectively.

Within the realm of knowledge, critical pedagogy will address how knowledge is legitimated and regulated within cyberspace, and how modes of regulation and legitimation in cyberspace may vary from those that prevail in more traditional spaces associated with the book. On the face of it, there appear to be significant differences between forms of self-regulated and self-monitoring collaborative practices of knowledge production within virtual communities of scholars involved in on-line modes of publishing by electronic journals, and more conventional forms and social relations of regulation associated with print-based scholarly journals. And, as noted earlier, it seems quite plausible to think of discussion groups, conference groups, and a whole range of other kinds of user groups within cyberspace developing procedures for regulating what gets discussed and legitimating what comes to be taken up as "knowledge," in accordance with purpose-driven and interest or desire-serving ends. The question is how far we might be able to observe or create qualitatively different practices of regulation and legitimation of knowledge in cyberspace from those that prevail in "bookspace": recognizing that just as bookspace is not monopolized by any one mode of regulation and any one set of legitimation practices and relations, neither does/will cyberspace reflect a total homogeneity.

Sceptics may point to extant texts and practices already well-established within cyberspace environments which approximate closely to models of regulation and control associated with "bookspace"—such as software packages of Great Books, Classics, and encyclopedias, or "Project Gutenberg." Against such observations we would argue that many other texts exist within open access user spaces that can be engaged, edited, and appropriated on-line: re-authoring and otherwise using them in accordance with user needs and interests. Indeed, and subject to the reasonable limitations of copyright and intellectual property laws, even the "great works" available on-line can be downloaded and manipulated and "played with" in ways that contest or subvert authorial regulation and control, beyond options readily available with conventional printed texts. In any event, there is important work to be undertaken by critical pedagogy in the realm of knowledge. The key point is that cyberspace is not (yet) a *fait accompli*. It is still open to being made, in ways that bookspace no longer is. "Making cyberspace" along different lines of knowledge regulation and control from those of bookspace is an historical option which can be taken up within transformative practice agendas of critical literacy.

Recalling Gee's account of Discourse noted above, we recognize that knowledge is always a function of Discourse. Within a Discourse, particular beliefs, values, theories, information, and so on become legitimated as knowledge. Discourses are necessarily bounded and regulating. Hence, participation

LANKSHEAR, PETERS, AND KNOBEL

within particular Discourses presupposes, among other things, being subject-ed to—and acceding to—their distinctive constructions, legitimations, and (modes of) regulation of knowledge.

Within the realm of knowledge, critical pedagogy will involve learners performing "anatomies" of Discourses in cyberspace, to discern and analyze their distinctive legitimations and regulations of knowledge. "Anatomies" will disclose the purposes, goals, and values of Discourses, and their concomitant modes and means for regulating, controlling, and sanctioning *what* counts as knowledge within their purview. "Anatomies" will also examine *why* some beliefs and information count as knowledge within given Discourses while others do not, and will provide a basis for examining who stands to benefit from accepting these discursive constructions of knowledge and who will likely be disadvantaged. Such critical practices of "anatomy" further make *explicit* the contingent and historical (non necessary, non transcendent) and in-escapably ideological character of (all) Discourses and hierarchical *orders* of Discourse—from dominant Discourses to subordinate Discourses—within everyday life, and systematic patterns of advantage and disadvantage thereby established and maintained (Gee 1991; Fairclough 1989, 1992).

These ideas apply also to practices of critical pedagogy within the realm of understanding. The task here is to develop and apply meta-level awareness of discursive practices in cyberspace, so that learners can be reflexive about their own practices as members of self-regulating and self-monitoring groups/virtual communities; so that they can exercise reflective choices about which cyberspace Discourses they will join and remain in; and so that they can envisage and implement informed practices of Discourse critique and transformation, within and without cyberspace environments. This calls for generating and seizing opportunities for enabling learners to make *as explicit as possible* their understanding of social practice, subjectivity and identity, modes of regulation and control, processes of legitimation, patterns of social advantage and disadvantage; how these are related; and how they and our participation in them are historical and contingent, and, to that extent, amenable to change.

2. Some Practical Developments

There are many possibilities for extending critical pedagogy into cyberspace environments under classroom conditions. We will discuss briefly a small sample of these under two headings.

(i) Networked learning in classrooms: "wiring" critical pedagogy

Classrooms from elementary through tertiary levels are increasingly being equipped with computer hardware and software. Of course, considerable in-equalities in quantity and quality of provision are evident from school to school, community to community (c.f., Papert 1993). These differences notwithstanding, there are important points that should be observed with regard to extending practices of critical pedagogy into cyberspace.

Having electronic gadgetry available by no means guarantees that students will be exposed to cyberspace environments. Still less does it guarantee they will have opportunities to interact in cyberspace from a critical pedagogical perspective. Large quantities of electronic hardware and software are currently being employed within pedagogical and curricular practices that merely reinvent the enclosures of bookspace within the domain of digital text. In part, the kind of critical practice we envisage calls for appropriate hardware, software, and access opportunities. Beyond this, however, it presupposes certain "awarenesses" and dispositions on the part of members of classroom learning communities.

An orienting comment from Taylor and Saarinen provides a useful starting point here:

> In the intertextuality of cyberspace, surface does not hide depth; rather windows open to other windows whose surfaces disclose other surfaces. As this technology is adapted by the telecommunications industry, unprecedented possibilities for the dissemination of information emerge. The restrictions of limited newspaper space and air time give way to a lateral extension in which topics expand without limit. For people who are interested, a simple click enables further consideration of a broad range of topics and issues. Furthermore, [in cyberspace] the passivity of traditional televisual media [and, we would add, much traditional practice using conventional printed texts] gives way to interactive dialogues in which the reader/listener does not simply accept what is given but asks questions and even offers reactions and responses. Within this communication network, superficiality [surface] allows for a "depth" that has never before been possible (1994: Superficiality 4).

At the infrastructural level, accessing the potential of cyberspace currently calls for a minimum of 486 processor speed (or equivalent), windows-type applications, CD-ROM and sound and video card facilities, and a modem. It is possible to obtain these needs at less than the equivalent price of a basic PC a few years ago. The practical point is to invest available funding wisely. It is very likely that in many classrooms there will be students whose knowledge of such matters is in advance of the teacher's. This provides an excellent basis from which to begin democratizing knowledge and authority relations: allowing "organic" student knowledge to assume high ground in important decision-making processes pertaining to resourcing critical pedagogy. This does not mean simply accepting student knowledge on face value but, when appropriate, taking advice from learners and extending to them responsibility for checking out options. Inviting students to justify their ideas and preferences will provide pedagogical opportunities for making explicit the relationship between technologies and the Discourses to which they are integral. From the outset, then, critiques of reified technicist thinking can be set in train.

Affordable access to global electronic mailing and cyberspace networks—such as the Internet and its myriad nets—through a modem is also optimal. (NB. During the period between the initial writing of this chapter and the proof reading phase, initiatives to network schools have unfolded dramatically. Shortly before this book went to press, President Clinton's 'Technology Literacy Challenge" was announced, on 15 February 1996. The $2 billion 5 year package challenges "the private sector, schools, teachers, parents, students, community groups, state and local governments, and the federal government" to meet the goal of making all US children technologically literate "by the dawn of the 21st century". The strategy comprises four "pillars" that will ensure all teachers receive the necessary training and support "to help students learn via computers and the information superhighway", develop "effective and engaging software and on-line learning resources" as integral elements of school curricula, provide all teachers and students with access to modern computers, and connect every US classroom to the information superhighway—Winters, 15 February 1996. Other countries, like Australia, are playing "catch up", although without promulgating anything to date on a proportionate scale to the Clinton proposal. Large scale initiatives notwithstanding, dramatic inequalities between schools and school districts are legion, and are likely to exist for some time, and many schools will be obliged to call on their entreprenuerial capacities to provide network capacity.) Where schools are not networked as part of their regular resourcing, it may be necessary for teachers and students to explore ways of obtaining at least some degree of access. Various forms of strategic and/or entrepreneurial activity might be employed here. For example, teachers who are involved in graduate programs may be able to obtain "dial-in" facilities through their institution, or else they might seek to have their classroom integrated into research and development projects through which access is made available. Alternatively, the class might pursue entrepreneurial methods, such as negotiating partnerships with networked corporations, or with telecommunications and/or electronics companies. In addition, classes might subscribe to bulletin board servers, rather than to Vax/Unix servers directly. A wide range of servers are available at very reasonable rates, and others are free.

Relevant knowledge and technical skill for accessing "spaces on the Net," using electronic mail, cutting and pasting text, sound and images, generating graphics, converting text to sound and sound to text, and morphing, etc., are also required. Here again the knowledge of students may well outstrip those of teachers—with the general opportunities and benefits noted earlier potentially available (c.f., Papert 1993; Perelman 1992). There is, however, more to this than technicist know-how alone. The critical pedagogy potential of cyberspace depends on teachers and students understanding that "being wired for critical pedagogy" involves much more than simply hooking hardware and software up

182

to terminals and electricity. At its most simple it means being able to conceptualize and approach interactions and activities in cyberspace as forms of engagement which offer intellectual and personal access to diverse discursive practices, diverse discursive productions, and diverse discursive communities.

This critical insight will become better and more explicitly understood as teachers and students progressively engage in actual practices within cyberspace. There are some reasonably obvious and fruitful places and ways for getting started which are worth noting here.

The crucial operating principle is to network the classroom to a range of local, regional, national, and world-wide virtual communities. These communities should provide for variety in terms of Discourses, subjectivity and identity. At its most straightforward, this might be done by establishing email connections with students in other schools, near and far. More ambitious options could include using cyberspace to develop collaborative learning across contexts of cultural and social difference and diversity, along the lines described by Taylor and Saarinen: where the authors jointly developed and "taught" a course involving their respective students in a North American and a Finnish university. Other options are to post messages relevant to classroom learning themes to existing message boards on Web sites, discussion lists, EdMOOs (e.g., Empire Internet Schoolhouse, K12net, KIDLINK, schoolNET, etc.), and to participate in dialogue around questions and issues within that virtual community. As a variation the class might generate a new discussion list on the Net, instigating its own purposes, values, and modes of interaction, as an experiment in creating a space of discursive practice and production. Within these virtual communities, students and teachers together can engage in dialogue across difference, seeking out commonalities, experimenting with identities, tracing borders, and moving in and out of different Discourse communities.

As a variation on active participation, a class might simply log into a range of cyber-spaces, download interactions over a period of time, and use these in the manner of Freirean "codifications" (Freire 1973) to interrogate the regulation of information and knowledge, to trace lines of legitimation, and to undertake "anatomies" of the Discourses involved in pursuit of explicit understandings.

At a sophisticated level, practicing critical pedagogy in cyberspace may involve grasping and operating from some highly complex epistemological and ontological insights and meta-level understandings. Taylor and Saarinen offer two provocative stimuli here.

> When depth gives way to surface, under-standing becomes inter-standing. To comprehend is no longer to grasp what lies **beneath** but to grasp what lies **between**. (1994: Interstanding 1)
> Compu-telecommunications technology involves an epistemological shift no less radical than Kant's Copernican revolution. The very forms

through which we perceive and categories with which we think are transformed by the changing technologies of knowledge production. Things give way to events, identities to differences, and substances to relations. Everything is simultaneously interconnected and in flux. (1994: Interstanding 3)

The processes integral to operating with the space-time compressions of cyberspace and the rapid sequences of cyberspatial screen shifts and hyper/intertextual maneuvres made available by "windows," reflect the very epistemology and ontology of dynamism, relatedness, "mutability," and anti-reification that has characterized critical pedagogy from its Freirean origins (and even earlier, as in the theories of the Frankfurt School). Critical understandings of social phenomena and social "facts" stress the importance of grasping the operation of discursive processes and relations, which deliver up power, knowledge, cultures, hierarchies, and the like, as dynamic *productions*: not as autonomous existents, finite properties, or transcendent qualities. Our journeys in cyberspace and our critical reflections upon them could be brought into "conversation" with the kinds of categories and constructs that prevail in the positivist world of controlled experiments and linear causal relations between independent and dependent variables. In exercises of "critical pedagogy across the curriculum" students might consider the implications of treating science, economics, and other curriculum subjects to the kinds of Discourse "anatomies" they have developed and practiced in other curricular and noncurricular contexts of cyberspace.

184

(ii) Transforming social practices and relations in "real" space and time.

As intimated already at several points, critical pedagogy in cyberspace presents exciting possibilities for democratizing classroom learning. While the potential of cyberspace may well point toward prospects for deschooling society in radical ways, we are not advocating anything like that here. Neither are we suggesting that basic skills and competencies be thrown over to thoroughgoing critical approaches to learning—although we agree with those who argue that critical forms of engagement can be introduced at earlier levels and more "basic" stages of learning than is often assumed.

The superabundance of information available in cyberspace frees the teacher up to a considerable extent from having to provide content. This "freedom" does not of itself preclude the possibility that teachers may nonetheless take it upon themselves to proffer "authoritative" interpretations, frame discussion tightly, point to the "moral" of the various "stories," distil themes, and bring "lessons" to "the foreseen close." To do so, however, would defeat the potential of critical pedagogy in cyberspace.

Rather, cyberspace should be employed by critical teachers to provide contexts in which they can assume a maximally *generic* role: where they devote their energies and understanding principally to maintaining settings where learners (including the teacher) practice "Discourse anatomy," and where the emphasis is on rendering the implicit explicit.

The teacher should aim to keep in front of students the task of subjecting what they encounter in cyberspace to general forms of critical interrogation. Fundamental questions which make up much of the stock and trade of learners in the process of practicing critique and "anatomy" might include: what is this practice?; where does it come from?; what are its purposes?; what does it make of participants?; what forms of subjectivity and what kinds of identities are associated with it?; what alternative forms of practice exist here, or might exist?; who benefits from the practice as currently constituted?; who controls and regulates knowledge and information within this practice, and by what means?; what counts as knowledge and information here, and why?; which practices "go together" and which do not?; why not?; what sorts of combinations of practices might be possible, interesting, challenging?; what patterns are evident between patterns of values and beliefs and discursive histories—across time and place?: and so on. The aim will be for students to employ such questions as a means for making their own practices and those of others more explicit, together with exploring the historicity and contingency of social practices. It is in such acts of interrogation and seeking to make what is implicit explicit, to the point where individuals become reflexive and self-regulating in their practices of reflection and action, and not in specific "answers," that the objectives of critical pedagogy should be sought.

Just as critical pedagogy in cyberspace provides possibilities for transforming classroom practice along more democratic lines, so the insights, information, and exposure to differences and experiences of solidarity gleaned from encounters in cyberspace enhance the prospects of individual and collective action aimed at transforming social practices and relations outside the classroom.

Many discussion groups are based around social movements and forms of cultural politics—such as networks concerned with issues of ecology, sexuality, gender, alternative and counter cultures, human rights, and access to and manipulation of information. Where mis-information and dis-information are detected, opportunities can be created to "post" a critique in conventional print space as well as in cyberspace. The Net provides stimuli as well as support for experimenting with diverse kinds of Discourse construction, interpersonal relationships, and border crossings (Giroux 1992) at the level of identity and subjectivity. One indicator of successful critical pedagogy in cyberspace will be the extent to which students freely and willingly extend their critical practice into public and private spheres. This, we believe, is much more likely to happen where educators observe the "generic" stance advocated here, and refrain as far as possible from assuming rights and responsibilities that prevail in modernist enclosures based upon the book. The invitation to pursue critical literacy in cyberspace is an invitation to do precisely this.

185

REFERENCES

Aronowitz, S. and Giroux, H. (1988). Schooling, culture and literacy in the age of broken dreams. *Harvard Educational Review* 58, 2.

Barker, F. (1984). *The Tremulous Private Body: Essays on Subjection*. London: Methuen.

Bee, B. (1984). *Women's Work, Women's Lives*. Sydney: NSW Department of TAFE.

Bee, B. (1989). *Women and Work Literacy Resources*. Sydney: NSW Department of TAFE.

Bell, D. (1973). *The Coming of Post-Industrial Society: A Venture in Social Forecasting*. New York: Basic Books.

Benyon-Davies, P. (1993). *Information Systems Development: An Introduction to Systems Engineering*. London: MacMillan.

Brady, J. and Hernández, A. (1993). Feminist literacies: Toward emancipatory possibilities of solidarity. In C. Lankshear and P. McLaren (eds.) *Critical Literacy: Politics, Praxis and the Postmodern*. Albany, NY: SUNY Press.

Castells, M. (1989). *The Informational City: Information Technology, Economic Restructuring, and the Urban-Regional Process*. Oxford: Blackwell.

Delany, P. and Landow, G. (1993). Managing the digital word: The text in an age of electronic reproduction". In Landow and Delany *op. cit.*

Deleuze, G. and Guattari, F. (1983). *Anti-Oedipus: Capitalism and Schizophrenia*. Minneapolis: University of Minnesota Press.

Dery, M. (1994). Flame wars. In his (ed.) *Flame Wars: The Discourse of Cyberculture*. Durham and London: Duke University Press.

Dewey, J. (1916). *Democracy and Education*. New York: MacMillan.

Dibbell, J. (1994). A rape in cyberspace; or, how an evil clown, a Haitian trickster spirit, two wizards, and a cast of dozens turned a database into a society. In M. Dery (ed.) *Flame Wars: The Discourse of Cyberculture*. Durham and London: Duke University Press.

Eco, U. (1989). *The Open Work*. Cambridge, MA: Harvard University Press.

Ellsworth, E. (1989). Why doesn't this feel empowering? Working through the repressive myths of critical pedagogy. *Harvard Educational Review* 59, 3.

Elsasser, N. and Irvine, P. (1985). English and Creole: The dialectics of choice in a college writing program. *Harvard Educational Review* 55, 4.

Fairclough, N. (1989). *Language and Power*. London: Longmans.

Fairclough, N. (1992). *Discourse and Social Change*. Oxford: Polity Press.

Freire, P. (1970). *Pedagogy of the Oppressed*. New York: Seabury.

Freire, P. (1973). *Education for Critical Consciousness*. New York: Seabury.

Gee, J. (1990). *Social Linguistics and Literacies: Ideology in Discourses*. London: Falmer Press.

Gee, J. (1991). What is literacy? In C. Mitchell and K. Weiler (eds) *Rewriting Literacy: Culture and the Discourse of the Other*. New York: Bergin and Garvey.

Gee, J. (1993). Tuning into forms of life. *Education Australia*, 19–20: 13–14.

Gee, J. and Lankshear, C. (1995). The new work order: Critical language awareness and "fast capitalist" texts. *Discourse* 16, 1.

Gibson, William. (1984) *Neuromancer*. New York: Paladin.

Giroux, H. (1988). *Schooling and the Struggle for Public Life*. Minneapolis: University of Minnesota Press.

186

Giroux, H. (1991). Modernism, postmodernism and feminism. In his (ed.) *Postmodernism, Feminism and Cultural Politics*. Albany, NY: SUNY Press.

Giroux, H. (1992). *Border Crossings*. London: Routledge.

Giroux, H. (1993). Literacy and the politics of difference. In C. Lankshear and P. McLaren (eds.) *op. cit.*

Giroux, H. and McLaren, P. eds. (1989). *Critical Pedagogy, the State, and Cultural Struggle*. Albany, NY: SUNY Press.

Grossberg, L. (1992). *We Gotta Get Out of this Place*. London: Routledge.

Grossberg, L. and Nelson, C. (1988). Introduction: The territory of Marxism. In their (ed.) *Marxism and the Interpretation of Culture*. Urbana: University of Illinois Press.

Haraway, D. (1985). A manifesto for cyborgs: Science, technology and socialist feminism in the 1980s. *Socialist Review* 15.

Haraway, D. (1990). *Simians, Cyborgs and Women*. New York: Routledge.

Harvey, D. (1989). *The Condition of Postmodernity*. Oxford: Blackwell.

Hinkson, J. (1991). *Postmodernity: State and Education*. Geelong: Deakin University Press.

Hirst, P. (1974). *Knowledge and the Curriculum*. London: Routledge and Kegan Paul.

Illich, I. (1971). *Deschooling Society*. New York: Harper and Row.

Jameson, F. (1984). Postmodernism or the cultural logic of late capitalism. *New Left Review* 146.

Kress, G. (1985). *Linguistic Processes in Sociocultural Practice*. Geelong: Deakin University Press.

Kress, G. ed. (1988). *Communication and Culture*. Kensington, NSW: University of New South Wales Press.

Landow, G. (1992) *Hypertext: The Convergence of Contemporary Critical Theory and Technology*. Baltimore: John Hopkins University Press.

Landow, G. and Delany, P. (1993). *The Digital Word: Text-Based Computing in the Humanities*. Cambridge, Mass.: MIT Press.

Lanham, Richard A. (1993) *The Electronic Word: Democracy, Technology and the Arts*. Chicago and London: The University of Chicago Press.

LeCompte, M. and deMarrais, K. (1992). The disempowering of empowerment: From social revolution to classroom rhetoric. *Educational Foundations* 6, 3.

Lyotard, J-F. (1984). *The Postmodern Condition: A Report on Knowledge*. Minneapolis: University of Minnesota Press.

Machlup, F. (1973). *The Production and Distribution of Knowledge in the United States*. Princeton, NJ: Princeton University Press.

McLaren, P. (1986). Postmodernity and the death of politics: A Brazilian reprieve. *Educational Theory* 36, 4.

McLaren, P. (1988). Culture or canon? *Harvard Educational Review* 58, 2.

McLaren, P. (1989). *Life in Schools*. New York: Longman.

McLaren, P. (1994). *Critical Pedagogy and Predatory Culture*. London: Routledge.

McLaren, P. and Lankshear, C. (1993). Critical literacy and the postmodern turn. In their (ed.) *Critical Literacy: Politics, Praxis and the Postmodern*. Albany, NY: SUNY Press.

McLuhan, M. (1968). *War and Peace in the Global Village*. New York: Bantam.

McLuhan, M. and Powers, B. (1992). *The Global Village: Transformations in World Life and Media in the 21st Century*. Oxford: Oxford University Press.

Odlyzko, A. (1994) Tragic Loss or Good Riddance? The Impending Demise of Traditional Scholarly Journals. *Surfaces*, IV, 105.

Okerson, A. (1994) Oh Lord, Won't You Buy Me a Mercedes Benz. Or, There Is a There There. *Surfaces,* IV, 102.

Papert, S. (1993). *The Children's Machine: Rethinking School in the Age of the Computer.* New York: Basic Books.

Perelman, L. (1992). *School's Out.* New York: Avon Books.

Peters, M. and Lankshear, C. (1994) Critical literacy in cyberspace. Paper presented to the Philosophy of Education Society of Australasia Annual Conference. Auckland: University of Auckland, November 9–11.

Poster, M. (1990). *The Mode of Information: Poststructuralism and Social Context.* Cambridge: Polity Press.

Pusey, M. (1991). *Economic Rationalism in Canberra.* New York: Cambridge University Press.

Rheingold, H. (1991). *Virtual Reality.* London: Secker and Warburg.

Rheingold, H. (1994). *Virtual Community.* London: Secker and Warburg.

Rockhill, K. (1993). (Dis)connecting literacy and sexuality: Speaking the unspeakable in the classroom. In C. Lankshear and P. McLaren (eds.) *op. cit.*

Rose, M. (1991). *Post-Industrialism and Postmodernism.* London: Routledge.

Ross, A. (1991). *Strange Weather: Culture, Science, and Technology in the Age of Limits.* London: Verso.

Rushkoff, D. (1994). *Cyberia: Life in the trenches of Hyperspace.* San Francisco: Harper.

Scheffler, I. (1965). *Conditions of Knowledge.* Glenview, Ill: Scott-Foresman.

Schumaker, E. F. (1975). *Small Is Beautiful: Economics As If People Mattered.* New York: Harper and Row.

Shor, I. (1980). *Critical Teaching and Everyday Life.* Boston: South End Press.

Shor, I. (1992). *Empowering Education: Critical Teaching for Social Change.* Chicago: University of Chicago Press.

Shor, I. ed. (1987). *Freire for the Classroom.* Portsmouth, NH: Boynton/Cook.

Shor, I. and Freire, P. (1987). *A Pedagogy for Liberation: Dialogues on Transforming Education.* Westport, Conn: Greenwood, Bergin and Garvey.

Smith, R. (1994) Cyberpunk Nurseries: Computer Game Playing among Young Children and Adolescents. Research Grant Application, Brisbane, Griffith University, Faculty of Arts and Humanities.

Stone, A. (1991) Will the Real Body Please Stand Up?: Boundary Stories about Virtual Cultures. In M. Benedikt (Ed.) *op. cit.*

Taylor, M. and Saarinen, E. (1994). *Imagologies: Media Philosophy.* London: Routledge.

Touraine, A. (1974). *The Post Industrial Society: Tomorrow's Social History.* London: Wildwood House.

Wark, M. (1993). Third nature. *Cultural Studies* 6, 2.

Weiler, K. (1991). Freire and a feminist pedagogy of difference. *Harvard Educational Review* 61, 4.

Winters, K. (15 February 1996). America's technology literacy challenge. U.S. Department of Education, Office of the Under Secretary, k.winters@inet.ed.gov, posted on acw-l@unicom.acs.ttu.edu on 17 February 1996.

Wittgenstein, L. (1953). *Philosophical Investigations.* Oxford: Blackwell.

INDEX

195